The Vital Missing Link to the Whole Armor of God

The Father's Gift of Health, Wholeness, Fruitfulness, Grace, and

Protection, and Energy, through Crystals

Birthing Forth the Treasures of the Father's Heart

Jesus Rocks!
Black & White Print Version

By T.R. Green

Birthing Forth the Treasures of The Father's Heart
Jesus Rocks! Black & White Print Version

ISBN E-book Standard Addition # **978-1-7344532-0-1**

ISBN Printed Book # **978-1-7344532-3-2**

Table of Contents

Chapter 6: Crystals: The Vital Missing Link to the Whole Armor of God in Our Life

Dedication

May this book help you to know and understand the better you, with the use of crystals. May you receive all the health benefits of crystals. May you receive healing spiritually, mentally, emotionally, and physically. May you have your adventures with crystals through the Father.

Acknowledgments

I want to acknowledge those who received the open revelations, that the Father (Jehovah, Yod, Hey, Vav, Hey, Yahweh), Jesus (Yeshua), and Holy Spirit (Ruach) has given me.

I want to acknowledge my wonderful husband, who has supported me on this journey and recognized what the Father has been speaking to me. I want to thank my husband for letting me pursue my ministry, business, and the call of the Father in my life.

You have been the provider for our household since our marriage, and I thank you for being such an amazing husband.

I want to acknowledge those who have stood by me and supported me and recognized the Father's mandate of crystals on my life. You stood by my side, no matter the opposition we faced.

I want to thank those who supported me as a Certified Crystal Healer.

I would like to thank those who have supported me in my business, and who have helped me to grow my business and pushed me to fulfill the vision, the Father has called me to do

I want to thank those who have given donations for this book to be and my business.

I want to thank those who encouraged me to write this book because of the many treasures and revelations it holds.

I want to acknowledge the purchaser of this book., may you receive the many blessings of this book, and may you have your eyes to see and your ears to hear the revelations of crystals in the word of God.

I want to thank those whom the Father has sent to confirm the things he has spoken unto me.

This is Amazing Grace!

This is amazing grace.
I have the rock on my side.
When everything's not going on right.
This is amazing grace!
I don't react like the past,
when everything's not going on right!
This is amazing grace!
My weaknesses start to fade,
when good vibrations start to come my way!
This is Amazing Grace!
He's the rock on which I stand.
I'm not confused about his plan.
Christ the Rock, Living Rock, Christ the Rock!
Christ the Rock, Living Rock, Christ the Rock!
Song by T.R. Green

Introduction

When we think about crystals or gemstones, what comes to mind? Is it the beauty each one carries? Is it the shimmering light that flows through the stone? Maybe in gemstones, we look at how crystal clear the gem is and the depths of how each gemstone is cut and structured. When we look deep within it, you see it rainbows and rays of colors. We might like the way it is shaped or cut. It may look beautiful on us like a necklace, ring, anklet, bracelet, or maybe a crown like the kings and queens wear. There are many uses of these gemstones and crystals the Lord wants to restore to men and women to help benefit them. These stones and crystals are not on this earth just for their beauty and radiant light. Stones and crystals are here because the Lord has made each one with its own characteristics, attributes, and functions to be used to help us as humans. **Prov.17:8 (KJV) says," 8 A gift is as a precious stone in the eyes of him that hath it: whithersoever it turneth, it prospereth."** Meaning each crystal is a gift because it prospers and completes the function that the Father called, commissioned, and ordained for it to do. We can also tell the crystals what to do according to God's word, or what we need them to do for us spiritually, mentally, and emotionally, and financially to the glory of God and they will obey because that is one of the functions that the Father originally intended for them to do. So, whether it is one crystal or more that we have, it will complete the job that it intends to do. **"You shall also decree a thing, and it shall be established to you. Light shall shine on your ways." Job 22:28 KJV**

The crystals protect the chakras, which we may know them as the wheels; they were wheels within a wheel that followed the living creatures wherever they went. **"19 And when the living creatures went, the wheels went by them:, and when the living creatures were lifted up from the earth, the wheels were lifted up. 20 Whithersoever the spirit was to go, they went, thither was their spirit to go; and the wheels were lifted up over against them: for the spirit of the living creature was in the wheels. 21 When those went, these went; and when those stood, these stood; and when those were lifted up from the earth, the wheels were lifted up over against them: for the spirit of the living creature was in the wheels." Ezekiel 1:19-21 (KJV)**

Well, we have them too as well within our bodies and on the outside of the body. Let us talk about the seven main wheels or chakras in this book because we are spiritual and energy beings. The wheels and the chakras are also known as energy centers or vortexes within the body. If one of them is off we don't know how a person may react, just by one of those wheels or chakras not being activated or balanced. But we have treasures of the Father that help keep the chakras and wheels within the body to stay in alignment, and they are called crystals and gemstones. Crystals are a vital missing link to the armor of God, that's why many people are constantly getting delivered from the same thing in different churches repeatedly. They are a part of mankind's armor in order to protect mankind's life. I go over each armor detail, the helmet of salvation, truth to cover thy loins, the shield of faith, etc. (Ephesians 6 :10-18) within this book. Every person whether saved or unsaved need crystals to protect their chakras or wheels. Jesus is restoring his name as the Rock which are the crystal and gemstones within the Father's heart.

The ancients of old used crystals to bring forth health, healing, prophecy, creativity, balance, protection, energy, wisdom and to grow spiritually. Amulets in ancient times, even in the bible we will go over some of the scriptures. Amulets, meaning something that is hung on and was employed to protect man, his possessions, and his houses. What did they protect people and property from? They protected them from evil influences of witchcraft, negative energies (demons) and other evil powers. It is true that witches and warlocks used them also for wrong and to protect their own selves from the evil, and the demons that surrounded them they created around for themselves. Crystal works in conjunction to protect people from witches and warlocks by manifesting the word of God to protect them, their family, their households, surroundings, and environments. The original intent of the Father was and is now to use them for good. How can we call something that the Lord put on earth as good, evil? Maybe because all we hear are negative reports of people that use them like witches, warlocks, and normal people using them to bring harm against other people by putting evil spells on people during prayer or mixing things together to do harm to a person, but it's not the person themselves doing it, it's the demonic spirit, or negative energies surrounding them, impacting their decisions, or familiar spirits

in their bloodline from generation down to generation. Someone could have had a spell put on themselves from someone else without even knowing it.

*We never know the background of the person's life that has done these things, but when we walk in love, authority, and the glory (light) of God it dispels the darkness. You should not be fearful or weary because we are in Christ Jesus himself and everything is made out of him through the Father **Prov 12:16 (KJV) says**, **"With him is strength and wisdom: the deceived and the deceiver are his,"** meaning Satan, the fallen angels, and those under Satan's influence, can only do what the Father allows them to do, just like in the book of Job (see Job 1-12 (KJV)); so do not be worried God is in full control. We see in 2 Kings Chapter 18 it talks about the false prophets of Balaam verses Elijah that the LORD himself showed himself to fight on behalf of Elijah the Prophet.*

"19 Now therefore send, and gather to me all **Israel unto mount Carmel, and the prophets of Baal four hundred and fifty, and the prophets of the groves four hundred, which eat at Jezebel's table.**

20 So Ahab sent unto all the children of Israel and gathered the prophets together unto mount Carmel.

21 And Elijah came unto all the people, and said, How long halt ye between two opinions? if the Lord be God, follow him: but if Baal, then follow him. And the people answered him not a word.

22 Then said Elijah unto the people, I, even I only, remain a prophet of the Lord; but Baal's prophets are four hundred and fifty men.

23 Let them therefore give us two bullocks; and let them choose one bullock for themselves, and cut it in pieces, and lay it on wood, and put no fire under: and I will dress the other bullock, and lay it on wood, and put no fire under:

24 And call ye on the name of your gods, and I will call on the name of the Lord: and the God that answereth by fire, let him be God. And all the people answered and said, It is well-spoken.

25 And Elijah said unto the prophets of Baal, Choose you one bullock for yourselves, and dress it first; for ye are many; and call on the name of your gods, but put no fire under.

26 And they took the bullock which was given them, and they dressed it, and called on the name of Baal from morning even until noon, saying, O Baal, hear us. But there was no voice, nor any that answered. And they leaped upon the altar which was made.

27 And it came to pass at noon, that Elijah mocked them, and said, Cry aloud: for he is a god; either he is talking, or he is pursuing, or he is in a journey, or peradventure he sleepeth, and must be awaked.

28 And they cried aloud, and cut themselves after their manner with knives and lancets, till the blood gushed out upon them.

29 And it came to pass, when midday was past, and they prophesied until the time of the offering of the evening sacrifice, that there was neither voice, nor any to answer, nor any that regarded.

30 And Elijah said unto all the people, Come near unto me. And all the people came near to him. And he repaired the altar of the Lord that was broken down.

31 And Elijah took twelve stones, according to the number of the tribes of the sons of Jacob, unto whom the word of the Lord came, saying, Israel shall be thy name:

32 And with the stones he built an altar in the name of the Lord: and he made a trench about the altar, as great as would contain two measures of seed.

33 And he put the wood in order, and cut the bullock in pieces, and laid him on the wood, and said, Fill four barrels with water, and pour it on the burnt sacrifice, and on the wood.

34 And he said, Do it the second time. And they did it the second time. And he said, Do it the third time. And they did it the third time.

35 And the water ran round about the altar; and he filled the trench also with water.

36 And it came to pass at the time of the offering of the evening sacrifice, that Elijah the prophet came near, and said, Lord God of Abraham, Isaac, and of Israel, let it be known this day that thou art God in Israel, and that I am thy servant, and that I have done all these things at thy word.

37 Hear me, O Lord, hear me, that this people may know that thou art the Lord God, and that thou hast turned their heart back again.

38 Then the fire of the Lord fell, and consumed the burnt sacrifice, and the wood, and the stones, and the dust, and licked up the water that was in the trench.

39 And when all the people saw it, they fell on their faces: and they said, The Lord, he is the God; the Lord, he is the God." 1 Kings 18: 19 - 39 KJV

So we see when it comes to coming against witches or warlocks that have crystals to use them against God's people, and good people who use crystals,

their power will not work because the crystals will perform and protect the Sons of God and every individual who is good because of his love for those who walk uprightly before him. We see in this scripture passage in 1 Kings 18 KJV that Elijah took 12 stones representing the 12 tribes of Israel. He did that under the instruction of the Lord, and <u>the stones on the altar</u> showed the manifestation power of God Almighty himself. That's when it comes to the people of God using crystals for his original purpose and intent that crystals will protect those operating out of his light, power, righteousness, and goodness, and love versus those who use crystals to do evil or have made a covenant with demonic spirits or demonic entities. Those who use it for evil the Lord will deal with them and send judgment in his timing if they don't hearken to his voice to turn from evil. It's Light against darkness. Good versus Evil. The Lord will always defend those who do good.

But love conquers all and changes a person. Truth be told, people worldwide are using crystals for benefits of health, healing, creativity, fruitfulness, prosperity, and balance and to protect themselves from evil, and it has fulfilled these things for them. The Lord wants to restore these gifts back into the church to help the Body of Christ because of his love for his children and all mankind. Other people are reaping the benefits of the crystals, the Father (Jehovah, Yod Hey Vav Hey, Yahweh, Yah) wants to restore to the body of Christ of its original intent he had for the use of crystals. According to the Jewish Encyclopedia, Abraham wore a jewel on his neck, which was initially called an amulet (meaning to be hung on), and it healed every sick person that looked upon it. You can use each crystal; however, you want for yourself. They can help you as an offence because they increase, life, deliverance fruitfulness (love, joy, peace, patience, kindness, and goodness, and self-control) in you that the Father originally intended for us to have through his son Christ Jesus. There are many other benefits that I will explain in this book.

We know Christ is the mediator of all things. (1Tim 2:5 (KJV)) We see the priest wore precious metals on their breastplate. We know they used the Urim and Thummim for divination. Divination is the same thing as a prophecy because prophecy is bubbling forth a prophetic word, meaning you can tell the past, present, and future. We know the ten commandments were written on a sapphire stone. We know the stones will praise the Lord if a man holds their peace. We know they will be used as a witness. We know they keep a record of what took place on earth. We know that they will protect us. We know they bring healing. We know they will minister to us. We know they will give us water if needed at the command of the Lord. We know they will cry out. You may say, "I never known for them to do these things." I'm glad you said that, it's my prayer that by the end of this book you will know the truth and it will set you free. We know the bible reveals hidden secrets and mysteries. Scriptures have layers after layers of meaning that the Father reveals about crystals, stones, and rocks. All other

countries' cultures, people have taken advantage of the benefits of using crystals, stones, and rocks for good because of their benefits, so should we. Besides, they are the Lord because he dwells in them, and they represent him and his ways. That's why the Lord gave us discernment to know both good from evil and to test the spirits to see if they are of God. Christ wants to restore these treasures because he wants his people to accelerate in the realm of the spirit, in order to advance his kingdom.

The bible gives deeper meanings and prophecies through stories as you read them. For instance, (Read Acts Chapter 10 KJV) Cornelius prayed to the Lord and did alms for people. He feared God, and an Angel told him to send men to Joppa to look for a man named Peter. During this transition, the Lord had to break the religious mindset that the Jews made that Jews couldn't enter the home of a non-Jew or they would become contaminated and unclean, so that tradition made peter prejudice towards other people outside the Jewish culture so the Lord had to break that off him because it would do more damage than good with that type of mindset. Christ loves all men. So, the Lord put Peter into a trance while being hungry and showed all manner of different kinds of four-footed beasts, which represented the different nations and people outside of the Jewish nationality, so the Lord told him to rise, Peter, kill and eat. Then Peter told the Lord not so Lord he had never eaten anything common or unclean. The Lord told him to kill and eat, and Peter said not so Lord, so the Lord told him a second time, What God hath cleansed, that call not thou common. The different animals represented the different nations outside of The Jews, and one of the nationalities was the nationality of Cornelius, and the Lord knew more than likely he would come across different foods to eat that was considered unclean to him by meeting up with other people from different nationalities.

The Lord knew we would also be in a time now where people are going by the law and works and stating that you have to do the law and not eat unclean foods in order to get into the kingdom, or have a deeper relationship with the Father which is so untrue. The Father had the list of unclean foods in the law because they are unhealthy for the body, and he knew it could affect your body in a different way by lowering your frequency and vibration. So, you may feel more sluggish or tired you eat unclean food all the time because of the fat that's in it. Some people don't feel any difference, Hallelujah! But, that will never dictate your relationship with the Father. Jesus became the law for us to set us free, some people may not eat pork because it's unhealthy, some may eat it because it's good and they like it. The Father loves us all as his children; no person is better than the other. Now, unfortunately, this has become a heated debate, which it should not be. But, that's why the Lord had to correct Peter and tell him those animals were clean and those nationalities are clean also because of Christ's blood that was slain from the beginning of the world.

The Lord is so awesome and speaks in so many ways. He speaks through nature, birds, the earth, and other things, which I will explain all these things in this book on my walk with the Father and Christ himself through Holy Spirit. He is so amazing and majestic. Everything praises him and lifts him up. **Let everything that has breath praise the Lord Psalm 150:6 (KJV)**

Chapter 1: The Importance of Crystals

There are many testimonies, signs, and wonders that the Father has shown us in heaven above, many victories he has won for his children in the bible. There have been hidden treasures that are alive that the Father wants to restore to his children that have been lost to help with health, energy, prosperity, healing physically, mentally, emotionally, and spiritually. They are alive like all things are alive, and they are ready to serve, just like the angels. The ancients of old used them, the Christians of old used them, other civilizations used them, but because man has called them evil, when in fact they aren't. It has left people and the church powerless and suffering. It is the evil intentions that people intend for them to do that they fulfill that makes them look evil when all they are doing is one of the functions the Father has told them to do, which I show scriptures on later. It just so happened that man has used these things for evil and corruption because of Satan and his troop that fell from heaven. Everything that the Father made was good and used for good until sin entered the world through the fall of Satan and the fallen angels that went with him. Crystals work with your energy field/or aura to birth forth their benefits by aligning its frequency and vibrations with yours to bring forth healing, protection, and other attributes.

The Father wants to restore the crystals back to his original intent, which is for good and to advance Christ Kingdom. He wants to restore the crystals he had for mankind so that we can benefit from them. It's his gift to mankind and other creation. "**Who is the rock except our LORD which it states in Psalms 18:31 (ESV) For who is God save the LORD? or who is a Rock save our God?"** <u>CHRIST IS THAT ROCK</u>. **"In the beginning was the word, the word was with God; the word was God. "John 1:1 (KJV)** We see in the beginning Christ was with the Father, and when he spoke, things were created as in heaven so down here on earth, and everything he created has his own characteristic and attribute because Christ is all in all. "**Who is the image of the invisible God, <u>the firstborn of every creature:</u> For by him were all things created, that are in heaven, and that are in earth, visible and invisible, whether they be thrones, or dominions, or principalities, or powers: all things were created by him, and for him: 17 And he is before all things, and by him all things consist. When** they say every creature, he means all things living." **Colossians 1:15-17 (KJV)** Human beings are the closest resemblance to him and have his character and nature, all other creation who may not resemble his face but their character, nature, personality, and what they do reflects him. **"For in him, we live and move and have our being.' As some of your own poets have said, 'We are his offspring." Acts 17:48 (KJV)** All things are alive, whether seen or unseen, they take up a form of some type of frequency or vibration, which is broken down into matter. It's all alive because it's in him. He is science. He's the invisible of all things. He's I AM that I AM. He is the air that we breathe.

The Father wants to restore all things he created back into its rightful place and original order. What is that order? To expand the kingdom of God through the Sons of God, which is you and me. One of the first and foremost things he wants to be restored is Crystals. Crystals have been used for centuries by ancient civilizations for healing, restoration, creativity, protection. But because the enemy used it for evil, some people said it was demonic. Did they not forget Christ is all in all! So, we must restore them back to their original purpose and intent of the Father, which is to do good. That's why there are many in the church sick, going through spiritual warfare, oppressed, and not increasing in the gifts the Lord has placed initially for them. People say oh...but that's witchcraft. It's not witchcraft when you use them for the Father's original purpose, which is to do good and bring forth the kingdom of God. That's why we restore the crystals back to their rightful place to do what the Father intended for them to do. That's why you pray over them and consecrate them back to the Lord and tell him they are used for his purposes that he originally intended for them to be used for. Just because they use it for evil, that means, we are to use it for good, to expand Christ's kingdom. Love prevails above else. Truth be told, if it were so bad, why are there individual crystals assigned to protect you from witchcraft, and spells like the crystal called sapphire, ruby, amethyst, and black tourmaline.

We must take advantage of the treasures the Father has given us all to use for good and not evil, that's how you counteract the enemy. If the enemy used it for evil, we know the Father wants to use it for good. Jesus said in Matthew, **"If ye then, being evil, know how to give good gifts unto your children, how much more shall your Father which is in heaven give good things to them that ask him? Matt 7:11 (KJV)** and in James it says, **every good gift and every perfect gift is from above, and cometh down from the Father of lights, with whom is no variableness, neither shadow of." James 1:17 (KJV)** As stated before in **Prov.17:8 (KJV) says, "8A gift is as a precious stone in the eyes of him that hath it: whithersoever it turneth, it prospereth."** Meaning each crystal is a gift because it prospers and completes the function that the Father called, commissioned, and ordained for it to do. If we tell individual crystals to do a particular task, they will obey you if it's what the

Father created them to do. This is whether a person is good or bad. It has to do what it is told to do, or it's breaking the protocol of what the Father has called, commissioned, and ordained for it to do. Meaning it must fulfill its purpose.

<u>We never use these gifts to control a person because Christ gave man free will</u>. We don't use crystals to make a person fall in love with you. But we can cause demonic influence to cease by collaborating with the Lord to bring heaven down into the atmosphere. We know heaven is inside us, but we want the frequencies, vibrations, and energies of the Father, the Son, and the Holy Ghost to surround us. We have let man out of the goodness of their hearts tell us these things are evil and not to use them any longer because people were using them for evil and to just stick with the gemstones, which are purified crystals. Satan only mimics God and try to be like him. He mimics everything the Father does, but he twists and perverts it. Meaning he uses it to do evil. The Lord created crystals, stones, and rocks for us to use, and to have dominion over things. Crystals, stones, and rocks are alive and vital. God told mankind to have dominion over the earth**. (Genesis 1:26). Then God said, "Let us make mankind in our image, in our likeness, so that they may rule over the fish in the sea and the birds in the sky, over the livestock and all the wild animals, and over all the creatures that move along the ground**." Genesis 1:26 (NIV). Crystals are part of the earth. But I'd rather say to co-labor with them because they are alive like every other being. It's up to a person whether they use it for good or whether they use it for evil. The bottom line is, it's **good** versus **evil**. Light versus darkness. Right versus wrong. Corruption versus incorruption. Who side will you be on, the Lord's side or Satan?

The Father doesn't want us to get into works; he wants sincere hearts of love. He wants us to commune with him, his son Jesus, and the Holy Spirit. Crystals help assist individuals in hearing the Father, the Son, and the Holy Spirit more clearly, just like the angels do. The Father wants to have fun with his children. But this can only happen if we would let him. Even if people use them for evil because of the influence of Satan to use them for evil, then we know it's not them but the demonic spirit and negative energy influencing that person. **"12 For we wrestle not against flesh and blood, but against principalities, against powers, against the rulers of the darkness of this world, against spiritual wickedness in high places." Ephesians 6:12 (KJV)** And that's okay because the bible talks about that. But God is still in control. In Job, it says, **"16 With him is strength and wisdom: the deceived and the deceiver are his." Job 12:16 (KJV)** So they can only do what the Lord allows them to do, and just like with Job, Satan was only allowed to do to Job what God allowed. **(Job 1:1-8 (KJV)** But, thanks be to God, we have prayer and the extra benefits of crystals to help us. In this book, you will learn the different attributes and uses of crystals. You will know their functions, their personalities/or character, and how it

correlates to help us bear fruit (love, joy, peace, patience, kindness, goodness, and self-control). We will learn how they bring forth healing. We will learn crystal functions and their characteristics because they are alive, just like the angels and everything else on the earth.

Crystals have their own functions and characteristics and are very much alive. They give out different frequencies and vibrations. John even knew that rocks could raise up children unto Abraham in **Matt. 3:7-12 (KJV)** if you read it, he was not just talking about the men as stones who he was baptizing being able to raise up children unto Abraham; it had a deeper meaning because the Lord knew there would be a time such as this to come. It was the stones on the priest breastplate. The Pharisees and Sadducees came to be spectators of John

's baptizing, John knew their heart and knew the evil intentions and pride of the Sadducees. The Pharisees and the Sadducees didn't believe they needed to be baptized unto repentance because they had faith in Abraham, and they believed in the law and works. Inside their hearts wasn't sincere fruit of love, joy, peace, patience, kindness, goodness, and self-control. They had these fruits, but much of it was not sincere, it was just a form of an appearance of godliness. Haven't we all been guilty of this. Thank God for Jesus's blood. But they didn't know the new thing the Lord was birthing forth into the earth in order for men to bear fruit before Christ came on the scene. When he said, out these stones, God can raise children unto Abraham, he not only meant the men he baptized would be able to raise up children and teach others how to walk in faith like Abraham and to minister to them; but also the Lord showed me him pointing to the stones on the priest breastplate because the priest had 12 different stones assigned to each one of the 12 tribes of Israel on their breastplates, each stone representing one of the tribes. Each stone, the priest, wore brung forth different fruits of the sons of Jacob and counteracted each son of Jacob weaknesses or sins so that it would break the curse that was in the bloodline from generation down to generation, which we will talk about in another chapter in more detail.

For example, Issachar: Sapphire Blue Sapphire increases/enhances intuition, mental clarity, and spiritual power, all of which can assist in personal and spiritual growth. Sapphire brings forth spiritual healing and spiritual truth. It brings forth faithfulness and brings for joy, peace, and wisdom. Each crystal that described their lifestyle or what they represented in life was the stone for each son of Israel. Another example was Joseph's stone that represents him, which is named black onyx. We know Joseph went through some trials that could stress a person and drain a person spiritually, mentally, and emotionally; he was kidnapped, traded as a slave, falsely accused of rape, etc. But he had a great destiny. Some of the benefits of black onyx are, it's a powerful protection stone, it shields you

from all negative energy, and helps to prevent the drain of personal energy. Black Onyx aids the development of emotional and physical strength and stamina, especially when support is needed during times of stress, confusion, or grief. It gives courage, endurance, and patience. It reminds you to let go of the things of the past in order to move forward. It is excellent for those starting up businesses. We know Joseph became the next highest man to go to if Pharaoh wasn't around. God speaks once yea twice, but do men perceive it. (Job 33:14 KJV) That even if they had one stone, it would show them what to do under the instruction of the Lord. People wouldn't need to go to the priest for direction or prophecy. Just one crystal by itself can direct and counteract our weaknesses — all by faith.

*Let's go back to John, talking to the Pharisees and Sadducees. "**7 But when he (John) saw many of the Pharisees and Sadducees coming to where he was baptizing, he said to them: "You brood of vipers! Who warned you to flee from the coming wrath? 8 Produce fruit in keeping with repentance. 9 And do not think you can say to yourselves, 'We have Abraham as our father.' <u>I tell you that out of these stones God can raise up children for Abraham.</u> 10 The ax is already at the root of the trees, and every tree that does not produce good fruit will be cut down and thrown into the fire. 11 "I baptize you with water for repentance. But after me comes one who is more powerful than I, whose sandals I am not worthy to carry. He will baptize you with the Holy Spirit and fire. 12 His winnowing fork is in his hand, and he will clear his threshing floor, gathering his wheat into the barn and burning up the chaff with unquenchable fire." Matt 3:7-12 NIV** John knew that each stone has its own character, nature, attributes, and gives messages just like angels. Remember, "speak to the earth, and it will teach you" (Job 12:8 KJV) crystals are part of the earth.*

The only thing a person needs to use to communicate was just one of the gemstones of the priest breastplate in order to know the word of the Lord. Some crystal's characteristics are faith, some joy, some love, some peace, they relay messages, and teaches you new things. Some heal, destroy the works of the enemy both at the same time. But many of them are diverse in their own way because one can bring joy and love, and actually heal your sinuses, your throat, they can help heal your bones, and at the same time protect you from witchcraft, they heal physically mentally and emotionally. Some transmute doubt into faith. They transmute negative energy and turn them into positive energy. Awesome! Like the Lord, Jesus told me, even though their small, they pack a lot of power. *** <u>I also want to explain that this is not to replace any of your medications, consult with a doctor before using the crystals, gemstones, etc. This is only to help give you the knowledge on helping you to benefit in different areas of your life and in your body physically, mentally, emotionally, and spiritually.</u> I have seen the healing power of crystals in my life and in the lives of others. Everyone is different. Healing is one of the gifts I flow in, but sometimes if it doesn't flow through me correctly, it could be something blocking me or a limit I put on myself

that caused me not to be able to lay hands on somebody and for them to receive healing. Or the Lord may say it's just not the time for that person's healing, or they need to go to an actual medical doctor or another specialist. My prophetic gifts increased dramatically using crystals.

Chapter 2: Christ Being the Rock of All Rocks (Crystals, Stones, Rocks, and Gemstones)

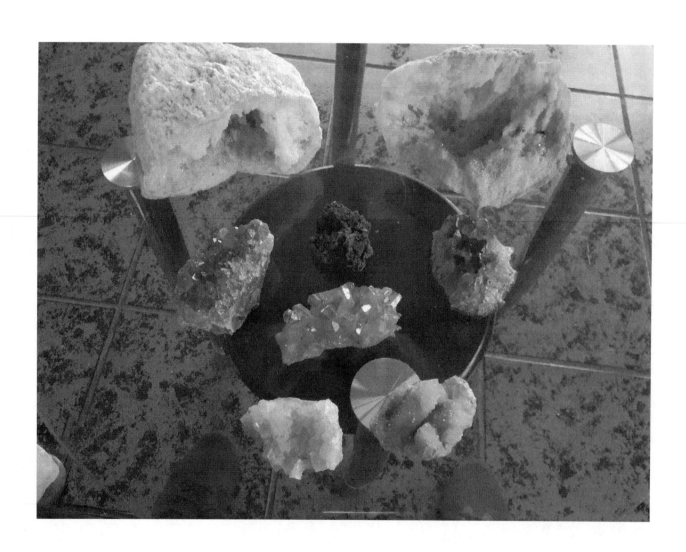

The Father gave Christ as a gift for us to receive and have everlasting life, and to remove our sins. All through the bible, Christ is known as the rock because of the multifaceted characteristics that rocks/stones/crystals can do. We see Christ as the rock in the book of Daniel Chapter 2 (KJV) with the statue of King Nebuchadnezzar and the other kingdoms. King Nebuchadnezzar's head on the statue was gold representing his kingdom Babylon, then his chest and arm made up of silver representing the Medo-Persia Kingdom, next the brass belly and thighs represent the Grecians Kingdom, as you go down you see legs of Iron which represented the Kingdom of Rome. The feet of iron and clay represent the divided kingdoms of the world. A stone was cut out of the mountains without hands. The stone broke in pieces all the kingdoms and consumed them. All were destroyed by one rocked carved out of the mountain without hands, and that rock is Christ, and his kingdom will consume and destroyed all the other kingdoms. And we will talk more about the different things that small living rock accomplished, which is himself Christ Jesus. It shows that though it was small, it destroyed kingdoms, and that shows you can remove the kingdom of darkness and its demonic forces by using the stones. You don't even have to fight; they do the work for you, through your intentions. If you pray and decree and declare the word of God according to God's divine will, then they will obey. They have the gift of grace, which came through Christ the Living Rock. That's why Christ is known himself as a rock because he is the Living Rock of all living rocks. David said, **"For who is God save the LORD? or who is a rock save our God?" Psalms 18:31 (KJV)**

We see David took one small stone and killed the giant Goliath, who was over 9ft. David magnified the Lord and knew if he protected him from the bear and the lion, then God he would protect Israel and win the battle for them, David says, **"You come against me with sword and spear and javelin, but I come against you in the name of the Lord Almighty, the God of the armies of Israel, whom you have defied. 46 This day the Lord will deliver you into my hands, and I'll strike you down and cut off your head. This very day I will give the carcasses of the Philistine army to the birds and the wild animals, and the whole world will know that there is a God in Israel. 47 All those gathered here will know that it is not by sword or spear that the Lord saves; for the battle is the Lord's, and he will give all of you into our hands." 1 Samuel 17:45-47 (KJV)** *Just as David stated, the Lord performed through a tiny stone. It struck Goliath and sunk into his head by the power within it which is Christ the Rock" Hallelujah. Christ is the rock of all rocks. Christ is the living stone.* **1 Peter 2:3,4 (KJV)** *says,* **"If so being ye have tasted that the Lord is gracious. To whom coming, as unto a living stone, disallowed indeed of men, but chosen of God, and precious,"** *in the NIV Version Stone is capitalized because Christ is the chief of all stones. Then further down the next verse calls us lively stones, its states in verse* **"5 Ye also as lively stones, are built up a spiritual house, and holy priesthood, to offer up spiritual sacrifices, acceptable to God by Jesus Christ." 1 Peter 2:5 (KJV)**

*We see in verse 5 stone was lower case. It's not just calling us lively stones cause of our bone structure in our body or calling Jesus a living stone because he came as the Father in the form of an earthly man with bones. But each Crystal, stone, or rock have their own facets, uniqueness, characteristics (love, joy, peace, etc.), functions (heal, physically, mentally, and emotionally), and duty (protect offensively and defensively), by the Father through Christ Jesus. Christ is the Rock of all Rocks because he has birth forth the diversity of each rock/stone/crystal/gem in the representation of him. Every function they do, Christ does it all. Even though you may not recognize the name of a particular stone by its shape and color, each stone, crystal, or clusters are uniquely designed with their own signature or fingerprint because of their size, or shape, or color may be different from the others. You may have some stones with the same name but a different color. Like you have the crystal named Carnelian, but you have some that are light orange, some almost dark red. The characteristics, benefits, and functions of the light orange carnelian differ from a dark orange carnelian stone. For example, an orange carnelian is assigned to the Sacral Chakra/Wheel, and a red carnelian is assigned to the Root Chakra/Wheel. Even when you separate the orange carnelian stones in a group, each one has the same exact function, but it has **its** own signature because something may be slightly different about the shape. Here's another scripture that describes the different diversities and characteristics of rocks and how they relate to us benefiting from them.*

"13 Hear, ye that are far off, what I have done; and, ye that are near, acknowledge my might. 14 The sinners in Zion are afraid; fearfulness hath surprised the hypocrites. Who among us shall dwell with the devouring fire? who among us shall dwell with everlasting burnings? 15 He that walketh righteously, and speaketh uprightly; he that despiseth the gain of oppressions, that shaketh his hands from holding of bribes, that stoppeth his ears from hearing of blood, and shutteth his eyes from seeing evil; <u>16 He shall dwell on high: his place of defence shall be the munitions of rocks:</u> bread shall be given him; his waters shall be sure. 17 Thine eyes shall see the king in his beauty: they shall behold the land that is very far off." Is. 33:13-17 (KJV)

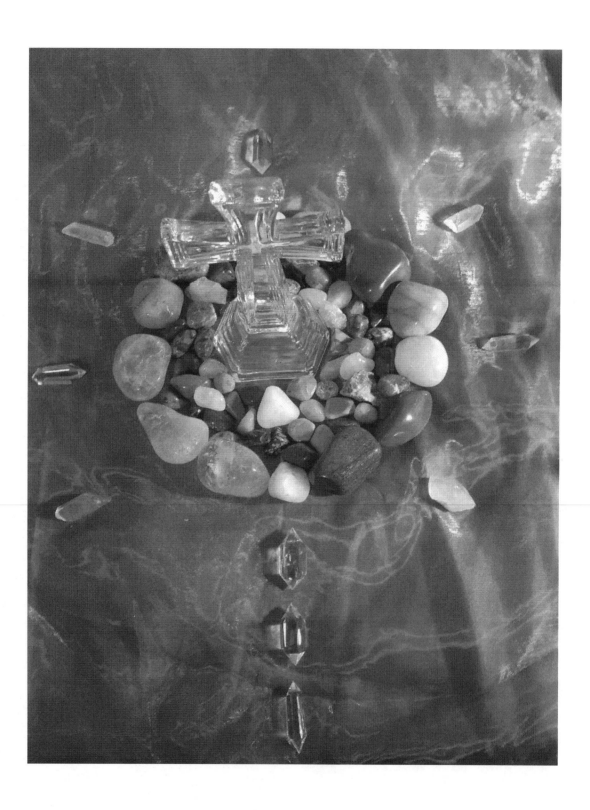

We see here that Christ gives a distinction of who will see him, we know it will be the pure in heart, those that do good and turn away from evil deeds, those

who walketh righteously. We see Christ talks about the defense being the munition of rocks. He wasn't just talking about a fortress, as some say, each rock that created that fortress is different. During the war, people hide behind trenches of rocks opposite of the side of their opponents during the war. Though they hide behind the different rocks, each rock still has its own functions, and minerals, and signature, yet those rocks would protect the soldiers. But if those rocks would hide and protect the soldiers from being hit by a bullet, arrow, etc., just like the fortress would, but in a different way; How much more will the different Crystals, stones, gemstones protect you through Christ who is the Rock of all rocks and mediator between the Father and Man. The munition of rocks is different diversity of rocks, their different function, benefits, offense, and defense used as weapons and shields to protect a person spiritually, mentally, emotionally, physically, and financially. That's the mystery revealed.

Some people used rocks to make axes and make the spearhead out of rocks to protect them from the opposer if it tried to come near them. But the point I'm trying to make is, how much more will the crystals protect you. What are the weapons and shields you have from the crystals, is it fruitfulness, love, joy, peace, patience, kindness, goodness, faithfulness, gentleness, and self - control against these there is no law? **(Gal 5:22,23 NLT)**, so, therefore, you are not moved by the trials in life. For instance, love could be a weapon against those who oppose you, it may convict their hearts of the darkness in their hearts, and they may repent and see you now in a good way because love conquers all. Another good use of crystals is that they transmute negative energy into positive energy as a shield round about you. Crystals help remove negative energy or demonic spirits by bringing forth an increase of angels to fight and destroy demonic spirits as a weapon. Maybe your weapon or shield is healthy because it protects you from sickness and disease. Maybe your shield and protection are discernment and wisdom, so you know how to bring peace or avoid negative situations. Crystals increase your intuition and bring forth the increase in the seer realm (see, hear, smell, touch, feel), or the prophetic; they help you offensively and defensively. They reveal the truth, help you grow spiritually, mentally, and emotionally through Christ the Rock.

That's why Christ Jesus is known as the Rock if you look back in **Isaiah 33:16 (KJV) he said, "those who live righteously shall dwell on high, his place of defense shall be the munition of rocks, but it says bread shall be given him who is the living bread Christ, and waters shall be sure."** What are those waters? Living waters through Holy spirit, his word, speaking life over yourself. Though people may misuse Jehovah's (Yahweh, YOD HEY VAV HEY) gift which is his son the Rock (crystal, stone, gemstone, or rock) in the wrong way by the grace his son gives through the rock or crystal, it's okay; God is in full control. **Job 12:16 (KJV) says, 16 "With him is strength and wisdom: the deceived and the deceiver are his."** People who do evil things purposely are doing it by demonic influence or possession; we know that's not them but a demonic spirit

because some have made covenants with Satan. If a demonic spirit is broken down into matter, it is negative energy, and when you break it down more, then you will see positive Ions. Even though positive ions sound like they are right, scientifically, we know they are wrong. Positive ions is negative energy that weighs people down. That's why many people feel burdened or weighed down. That's why we bind negative spirits, negative energies, and command demonic spirits, and negative energy to go. And loose the energies, frequencies, and vibrations of the Father, the Son, and the Holy Ghost, or loose what the spirit tells you to loose. But, the crystals do it by itself. When I needed fear to be removed, all I needed was amethyst, and it removed (bind) fear and stress, and it gave me peace (to loose) instead. Wow!

"1Truly my soul waiteth upon God: from him cometh my salvation.

2 He only is my rock and my salvation; he is my defence; I shall not be greatly moved.

3 How long will ye imagine mischief against a man? ye shall be slain all of you: as a bowing wall shall ye be, and as a tottering fence.

4 They only consult to cast him down from his excellency: they delight in lies: they bless with their mouth, but they curse inwardly. Selah.

5 My soul, wait thou only upon God; for my expectation is from him.

6 He only is my rock and my salvation: he is my defense; I shall not be moved." Psalms 62:1-7 (KJV)

Crystals are so unique; they have certain ones whose jobs are to bind and to transmute negative energy into positive energy. There are crystals assigned to break soul ties. There are some crystals that keep demonic spirits out of your house. Their uses are many. They have crystals assigned to break witchcraft. They have crystal assigned to help remove negative thoughts from our minds and impart positive thoughts. We will talk about this also in a later chapter. Christ is in all things; he is in full control. It's because of the fall of Satan that sin entered the world. But the Father knew what Satan was up to before Satan knew himself because the Father knows the end of all things from the beginning. By the sins of man, things have become corrupted, unhealthy, polluted, abused, misused, and used for wrong purposes by the influence of Satan and the other fallen angels that fell with him out of heaven and chose to work for him. Even though people may misuse crystals for doing wrong, it's okay, because again, Christ is in full control. Hallelujah!! 1 Cor 11 KJV, shows that Christ is the head of every man. **"But I would have you know, that the head of every man is Christ; and the head of the woman is the man; and the head of Christ is God." 1 Cor11:3 (KJV)** We see that Christ is the King of Kings and the Lord of Lords. Bread of Life, he's the Living stone of all stones because he's in all. We will see

later on, the different characteristics of some crystals their functions and how they help bring healing.

Chapter 3: Crystals Are Alive

Crystals hear, speak, witness, and keep a record

Crystals speak although you may not necessarily hear them, they speak to you through energy, frequency, and vibration as their own language. They help you hear in the realm of the spirit more. Just like with a radio station, without the clear quartz crystal, you wouldn't be able to hear the radio station clearly. The crystal work with the frequency of the antenna for you to hear the radio. You wouldn't be able to hear the radio station any other way without the crystal quartz because its frequencies get in tune with the radio station's satellite frequency. "**2 Day unto day uttereth speech, and night unto night sheweth knowledge.3 There is no speech nor language, where their voice is not heard." Ps. 19:2,3 (KJV)** Meaning all things seen that you may not hear, speaks like the stars, the moon and they give off frequencies, vibrations, energies, that you may not hear in the physical, but their existence tells prophecy of the coming of Christ and future events to take place. The Zodiac is based on the twelve tribes of Israel and gives the prophecy, which is a witness of the coming messiah, the stars prophesy about Jesus. Even by the meaning of their names tells messages of the Lord. Yet they speak. They make sure the prophecies come to past in the universe and the earth. You may see a cloud in the shape of the cross, with the shape of a man's body, though it may not speak in the natural language that I usually hear, I know its pictorial language represents Christ's death and his resurrection to remove all sin from man. And we know it represents the gift of Holy Spirit who is now able to dwell inside of man once they are reborn.

I love the book of Job because it reveals so much knowledge, at first, I didn't like to read it because it was always about the woe is me, and most people who read it always were going through trials and tribulations. I would always try to skip over Job unless the Lord led me to it to read, which he did, so I couldn't get around it, unfortunately. So, I would always read it once a year just so I could have my whole bible read every year. But now I see why people have come to appreciate Job in moments when opposition comes, the Lord comforts, but the Lord also reveals secrets, mysteries, and truth in Job. Let's talk about Jobs's opposition with Zophar and how it relates to receiving messages from crystals and Christ our rock, Hallelujah!! I'm excited!

And Job answered and said,

*"**2 No doubt but ye are the people, and wisdom shall die with you.**

3 But I have understanding as well as you; I am not inferior to you: yea, who knoweth not such things as these?

4 I am as one mocked of his neighbour, who calleth upon God, and he answereth him: the just upright man is laughed to scorn.*

5 He that is ready to slip with his feet is as a lamp despised in the thought of him that is at ease.

6 The tabernacles of robbers prosper, and they that provoke God are secure; into whose hand God bringeth abundantly.

7 But ask now the beasts, and they shall teach thee; and the fowls of the air, and they shall tell thee:

8 Or speak to the earth, and it shall teach thee: *and the fishes of the sea* **shall declare unto thee.**

9 Who knoweth not in all these that the hand of the Lord hath wrought this?

10 In whose hand is the soul of every living thing, and the breath of all mankind.

11 Doth not the ear try words? and the mouth taste his meat?

12 With the ancient is wisdom; and in length of days understanding.

13 With him is wisdom and strength, he hath counsel and understanding." **Job 12:2-13 (KJV)**

   Though Job accusers or brethern were men full of knowledge and understanding, Job gave them honor for who they are; also, he recognized who he was in Christ and the knowledge he had of the Father as well. This knowledge was revealed through the close relationship he had with the Father. He also humbled himself and even told them in humility, I'm not inferior to you. So much courage he had, and humility he had, I love that about Job. Then Job begins to release truth he said, **"But ask now the beast, and they shall teach thee, and the fowls of the air, and they should tell thee:"** *Job 12:7 (KJV)*

   It has always been me and my husband's prayer every morning for the Lord to provide protection over our children and us. I literally never heard squirrels talk, I just always seen them skipping along the way and chewing on food, but this one time me and my husband was leaving out of the house to go to the van and this squirrel was literally on the tree looking at us and pointing to a dog, and you could hear its voice sound like a human voice all though not clear. He made his point across for us to watch out as a warning. My husband and I was in aww when we witnessed that. It threw me out of my element, I was like, "Did this just

happen?" It literally with his hand pointed to the dog! So, animals that you usually don't hear talk actually can talk to you. Just like the donkey talked to Balaam to let him know he couldn't pass the angel.

"27 When the donkey saw the angel of the Lord, it lay down under Balaam, and he was angry and beat it with his staff. 28 Then the Lord opened the donkey's mouth, and it said to Balaam, "What have I done to you to make you beat me these three times?"

29 Balaam answered the donkey, "You have made a fool of me! If only I had a sword in my hand, I would kill you right now."

30 The donkey said to Balaam, "Am I not your own donkey, which you have always ridden, to this day? Have I been in the habit of doing this to you?"

"No," he said.

31 Then the Lord opened Balaam's eyes, and he saw the angel of the Lord standing in the road with his sword drawn. So, he bowed low and fell facedown.

32 The angel of the Lord asked him, "Why have you beaten your donkey these three times? I have come here to oppose you because your path is a reckless one before me 33 The donkey saw me and turned away from me these three times. If it had not turned away, I would certainly have killed you by now, but I would have spared it." Numbers 22:21-35 (KJV)

Birds are one of the ways the Father speaks to me ever since I gave my life to Christ. Whenever I have seen a Blue Jay, I knew the Father was going to reveal to me that day an answer to a question, a secret, revelation, or something supernatural, a prophetic word to me directly, or send a man or woman of God to prophesy into my life. I want to make one thing clear. The Lord can use anyone or anything to give you a prophetic word; he can use someone in the grocery store, a psychic, someone on the street, or a regular person, he can use someone that is drunk to give a prophetic word. I have witnessed it. That's why he's God all by himself because all things are in him, and he's in full control of your destiny. We must show love and not be prejudice towards anyone. That is one thing the Lord has put on my heart to say to the believers of Christ. If we judge a person or turn away from somebody because they may not fit whom you would like them to be, then you can miss out on a blessing. We have been very prejudice in the church. People have callings, but just because they use their gifts through other avenues, doesn't mean for us to look down on them, they are still fulfilling their calling, they may not be born again just yet. They are still going by the book that is written of them, that the Lord chose for them. **"Then said I, Lo, I come: in the volume of the book it is written of me, I delight to do thy will, O my**

*God: yea,   thy   law is within   my   heart."
(Psalm 40:7,8 KJV)* Paul did mirror scrying with black obsidian in **1 Corinthians 13:12 (KJV)**. He looked in the black obsidian crystal glass, and it revealed truth and prophecy. I will explain that more in detail later on.

"12 For now we see through a glass, darkly; but then face to face: now I know in part; but then shall I know even as also I am known." 1 Corinthians 13:12 (KJV)

There are many born again psychics, but because of the state of the church, they stay at home because we tell them they can't be psychic or use crystal balls, oracle card reading, or do palm reading. There's a very fine line. Some are of the enemy; some are not. Everything the Lord put on this earth, he made it be used for his purpose of spreading the kingdom, not man's kingdom. The enemy has perverted so many things; that's why the Lord is restoring everything back to its original intent. We must break our pride, self-righteousness, and prejudice ways and learn sincere **love**.

I know born again believers in Christ (pastors included) that have gotten full detailed prophetic words from psychics about their calling in the Lord, and who they're God-ordained spouse was, and what the Lord was going to do in their life. Now they are fulfilling their ministry in Christ. I know believers in Christ who have gotten prophesied on what the Lord called them to do, and now they are fulfilling their calling in Christ Jesus. When the Lord started to tell me about crystals, the first thing I needed to know was about crystal balls. Whenever I see different colors, it represents the 7 spirits of God, or he may highlight certain scriptures in colors. I was reading an article about crystal balls because I knew that people would bring up crystal balls because crystals are used for divination or prophecy, and I wanted to know the truth for myself. So, I was reading an article on how John Dee found Queen Elizabeth's coin using the crystal ball, and I see in red a dot at the beginning of the sentence that said good spirits come in a relay's messages. So, I knew that was the Spirit of the Lord confirming, yes, they are used to reveal prophetic words through angels and other righteous beings. Just like the priest used the gemstones on the priest's breastplate for the use of divination (prophecy). If a person is influenced by a demonic spirit or negative energy and they channel through a demonic spirit, then you know that the crystal is being used for evil uses, and they are channeling or going through negative entities or energies. They have to do what a person tells them to do because that is one of their functions or protocols the Father has told it to do. We are going to talk about this further down in another chapter. When it comes down to crystal balls, I remember seeing a picture at my old church of Jesus holding the world in his hand and looking down into it. He gazes on the outside the earth through its aura, then he focuses further into the cloud, then into the land, then into the house, then into a person's heart or creations heart. Then he gazes more intently even down to the earth's core to see. Talk about 20/20 vision, where you

zoom into more details of things by what you see. Crystal balls were meant to bring clarity and prophecies. This was originally the Father's intent. The crystal balls are to help people see and prophesy and part of communing with the Father through Holy Spirit. Again, with what we will see with Apostle Paul. It was part of having a relationship with him through his son Jesus the Rock. Jesus is the door to the Father; he is the medium whom we go through in all things through the Father. The earth, crystals, sun, moon, and stars all work in conjunction to bring forth prophecies through Christ through the Father. People say that's fortune-telling, what do you think fortune-telling is? It's prophecy. We have to change our perception of things. But again, the enemy perverts everything and mimics everything that had a righteous intent for good and twists it for evil. You cannot be afraid to step outside the box when it comes to the things of God unless you don't grow spiritually, mentally, emotionally.

We often go into panic mode when we see crystal balls, we get afraid and in panic mode because how it has been portrayed in the media and yes from what the bible says. But it was men of old who used them just like the high priest, it may not have been in the same way, but it was still divination. So, we have been deceived in a lot of cases. So, in turn, God can use anyone and anything to speak and relay messages. It never fails when I see a blue jay, I know the Lord is going to reveal a secret or answer one of my prayers. Whenever I see a cardinal bird, I know the Lord is putting things in order and in direct alignment. I know he also is hearing my prayers and my conversation with him. It's been times where The Father would send a cardinal bird to confirm an answer that Holy Spirit just gave me within a split second the cardinal bird would appear at the same time Holy Spirit is giving the answer. Even if he doesn't release the answer right then and there, he will send the cardinal bird to let me know he's listening. I remember saying I couldn't eat after 10 am, and I started eating after 10 o'clock am, and the bird was chirping away louder and louder, telling me you know you are not supposed to be eating that, remember what you said. I couldn't believe it. I felt so guilty after that. I went to a meditation class, and the instructor said, did anyone have a bird give you a message. At the time, I thought she was talking about if we had a vision of birds during meditation. Holy Spirit reminded me, Terika remembers this morning the bird was chirping telling you and reminding you not to eat after 10 am, I said, "Yes, I do remember." So, I let the instructor know she wasn't crazy; it was me the bird had talked to because when she asked, no one encountered a bird talking to them.

This is the scripture I love, he says, **"Or speak to the earth, and it shall teach thee: and the fishes of the sea shall declare unto thee." Job 12:8 KJV** Wow! That is totally awesome. I remember after reading this scripture, I said okay, Lord, I'm going to speak to the earth like your scripture says to do. So, I said Earth, mother earth, teach me something that I don't know. I heard the

enemy say, *"You sound stupid; nothing's going to happen."* I had to kill that thought out of my mind. I honestly didn't know that the earth will teach you things if you ask, you may have known this, but I literally didn't know this until this scripture showed up. I knew you could learn about the ways on how things function on the earth by what they do, I knew you could tell the earth to things, and it will do it because the power the Lord gave to us as a man to have dominion. So that night, the earth answered my prayer. Why? The earth is in the Lord and is made out of him. *"**1 The earth is the Lord's, and the fulness thereof; the world, and they that dwell therein. "Psalm 24:1 (KJV) Job 12:10 (KJV)** says, "**10 In whose hand is the soul of every living thing, and the breath of all mankind."***

So, in my dream, my husband was on stage, I was dancing on the side, and I was feeling the different frequencies, vibrations, and energy as I spanned. Then, in the dream, it showed me a young lady that I went to high school with, that I needed to intercede for, and the funny thing was she was eating a dandelion, and it was good. So, I'm saying to myself, *"Lord dandelion is a type of weed flower, I know in the word of God weed represents sin."* So, I knew I had to pray, intercede, and stand in the gap for the removal of certain things of sin that was in her life and to pray for her salvation. But then the Holy Spirit said, *"Terika, it's a double meaning, she's eating on the dandelion for a reason also because she was eating it, and it was delicious."* So, I said, *"Okay, Lord."* So, I looked up dandelion and its benefits. One of the benefits is that it's known as the miracle weed in an article I read. The Lord is so funny he knows how to break a religious mindset off of me, thank you, Lord. I found out all this research about Dandelion, thank you Mother Earth for being alive and teaching me as the Bible says for you to do as part of the Kingdom of God.

1. Dandelion is known as a blood sugar balancer, and it helps diabetics.
2. Dandelion contains a substance known as alpha-glucosidase;
3. it is said to be nature's blood-sugar reducer. Wow!
4. Diabetes has been treated by dandelion for many years
5. People with diabetes should talk to their own physician to observe their blood sugar levels because of the effects dandelion root tea
6. It's so effective it reduces the medications for those who are diabetic
7. It's an energizer,
8. Anti-inflammatory
9. it reduces fatigue and increases your immune system.
10. It burns fat because of its effect on the liver.
11. Dandelion root boosts liver function and increases the rate of fat metabolism in two ways: by regulating the liver to produce more bile to send to the gallbladder, which in turn helps to burn fat, and second, it causes the gallbladder to contract and release its stored bile, therefore increasing fat metabolism.

12.   Dandelions can also help reset our hormone balance. Therefore, we stop keeping as much fat, heal our cells in order to multiply our energy levels, and speed up your metabolism so that weight melts off.

13.   It's known as an anti-cancer powerhouse.

14.   Dandelion's most exceptional therapeutic promise is its ability to fight cancer.

15.   Canadian scientists found out that after forty-eight hours of contact with dandelion extract, the cancer cells begin to perish. Research also found that dandelion was useful in cancer cells that were unaffected to chemotherapy.

16.   Tea, made from dandelion leaves, reduced the development of breast cancer cells, while a tea made from dandelion root, blocked the ability of cancer cells to invade healthy breast and prostate tissue.

17.   Also, dandelion root help to multiply the effectiveness of other cancer treatments used with it: blood purifier and immune booster.

18.   Studies found that dandelion drastically multiplied both red and white blood cell counts, making it a possible aid in the treatment of anemia, blood <u>purification</u>, and immune system modulation.

19.   It's known to have an advanced track record of boosting your health, especially against E. coli, Bacillus subtilis, and MRSA

20.   Studies have showed that an extract of dandelion root was able to selectively and quickly kill cancer cells without toxicity to <u>healthy cells</u>.

Researchers say dandelion root have "great potential as non-toxic and effective alternatives to conventional modes of chemotherapy available today." According to a study published in the journal Molecular Carcinogenesis, one of the ways that dandelion root seems to fight cancer is by making tumor cells more susceptible to the natural process known as apoptosis, which causes to kill their own selves. In a study published in Advances in Hematology, studies Researchers have added the role of superbug killer to the dandelion's impressive health-boosting resume; by this, it shows to be effective against the bacteria E. coli, Bacillus subtilis, and MRSA. It prevents osteoporosis. It improves your brain function and memory. It fights off urinary tract infections.

Wow! Talk about talking to the earth! All things on the earth are in the Lord and are here on earth for a reason. Nothing is without use. So how much more are the uses of crystals, they are part of the earth and have been on the earth for billions of years. They keep record in the earth, and if you speak to them directly, they will give you the answer and solution just like the earth. Because they are part of the earth, the earth is made out of them. They get direct orders from the Lord if you prayed over them and consecrated them to the Lord. David said, **"The LORD liveth; and blessed be my rock; and let the God of my salvation be exalted." Psalms 18:46** So if you decide to get them, make sure you pray over them and ask the Father to bless them and consecrate them unto himself and

anything that is not of him, any witchcraft, spell, demonic spirits, imbalances, or negative energies, for him to remove them from them. They have been touched by other people and their energy/and spirit, so that's why you pray and ask the Lord to cleanse them of anybody else's energy that has touched them, that you may get a bad vibe from.

*So, ask the crystal what's on the Lord's agenda for today, it just might tell you. Or ask a crystal a question, it may talk to you just like the angels or show you a vision. They minister to us just like the angels do. Even the ancient civilizations knew this. Even though they may not have been Jewish, Christ still revealed knowledge to all mankind and all nationalities. Even when it came to the fall of the tower of Babel, we know the Lord told secrets, revealed mysteries, knowledge, and understanding to all mankind before he changed their languages. That's why he changed their languages because when the mysteries and secrets were revealed about how the elements work, and how the cosmos work; Lord knew they would try to change the way heaven functioned, and they would try to change the way things worked, and operated, even exalt themselves above him, which we see today. That's why they said, let's make a name for ourselves. The Father knew they could mess up his original intent of the way the heavens or the universe are to function. And they would have exalted themselves above him and forget who made them. "**That's why the LORD said, as one people speaking the same language they have begun to do this, then nothing they plan to do will be impossible for them. Therefore, he confounded their language." Genesis 11:6 NIV** So all different nations had an understanding of mysteries and secrets, that's why Jesus said, "**And the eye cannot say unto the hand, I have no need of thee: nor again the head to the feet, I have no need of you." 1 Cor 12:21(KJV)** We can gain knowledge and information from each other so no one can exalt themselves above another person. Or one nationality can exalt itself against another nationality. Because we are all in him, and we get out knowledge from him. You will know if something is off because God gives us discernment and his word to find out the truth from error.*

If the earth can speak, if the animals can speak, numbers speak. We know the crystals are stones and are a major part of the earth and have been on the earth for millions of years if not, billions of years. They keep a record of what has been done on earth as well as in heaven. They give out vibrations. Just like in heaven, it talks about the heavens shaking. It's because different frequencies are coming together along with specific vibrations in the heavenly realm. And we know that as in the heavenly, then so it is on earth. That's why Jesus said when we pray, say, "Our Heavenly Father hallowed be thy name thy kingdom come, thy will be done, in earth as in, heaven, give us this day our daily bread. (Matthew 9:6-13 KJV) The earth is a replica of heaven. That's why when the rocks or mountains collide together; there is shaking and earthquakes from the vibrations and frequencies of the rocks colliding together. And it is powerful, yet scary if

you are going through that earthquake that's why we declare peace over that region.

*We also know in the throne room of the Father there is thunder and shakings. Jesus said if the disciples didn't praise him, the rocks would immediately cry out. Why? Rocks (crystals) have their own language through vibrations and frequency. They probably would have spoken in an actually heard language to hear them speak too. "Touching the King who can find him out." part of **Job 37:23 (KJV)** Even though we don't hear them, they can give a message. "**37 And when he was come nigh, even now at the descent of the mount of Olives, the whole multitude of the disciples began to rejoice and praise God with a loud voice for all the mighty works that they had seen;38 Saying, Blessed be the King that cometh in the name of the Lord: peace in heaven, and glory in the highest.39 And some of the Pharisees from among the multitude said unto him, Master, rebuke thy disciples.40 And he answered and said unto them, I tell you that, if these should hold their peace, the stones would immediately cry out.41 And when he was come near, he beheld the city, and wept over it,42 Saying, If thou hadst known, even thou, at least in this thy day, the things which belong unto thy peace!,but now they are hid from thine eyes. "Luke 19:37-41(KJV)** The rocks would cry out, sing praises as a witness of the King of Glory being there, the coming Messiah was right before them, the Savior of the world! Hallelujah!!!!!!!!!!*

During that time, heaven was releasing different frequencies and vibration unto man because heavens divine timetable was being revealed in heavens calendar. A significant event in history was happening in the earth. A shifting was taking place in the earth, and heaven was rejoicing, so the people on earth had to rejoice as well. So, the rocks would cry out and praise the Lord. The rocks are a witness and keep a record of things on earth and the records in heaven because they are linked through Christ, the Messiah, and Mediator. They will testify of Christ. Even in the book of Joshua when the Israelites start turning to other gods and Joshua renewed their covenant with the Lord, he also stated that the stone he placed, heard the words of the Lord (which means the word of God and the Father's Voice) and also that the stone would be against the Israelites if they turn back and start to serve other gods or deny the Father altogether.

*"**20 If you forsake the Lord and serve foreign gods, he will turn and bring disaster on you and make an end of you, after he has been good to you."***

*21 **But the people said to Joshua, "No! We will serve the Lord."***

*22 **Then Joshua said, "You are witnesses against yourselves that you have chosen to serve the Lord."***

"Yes, we are witnesses," they replied.

23 "Now then," said Joshua, "throw away the foreign gods that are among you and yield your hearts to the Lord, the God of Israel."

24 And the people said to Joshua, "We will serve the Lord our God and obey him."

25 On that day Joshua made a covenant for the people, and there at Shechem he reaffirmed for them decrees and laws. 26 And Joshua recorded these things in the Book of the Law of God. Then he took a large stone and set it up there under the oak near the holy place of the Lord.

27 "See!" he said to all the people. "This stone will be a witness against us. It has heard all the words the Lord has said to us. It will be a witness against you if you are untrue to your God."

28 Then Joshua dismissed the people, each to their own inheritance. Joshua." 24:20-29 (NIV)

So, we see that crystals are alive beings because they are witnesses. We see here that they keep record and knows what happens in history. In Joshua, it stated that the stone heard all the words of the Lord that were spoken to them. Jesus never said if the Sadducees will hear them cry out, but what he was saying was that they would cry out by their own language of frequencies and vibrations. Believe it or not, it can be by a physical voice if he wanted them to. The rocks (crystals) honor the King because they know he is in them as a whole. Crystals can relay a message and minister by a dream or vision, just like the angels do. Sometimes we hear angels speak sometimes we don't. It's the same with crystals. Their frequency becomes in tune with your frequency and vibration in order to keep your reception clearer to receive messages from heaven or what they can release. Their frequency and vibrations released are to help your body heal physically, mentally, emotionally, and spiritually. They are employed by the father to help us, to minister unto us, they give an increasing measure of grace on top of the grace Christ gave us because they are also what completes our armor, which we will talk about in another chapter. They give us unction and show us things. They teach us things. They are witnesses of the earth, and they also keep a record of what happened in the earth since they have been on this earth for millions of years. They are in Christ and are witnesses and helpers, just like the angels. They are collaborating with us to help us. We will talk more about the armor in another chapter.

Impart Living Waters of Christ

"They all ate the same spiritual food, and drank the same spiritual drink; for they drank from the spiritual rock that accompanied them, and that Rock was Christ." 1Cor 10:3-5 NIV *As spoken in the previous paragraphs, we learned that crystals hear. It was so funny because I was thinking about Moses losing the promise of God just because he didn't tell the rock for water to come out because the Lord was trying to show him part of the stones duties which is a manifestation which we will talk about later on in the book. So, I wanted to see proof that water can come out of the rock. So, I had a black tourmaline on my desk to protect me from harmful EMFs. So, I spoke to the black tourmaline and said, "Black Tourmaline, give me rivers of living water, I almost wanted to laugh because I was saying to myself, I know this is not about to happen, and it didn't.*

 Black Tourmaline

However, I noticed my lips started to close in a gentle way, and my throat just started to drink supernaturally. And I wanted to scream because of excitement, but I didn't want to spoil the moment, so I kept drinking in the realm of the spirit, living waters of Christ was flowing through my black tourmaline stone, and I was drinking the depths of Christ character that was within my black tourmaline. I felt so uplifted, calm, and full of so much joy that the more I drunk in the spirit, the more I got drunk in the Holy Ghost. "The kingdom of heaven is righteousness, peace, and joy in the Holy Ghost." (Romans 14:17 KJV) I started laughing so hard, and I couldn't contain it. I had overwhelming joy! I have noticed this with black tourmaline that it removes stress and tension. It uplifts and brings joy, peace of mind; I it removes distractions and stress very quickly. So, what I learned is depending on the character and fruit each crystal has, when you drink from it you will receive that perfect frequency of their character of fruit which we will talk about in the next paragraph. Jesus is awesome. So not only do we receive living waters through speaking in tongues and the word of God, but also through the crystals, especially when you understand the revelation that Christ himself is the rock which you carry or hold, and it follows you just like it did the Israelites.

Crystals have Characteristics

Crystals have characteristics. Some are known for joy, peace, love, compassion, patience, and protectors. We will talk about why they are known as

protectors in another chapter. Rubies are known for love, confidence,

courage, integrity, and honesty. Carbuncle (Garnet) has a characteristic

of intimacy and love. Rose quartz is known for love, kindness, and it's

very nurturing and caring. Celestite is known for the energy of calmness,

serenity, joy, purity, and peace. Citrine is known for the energy of joy,

a cheer upper for me, encourager, and high energy. Green Aventurine is known for abundance, life, joy, and prosperity. Prosperity doesn't only mean money, but prosperity also means fruitfulness. But it works for prosperity in both money and fruitfulness. Topaz cheers you up, brings laughter, and harmony.

Amethyst is known for relaxation, patience, clarity, and protection stone,

and it removes negative triggers. Black Tourmaline is known for patience and to relieve stress and a protector, and it's one of my favorites during tests and trials; it also brings laughter.

Crystals Sense - Protectors

Everything that you see, if you break them down, they are broken down into energy, matter, electrons, protons, positive ions, negative ions, etc. Crystals remove negative energies and thoughts from your body and your gateway/chakra/wheels of your body. And replace them with positive energy, just like Jesus did many of times. **"4 And when Jesus was come into Peter's house, he saw his wife's mother laid, and sick of a fever.**
15 And he touched her hand, and the fever left her: and she arose, and ministered unto them.16 When the even was come, they brought unto him many that were possessed with devils: and he cast out the spirits with his word, and healed all that were sick:17 That it might be fulfilled which was spoken by Esaias the prophet, saying, Himself took our infirmities, and bare our sicknesses." Matt.8:14-17(KJV) *We also see this on the cross by his stripes he took for every sin, sickness, infirmity, weakness, curses he took on himself that when he rose from the dead in exchange, man would be saved and set free from these things (demonic spirits, negative energies, curses where sickness and disease originally comes from) so that they would have life, and that more abundantly.*

It's like the woman with the issue of blood Jesus took on the nature of being the rock because of the awesome things that he created them to do. The woman kept paying doctors to help heal her, and she received no results. She touched Jesus and was immediately healed, and delivered, Jesus the rock felt positive energy (of the anointing and power), flow out of him in order to set her free.

"43 And a woman having an issue of blood twelve years, which had spent all her living upon physicians, neither could be healed of any,44 Came behind him, and touched the border of his garment: and immediately her issue of blood stanched.

45 And Jesus said, Who touched me? When all denied, Peter and they that were with him said, Master, the multitude throng thee and press thee, and sayest thou, Who touched me?

46 And Jesus said, Somebody hath touched me: for I perceive that virtue is gone out of me.

47 And when the woman saw that she was not hid, she came trembling and falling down before him. She declared unto him before all the people for what cause she had touched him and how she was healed immediately.

48 And he said unto her, Daughter, be of good comfort: thy faith hath made thee whole; go in peace." Luke 8:43-48 (KJV)

Jesus himself took on the woman's infirmity, and it diminished instantaneously because no sickness or disease could dwell on him or within himself because of the Splendor or the Light and frequency within him as God by himself through the Father; he automatically felt the frequency and vibrations of the woman's faith to be healed and set free at that time. So, in exchange, he took upon himself the negative energy (infirmity) from the places in her body that needed to be purified, healed, and then released and imparted the positive energy (healing). The frequency and vibrations worked in conjunction. Jesus took the infirmity from her because that was one of his functions and purposes here on earth as the Father Jehovah himself gave him, to bring healing and deliverance. Hallelujah! The same with some crystals, they take on the negative energy themselves (bind) and release (loose)positive energy unto the atmosphere or person. Some take on negative energy and purify it, purge, and turn it into positive energy at the same time. This is called transmutation. If you know the crystal/stone is made up of Christ himself, and you have faith that the crystal will manifest its function, as a protector, impart its characteristics of joy to increase joy within you through its vibrations and energy released, or whatever characteristic that particular crystal has, that the Father made it for, then you are good. One of the exciting things about this is that this helps your soul to be in subjection to Holy Spirit; you can ask Jesus or the crystal which is a reflection of Christ character of who he is; you will receive what you asked for in Jesus name.

"13 And whatsoever ye shall ask in my name, that will I do, that the Father may be glorified in the Son.14 If ye shall ask anything in my name, I will do it.15 If ye love me, keep my commandments. "John 14:13-15(KJV)

"For you shall have a covenant with the stones of the field, And the beasts of the field shall be at peace with you." Job 5:23 (NKJV).

They make a covenant with you! Wow!

Can somebody praise Jesus!!!! I will! Hallelujah!!

Crystals bring forth deliverance

We know if we break down power, we will get energy and energy into matter. We know that spirits are real, whether good spirits or evil spirits. Whether a demonic angel or a good angel. If you break them down, they are made up of energy, whether positive energy or negative energy. For example, if you break down a demonic spirit (evil spirit), you will get negative energy, which means you

will get positive ions. Positive ions scientifically speaking are harmful. That's why people feel weighed down or become sick because a demonic spirit has attached itself to the soul or one of the gateways through your energy field/electromagnetic field/or aura. In the old times, the only way doctors could find where a person had an infection or disease is located. They would have to use a pendulum. They would hold the pendulum over the body to find out where the sickness or illness was over the person. We have heard people state that people infected with cancer seen a small demon not even a foot-high run off a person once delivered. We know Jesus and the disciples faced demons all the time. If you break demonic spirits down, then you will get negative energy, and negative vibrations, and low frequencies.

*But the Father's promise is deliverance through his son Christ the Rock. When you feel weighed down, there's always a relief to where you feel lighter. You can use the picture for example. See the rainbow as yourself and your aura. When you are weighed down, heavy burdened or sick you have dark spots in your aura, and your aura is not its typical vibrant colors. But with crystals they help protect your aura and detox your body depending on which one you use. And they protect your organs and are there to assist your organs, they are assigned to, so they can be healed and restore properly. Plus, the added benefits of your whole being as spiritually, mentally, emotionally, and spiritually. So, the first picture if you are burdened, weighed down, and sick, this is how your aura your spiritual body look in the realm of the spirit. The second when is when your you are protected and working with crystals because they help you physically, mentally, emotionally, and spiritually, your aura is clear of any dark areas or tears in your aura; in the realm of the spirit your body is full of clear, vibrant colors. Some people will be able to restore their physical health, some may not, depending on the damage done to their bodies. Depending on the person's situation, everyone differs from one another. But the good thing is these minerals **ROCK because they are here to help bring deliverance!***

This is your aura and body when you feel heavy and weighed down, stressed, burdened, sick, or negative energies have filled your aura.

This is your aura when you are unburdened and not stressed. You feel lighter, free, calm, rejuvenated, healthy, and whole.

Chapter 4: The Value of Crystals, Gemstones, Stones & Rocks are Priceless.

For wisdom is more precious than rubies and nothing can be compared unto it. Prov.8:11 (KJV)

I love the above scripture because it talks about wisdom being worth more than the cost of rubies. Rubies are beautiful and shine from different angles depending on their cut. They are very expensive. Rubies are known for their love and wisdom. But we know the wisdom from God triumphs the wisdom of all things because he is in all things and knows the way all things operate because he is the source. But the reason why the cost of rubies is so high is not only for its beauty and radiant light that emits from it but because of the one crucial fruit that triumphs all fruit, which is love. But we need the wisdom from above to know how to love each fellow man, creation, ourselves, and God above all else **Rom 13:10 (KJV) says, "if you become love you have fulfilled the law."**

Love conquers sin in someone else's life and can change them. Love can heal a broken heart, but it takes wisdom to know how to react to an individual. When you put on jewels, they make you feel different without you even realizing it, and it's because when you put it on it is releasing its frequency and vibration of its character into your electromagnetic field/or aura. Not only that but look at the spiritual aspects of it and the physical aspects of it. Even when you wear specific colors, you feel different.

Emotional healing

Rubies bring forth love. *It helps to resolve conflicts and solve relationship problems.*
No matter how many times you may have been rejected, mistreated, or abused, instead of anger or negative energy manifesting, it allows by grace to transmute/or change those feelings into love. It helps you to love and appreciate yourself and whom you are becoming, this is what I have learned so far from wearing it. It encourages you to be in more of a courageous state of mind. It shows you the little small things that really matter. It promotes positive thinking. It brings about a more protective side of you, allowing you to take up for those who feel threatened, whether friends, strangers, children, animals, or the environment.

Mental healing

It helps to protect and sustain those with sensitive natures and/or inaccurate or falsified views of themselves or others. It overwhelms and overcomes any fear of being not pretty enough, unloved, and rejected. It's empowering for those who hold excess weight in the body in order to ground them in the physical world. It brings deliverance of destructive emotional holds. It is a reliable and powerful stone for growth and maturing in a more friendly attitude toward oneself and the physical body. It protects you from warfare.

It brings transformation of thought and intent into the physical manifestation in order to change one's world for good. It represents light in the darkness of one's life. It encourages you to follow your happiness, joy, and ecstasy.

Ruby assists in connecting one's energy to the earth for the purpose of refreshing and restoring one's energy centers (chakras, wheels, gateways). It is excellent for grounding and overcoming mental overload. It helps support you in times of stress and helps bring you peace of heart. It guards your heart if worn as a pendant. It's part of your armor gear. **"Above all else, guard your heart, for everything you do flows from it." Proverbs 4:23 NIV** It protects and guards your heart against the issues of life. We will talk more about using crystals as armor in another chapter.

Physical Healing

It strengthens the immune system, improves your blood circulation; it boosts your self-confidence and courage. Since ancient times, it has been used in the treatment of brain diseases. Also, it has been used in the treatment of mental illnesses. It clears your mind of negative thoughts. It helps regulate your

menstrual cycle. Relieve pain and tension in menstrual periods in women. It regulates blood pressure, protects against bone disease, reduces the psychological and physiological effects of menopause. It gives grace to those who struggle with difficulties and makes the body more energetic.

It helped me love myself and others. It made me appreciate the love of my family, friends, even people I don't know that I have seen in other places when I go running errands. It encourages me to see myself for who I am in the Lord. It brings forth enthusiasm and happiness. It gives me compassion and love for others and appreciates and sees the gifts in all creation for what the Father created them to be. It brings more of a motherly nurturing aspect of myself that I never saw before. It shows me that the small things are what matter and to take up for those, as stated earlier, who may not be able to defend themselves. It helps you take a stand in a more friendly manner than more of a stern manner.

So, we see here when you look at the impact that Ruby has, and it has many different benefits. And its benefits are at a high price. We see that rubies are next in line compared to wisdom, and I'm sure the Rubies are honored to be next in line compared to the wisdom of God. Because it took wisdom and understanding to create all things and know how everything functions, the bible talks about so many crystals and their health benefits, we just overlook the meanings and pay it no mind because of what we have been told. Let's dissect another bible passage in the book of Job about wisdom and its expense above crystals, and things on the earth God created for us to help benefit us. Their price is high because of its excellent benefits and their diverse effects in ancient times.

"12 But where shall wisdom be found? and where is the place of understanding?

13 Man knoweth not the price thereof; neither is it found in the land of the living.

14 The depth saith, It is not in me: and the sea saith, It is not with me.

15 It cannot be gotten for <u>gold</u>; neither shall <u>silver</u> be weighed for the price thereof.

16 It cannot be valued with the <u>gold</u> of Ophir, with the precious <u>onyx</u>, or the <u>sapphire</u>.

17 <u>The gold and the crystal cannot equal it</u>: and the <u>exchange of it shall not be for jewels of fine gold.</u>

18 No mention shall be made of <u>coral</u>, or of <u>pearls</u>: for the price of wisdom is <u>above rubies</u>.

19 The <u>topaz</u> of Ethiopia shall not equal it, neither shall it be valued with pure gold.

20 Whence then cometh wisdom? and where is the place of understanding?

21 Seeing it is hid from the eyes of all living, and kept close from the fowls of the air.

22 Destruction and death say, We have heard the fame thereof with our ears.

23 God understandeth the way thereof, and he knoweth the place thereof.

24 For he looketh to the ends of the earth, and seeth under the whole heaven;

25 To make the weight for the winds; and he weigheth the waters by measure.

26 When he made a decree for the rain, and a way for the lightning of the thunder:

27 Then did he see it, and declare it; he prepared it, yea, and searched it out.

28 And unto man he said, Behold, the fear of the Lord, that is wisdom; and to depart from evil is understanding." Job 28:12-28KJV

So, let's see the other benefits of other things that help benefit our body not only for their beauty but because of their healing power through their frequency and vibrations to bring forth health and wholeness to the body by working with our body. We will also see them bring forth protection.

Gold Benefits

1. Regulates Body Temperature - People who suffer with hot flashes or chills, or any other body problems caused by variations in the body, would benefit from wearing gold. A good example is women who suffer from Menopause.

2.Treats soreness and wounds - Since ancient times, the metal in its natural form was used to treat soreness and wounds. When applied to the sore area or a wound, it prevented infection and help heal the area.

3.Overall well-being - If you feel worn out, exhausted, or down, gold jewelry can cheer you up as it has high frequencies and positive energy that overcome any problems within the body or mind. By boosting oxygen flow through the body, it helps every part of the body to operate at its finest, therefore, making it easier to perform a task. Good blood circulation is an essential aspect of keeping away disease.

4.Treats Symptoms of Arthritis - Wearing 24- karat gold against the skin brings soothing effect and reduces arthritis symptoms.

5. Gold reduces stress and anxiety

6. Skin Treatment - Cleopatra used gold as an anti-aging solution, and it worked. It was conventional skin treatment during the Roman era, where gold salve was used to treat skin infections. Today, many dermatologists believe that gold has superb skin-healing powers. Many skin treatment products have gold as an ingredient. Just like the minerals in crystals and stones are used in today's medicine.

7. Gold boosts the immune system.

8. It assists in healing the nervous system as well as the endocrine system.

9. In Acupuncture

Silver Benefits

1. Powerful Immune Booster - Silver is a natural mineral that can super-charge your immune system and help you stay healthy. Research has shown that consuming silver daily is both safe and effective for boosting and maintaining a healthy immune system.

2. Silver destroys antibacterial bacteria in the body: While employed at UCLA Medical School in the 1980s, Larry C. Ford, MD, documented that silver can actually kill over 650 bacteria, fungus, parasites, molds, and fungi that have the potential to sprout diseases. At the same time, the tests established that silver has no known side effects.

3. Silver heals wounds and skin conditions - In 2012, a research article produced by Pharmacognosy Communications recommended that specific silver preparations should be considered for topical use to treat burns, thrush,

periodontitis, and other conditions. Silver also helps heal other skin conditions such as psoriasis and eczema.

4. It prevents and kills viruses - Martin Hum, from the Institute for Optimum Nutrition, lists silver as one of the natural remedies to stop viruses. The colloidal silver used in modern supplements is a suspension of pure metallic silver in water. It is thought to work by interfering with the enzymes that enable viruses, bacteria, and fungi to utilize oxygen. In other words, it suffocates and kills them.

5. Anti-Inflammatory

6. Silver even kills the deadly, drug-resistant MRSA pathogen, now responsible for up to 94,000 life-threatening infections.

7. Treats and prevents the common cold and flu:

8. Treats and fights against bronchitis and pneumonia: Silver is a remarkable mineral, which can help fight against bronchitis and pneumonia when ingested internally.

9. Purifies water

10. Better than an antibiotic: When an individual uses too many antibiotics over the course of time, they can develop a resistance to it. Silver doesn't create resistance or immunity in the organisms that are killed by it.

I know you have to be praising the Lord hearing these benefits. This information is so priceless when you think about it; we spend millions of dollars on medication when the Lord had what we needed here all along on earth to bring health and supernatural benefits and protection, let's go to the next thing on the list in Job. Are you shouting! Because I know I'm shouting right now, I'm super excited!! Hallelujah!!

 Onyx Benefits

1. Onyx helps you let go of unhealthy attachments/and or soul-ties to a past relationships

2. Releasing negativity - It is worn to release any sort of negativity from a person.

3. Helps you to let go of the past- Wearing the stone helps people get over their previous relationships, and to let go of the past. (Remember Joseph in the bible, he was forced to leave his Father and other relatives and friends. He had to leave the past behind in order to move forward. Read Genesis 37 KJV) This is typically for people who haven't been able to forget their previous relationships even if it ended years ago, or who are living more in the past than in the now

4. Separation - It helps one separate from people or situations that are unhappy, or troublesome.

5. This gemstone also helps a person change unhealthy, irregular, bad habits, and to become more focused and balanced. It helps the wearer stay free from any kind of stress and helps him or her makes quick, correct decisions that will effectively change his or her life for good.

6. Useful for Entrepreneurs- It is excellent for entrepreneurs who are thinking of or are in the process of starting a new business, it helps them make quick and sound decisions regarding their business, it also wards off negative opinions.

7. Increases your intuition and discernment

8. It helps you be put in divine alignment with the Father.

9. Deflecting Negativity- Negativity can make itself felt through different sources (negative relationships, negativity at work, etc.). Black Onyx helps in deflecting inner and outer negativity and protects the wearer from the evil eye, curses, or bad luck that is caused due to jealousy or negativity of some sort in the mind of others.

10. Protection from Evil Spirits - it helps ward off evil spirits from a person or from a person in his/or her family. It protects from black magic and dark sorcery, as well as evil spirits from a person's home and family.

11. Sharpens your senses

12. Physical Healing - it believed that this gemstone could heal eye disorders, teeth problems, epilepsy, feet trouble, bone issues, etc. For this reason, healers often advise their patients to wear a black onyx, as it starts to show the effects after continual use.

Sapphire Benefits

aka the magnificent and Holy Sapphire- Moses wrote the 10 Commandments on a Sapphire stone

2. Wisdom and Royalty

3. Faithfulness

4. Prophecy, clarity, and stimulates the mind's eye

5. Divine Favor

6. In Hebrew lore, King Solomon and Abraham both wore talismans of sapphire. In Christianity, it was used in ecclesiastical rings and was cherished by kings and nobility for its powers of protection and insight

7. As a talisman, Sapphire was thought to preserve chastity, discover fraud, and treachery, protect its wearer from poison, plague, fever, and skin diseases. It healed ailments of the eyes.

8. Assists in healing all parts of the body and soothes insomnia. Used externally as an elixir, sapphire water is considered an excellent purifier and should be used as the seasons change. Wow! Cures eye infections and improves eyesight, relieves heaviness, fever, nosebleeds, issues of the ears including infection, inner ear imbalances, and vertigo. It is beneficial to the thyroid, swollen glands, and in treating problems related to speech and communication. It helps the nervous system, treats blood disorders, dementia, and degenerative diseases.

9. High power in resisting black magic and ill-wishing.

10. Increased concentration

11. It will lose its luster if worn by an intemperate or impious person

12. It stimulates the mind's eye and throat

13. Stone of love and commitment

14. It can be highly effective aid in treatments for neuroses or even psychosis.

15. Releases Depression and lightens the mood brings calmness and truth. Many other benefits I just can't list.

Sapphires have many different colors; each color has its own vibrational strengths and benefits!

*The Father is the greatest mastermind. Thank you, Jehovah, Yahweh, Yod-Hey-Vav-Hey! Hallelujah! I want to elaborate on the depth and seriousness of the revelation on these crucial gifts that the Father has given unto us. It's merely priceless. Nothing can compare to the love and the protection the Father has for us by giving us things here on earth to benefit and help create. Job in verse 17 really hit home in the diverse benefits of crystals and gold together it says,"**17 The gold and the crystal cannot equal it: and the exchange of it shall not be for jewels of fine gold." (Job 28:17 KJV)** The reason why Job said this is because one tiny piece of gold has a high frequency along with its significant health benefits alone by itself, each crystal have their own frequencies and vibrations, characteristics, benefits, and healings (spiritually, mentally, emotionally and physically) themselves depending on which one you choose. So here you have two different things that came from the earth that have their own benefits, and if combined it has vast, dynamic benefits if used together, can you imagine the cost of that! Just think about 14 karat gold ruby rings, or 24 karat gold sapphire pendants or necklaces; they are combined as a protective shield, which we will talk about later. But then further, it reads that the exchange of wisdom shall not even be in exchange for jewels of fine gold. Meaning even with gold combined with the other different crystals and gemstones together, it has many different benefits. It still can't compare into the wisdom of the Father. The cost of the gold and any crystal combined is priceless, though expensive.*

Kings wore different gemstones on their crown to represent not only royalty, and dominion, but for the protection and the meaning of the Jewel and to activate the crown gateway. The gold crown of the kings and queens also activated the mind's eye for them to receive visions and understanding in biblical times when the holy spirit would come upon them, and every jewel had benefits to the king and / or queen. Depending on the ones they wore. We wonder why kings and queens had dreams and visions, and it was because they are set over the land to protect it and govern it because the Lord loves all nations and nationalities. He wants to restore them back to him and wants people to know who he is, the way, the truth, and the life. Amazing!! Like wow! Most holistic healers say combining gold with crystals and gemstones speeds the healing process even faster when combined with each other. That's why crystal jewelry (necklaces, rings, bracelets, etc.) itself is crucial.

Coral Benefits

1. *Fortifies the tooth enamel*
2. *Prevents bone loss and osteoporosis*
3. *Help with muscle contractions*

4. Prevents heart disease

5. Strengthens Bones

6. Lowers high blood pressure

7. Increases metabolism

8. Prevents gastric and colorectal cancers

9. Helps treat multiple sclerosis

10.   Reduces cramps, irritability, and PMS

Red Coral Gemstones -Warrior Stone

Red Coral

1. Victory over enemies and adversaries

2. Courage to overcome obstacles and enemies and ensures victory for the individual

3. It helps individuals overcome procrastination, hesitation, laziness, and gives the impetus and the individual to take tasks to their logical conclusion. It helps overcome delays.

4. It has a significant impact on mental health, helps people overcome symptoms of listlessness, depression, and despondency. It gives energy, vigor, and hope. It imparts courage and helps in overcoming fear and nervousness.

5. Great for boosting self-esteem

6. Miraculous effects of healing - it helps aid eruptions of the face. Therefore, it helps people who suffer from acne, skin ailments, boils, and yet it purifies the blood. Red Coral guards and protects against cuts, wounds, bruises, and injuries.

7. People with temperamental issues, lack of patience, and has anger problems can see self-improvement a lot in these areas after wearing Red Coral Gemstones

8. People in the army, armed forces, police, doctors, especially surgeons, chemical weapon manufacture or business, scientist, realty business find the red coral to be extraordinarily practical and beneficial.

9. The red coral provides reliable protection against the evil eye, hexing, and black magic, warfare, evil thoughts of others against you, that you may not be aware of.

10. It is known for and represents strength of marriage and long life of the spouse.

11. It possesses the innate ability to cure its wearer of most ailments, unhealthy influences, and from all evils that can otherwise harm them.

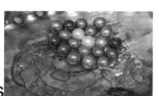

Pearl benefits

*1. Pearls help stop any harmful effects, or adverse effects of the moon, it helps in neutralizing the negative planetary influences on human beings. Because as you know in the book of Ephesians, it states, "**12 For we wrestle not against flesh and blood, but against principalities, against powers, against the rulers of the darkness of this world, against spiritual wickedness in high places." Eph.6:12 (KJV)** It reverses the effects it has on the body. It strengthens the mind force and increases good sleep. We have to remember what the bible says, "**the kingdom of heaven is like a merchant looking for fine pearls. When he found one of great value, he went away and sold everything he had and bought it." Matt.13:45-46 (KJV)** When you find out the benefits of crystals or stones, you sell everything you have for that stone because of the supernatural effects of it. Of course, it's just showing what people would do because of the vast benefits of the stone or crystals.*

2.  *Pearl increases the beauty and facial lusters in women*

3. Stone of purity and gentleness

4. It brings harmony between husband and wife

5. If used in combination with rudraksha, it helps solve problems related to depression and pessimism.

6. It helps in reducing discomforts during sleep

7. Pearl stone is recommended for those who get angry quickly and lose their temper.

8. Problems such as dysentery, throat trouble, eye trouble, is caused by affliction of the moon. These problems can be reduced by wearing pearl stone.

8. Pearl can be worn in combination with other stones for many other health-related diseases.

9. It helps in increasing memory and brain functions

10. It is said to bring prosperity

Topaz Benefits

1. Brings happiness

2. Provides inner peace and calmness of the mind

3. Eradicates negativity and evil

4. The wearer of topaz is said to experience relief from depression, worries, regrets, and despair linked from the past

5. It increases the power of concentration and enables the wearer to be more creative and ahead in academics.

6. It's linked with pride, sobriety, honesty, intelligence, dedication, kindness, and sincerity.

7. It's beneficial in assisting with liver problems, jaundice chronic memory loss, insomnia and aggressiveness

8. It's beneficial in the ailments of liver, fever, appetite, colds, coughs, and indigestion.

9. It cures mental disorders, suicidal tendencies, and nervous breakdowns. That's Priceless!

Crystals are and practical use for our day to day living

Here we see the healing power of crystals; we see this is nothing that the Father wanted us to stop using, he still wants them to be a practical use for us to use because of their different personalities, characteristics, attributes, and the healing power they impart. They help us increase in the fruit of the spirit (love,

joy, peace, patience, kindness, goodness, and self- control **see Gal 5:22-23 ESV**). *They help train us by the grace they impart into us through Christ Jesus by working with our electromagnetic or energy field/or aura into our gateways, chakra, or wheels. Ezekiel talks about the wheels, never knowing which way they would go.*

*"19 **And when the living creatures went, the wheels went by them, and when the living creatures were lifted up from the earth, the wheels were lifted up. 20 Whithersoever the spirit was to go, they went, thither was their spirit to go; and the wheels were lifted up over against them: for the spirit of the living creature was in the wheels. 21 When those went, these went; and when those stood, these stood; and when those were lifted up from the earth, the wheels were lifted up over against them: for the spirit of the living creature was in the wheels." Ezekiel 1:19-21 (KJV)*** *We are alive, and they are within our body and outside our body to help us live life to the fullest. Wherever we go, the wheels go with us. But they all must be balanced so we can operate efficiently in our day to day lives. It's just like when you never may know how Holy Spirit will move, and it's the same with them. If one of the wheels is underactive or inactive, a person can go into depression depending on the type of wheel that's out of balance or inactive. Or if one is overactive, like the throat chakra/wheel, then a person can be over-talkative, which, I will talk about later in the book, on how you can tell which chakras are out of alignment.*

We see they help us again offensively and defensively. They help us produce fruit by the grace the Father imparted unto them to work with our frequency and energy. We know, therefore, he said we should be like his treasure because he made us have our own personality, character, nature, and gave us specific duties and callings just like the crystals. **"For you are a holy people, who belong to the LORD your God. Of all the people on earth, the LORD your God has chosen you to be his own special treasure." Deuteronomy 7:6 (NLT)** *When we think of his own special treasure, think of us as believers in the body of Christ, we have our own fruitfulness, characteristics, personalities, and callings in the kingdom of God. We heal too, just like the crystals. We deliver people (set them free from bondage or afflicting spirits or negative energies), just like the crystals relieve/or deliver people. We are all a reflection of Christ's deity. Christ healed, set free, delivered people, gave messages, released wisdom, understanding, and guidance. So, do we as sons of God. Do you see the similarities? We will see the similarities crystals have with similar tasks like the angels do. When we say we should be unto God as his own special treasure, we just stop there as it's just us, but we fail to see the whole picture. It is just like when rubies can't compare unto wisdom, people say that's because wisdom is Christ or God, and he is above all, and they stop there. Instead of saying. wait a minute, hmmm...? what is the whole reason he is stressing this in scripture? Crystals have their own uniqueness and how they can be your friend because they are again in Christ, sent as gifts to*

help release another level of grace to help us go into perfection. That's why Jesus even compared the kingdom of heaven unto treasure hidden in a field, because of the many uses and benefits of the Father's treasures (crystals, stones, gemstones, or rocks). ***"The kingdom of heaven is like treasure hidden in a field. When a man found it, he hid it again, and then in his joy went and sold all he had and bought that field." Matt. 13:44 (KJV)***

The man that bought that field sold everything that he had because he knew the benefits the crystals would bring. Fruitfulness and prospering are priceless. I remember I had a dream, and I remember seeing my grandmother; she's a fantastic minister and Woman of God! Whenever I see her in the dream, the Lord has her to **represent** *Holy Spirit. So, I had a dream, and I saw this picture, and*

it had the celestite crystals   I had just bought two weeks prior, they were in a formation roundabout, like a circle but then it was another smaller formation at the bottom. And my grandmother, who represented Holy Spirit, said, "You are becoming this." And I said, "huh? that don't make no sense because you can't become crystals, and she said you are." So, I instantly woke up and said, "Lord, that can't be you sending me this message because I can't become a crystal." So, then I heard the Lord say, "Terika, you don't understand you are becoming and birthing forth the fruit celestite carries and its character and nature." ***"For you are a holy people, who belong to the LORD your God. Of all the people on earth, the LORD your God has chosen you to be his own special treasure." Deuteronomy 7:6 (NLT)*** *So he wants us to become like his special treasures. I said, oh. Okay, I understand. Celestite takes out worry, fear, tension, and anger; its personality or fruit it bears is purity, peace, and joy. It imparts purity, peace, and joy to the individual that uses it. Celestite also increases your hearing and gives you stronger intuition. They bring divine assistance.*

Jesus said, ***"Ye have not chosen me, but I have chosen you, and ordained you, that ye should go and bring forth fruit, and that your fruit should remain: that whatsoever ye shall ask of the Father in my name, he may give it to you." John 15:16 (KJV)*** *It's so funny because as many benefits crystals have, you can tell them through prayer to the Father on what you want them to do, and through the declaration of the word of God. We will break down this scripture in another chapter by Jesus being the Rock of all rocks. Jesus said in Matthew,* ***"Either make the tree good, and his fruit good; or else make the tree corrupt, and his fruit corrupt: for the tree is known by his fruit." Matt 12:33 (KJV), "A good man out of the good treasure of the heart***

bringeth forth good things: and an evil man out of the evil treasure bringeth forth evil things." Matt 12:35 (KJV) *That's why Christ said to keep your heart guarded.* **"Above all else, guard your heart, for everything you do flows from it" Prov. 4:23 (NIV)**

Isn't it funny, when you watch movies like Aqua man or superhero movies you notice a lot of times their hearts are guarded by a pendant or necklace, even the evil person they are combating in battle, have crystals or gems guarding their heart. If that crystal is removed, they would possibly, and more than likely end up bearing the opposite fruit that they are trying to bear, or they will lose strength or faith, or some type of supernatural ability. And they would operate outside of their character or personality. Because the heart has more electromagnetic fields coming from it than the brain itself. I remember my favorite cartoons was Duck Tales, you would see the wicked witch having a gemstone over her heart because it gave her supernatural capabilities, just think if it was broken or taken off, not only would the powers be broken but she possibly, and more than likely, would have turned good.

So, we can bear fruit from the crystals, praise the Lord. It's as if they add more grace to us through our everyday lives, they bear fruitfulness, that we want to have depending on what we lack. So, I'm glad the Lord interpreted the dream clearly. He also showed me to put that same formation down on my altar with clear quartz crystals surrounding the outside of celestite crystals. And I put a Herkimer diamond in the middle of the celestite because you always must have at least one crystal in the middle of the other surrounding crystals. The middle crystal amplifies the effect of the frequencies and vibrations of the surrounding stones and is the original intent of the crystal grid. It also is the overall result of all the crystals that surround it. It targets and is the main reason for the crystal grid. For instance, Herkimer Diamond is the hardest out of all the clear quartz stones, Herkimer crystal can receive and amplify the influence of other stones. It expands a small or soft energy stone, therefore giving it the strength and effects of a much larger stone. Herkimer Diamonds have a keep record; it accepts and keeps information that can be used later.

They may make a covenant with you to thoughts of love, well-being, or healing for others to draw on. We will talk about covenants or crystal programming later because it's in the Bible. Clear quartz has a high vibration and frequency. It's known to purify, cleanse, and amplify crystals and have high vibrations. So not only did I put Herkimer diamond in the middle of the crystal grid, but I also added clear quartz on the outside of all the celestites to increase the amplification of the celestite crystals. This is called crystal grids, when you have a group of crystals together in different shapes, forms, and patterns in order to manifest specific intentions, prayers, visions, and goals. The Father always knows the end from the beginning. I didn't have a crystal in the middle of all the celestites to amplify their effects, so I put a Herkimer Diamond in the middle, not realizing what I was doing,

but Holy Spirit was guiding me the whole time because I knew nothing about crystal grids at that time. He even gave me confirmation that I was on the right path during a prayer meeting we had later on that same day.

So, when I was connecting to the Zoom app in order to do prayer with my brothers and sisters in Christ in the Zoom app, I couldn't hear the prayer leader at all. I tried all I could do to connect to hear her and so I couldn't, so I turned off my kindle and used my cell phone which I totally don't like to use because it gets bad reception, but this time the reception was good, and I came in on them saying that an angel in the middle with a fiery sword going back and forth. Next, they said they saw surrounding the angel with the fiery sword, were other angels in a circle surrounding the angel with the fiery sword. And we were on the outside of the angels surrounding the angel with the fiery sword. The formation was the same formation of the top part of the crystal grid, but the smaller formation of the crystal grid I didn't see the correlation till they said they saw the pentagon and the white house we had to pray over our brother in Christ, President Trump, this was during the shutdown, someone said that the angels taking were taking off layers of tension, stress, frustration, and they saw the angels imparting the peace of Christ, joy, purity, and calmness to President Trump.

Then we also all in a circle pointed our hands towards President Trump. We imparted the frequencies and vibrations of Christ in us into President Trump for deliverance. So when I saw this prophecy and confirmation in fulfillment I got excited and couldn't contain myself, and I let them know what the Father showed me, and we were in awe of the Father, and laughing because the Lord is so prophetic, he always sends confirmation to let you know you are on the right path. So that small formation of celestite at the bottom didn't have a crystal in the middle to pull from because the celestite, which represents the angels surrounding President Trump they didn't need their fruit amplified. It was an exchange of them taking out the negative energy and vibrations and imparting the positive energy of their fruitfulness, character, and healing abilities physically, mentally, emotionally, and spiritually into President Trump. The clear quartz outside the second formation of President Trump represented all of us in the prayer group imparting frequencies, vibrations, and fruitfulness that we each had differently in each and every one of us through the anointing of God in order to bring forth deliverance to President Trump because the Lord told us in the realm of the spirit to point our hands towards President Trump in a circle so he could get set free through the anointing of God. So, I was able at this time to get confirmation from the Lord 3 times to let me know that the crystals are of him to help all mankind because again, he's the living rock of all living rocks. The formations that I made was a crystal grid for myself from Holy Spirit directly, and it was prophetic. The crystal grid was for myself and in order to reap the benefits of the crystals I used. Secondly, the Lord confirmed the visions that the prayer groups saw about the angel with the flaming sword being surrounded by other angels and us surrounding those angels by the top of the grid confirming the bottom grid being

for trump to receive deliverance from the angels and us during prayer. Thirdly, they call the stone celestite because the blue looks like the heavenly sky. We will talk about crystal grids in another chapter. On top of that, the same number on the crystal grid was the same number of each individual that was on the prayer call that night. I have a similar drawing, I couldn't remember the exact number, but this is so you can see how the crystal grid looked that the Lord showed me and had me to make.

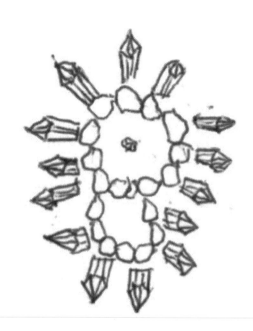

So, we see crystal assists us in bearing fruit. How many times have we screamed out loud or ask the Lord that we wanted to see an increase in love, joy, peace, etc., and we may not have got it right then and there? That has happened to me plenty of times. But now the Lord has given us a better and quicker way to expedite the process in bearing fruit. We see that John and Jesus pointed out the true value of crystals, gemstones, rocks, and that they are alive to help assist us in maturing spiritually, mentally, emotionally, and physically. Crystals help in expanding the kingdom of heaven, just like the angels do. We see this in these two bible passages that I'm going to go over. The first one is the one we read from earlier in Matthew:

"7 But when he (John) saw many of the Pharisees and Sadducees coming to where he was baptizing, he said to them: "You brood of vipers! Who warned you to flee from the coming wrath? 8 Produce fruit in keeping with repentance. 9 And do not think you can say to yourselves, 'We have Abraham as our father.' I tell you that out of these stones God can raise up children for Abraham. 10 The ax is already at the root of the trees, and every tree that does not produce good fruit will be cut down and thrown into the fire. 11 "I baptize you with water for repentance. But after me comes one who is more powerful than I, whose sandals I am not worthy to carry. He will baptize you with the Holy Spirit and fire. 12 His winnowing fork is in his hand, and he will clear his threshing floor, gathering his wheat into the barn and burning up the chaff with unquenchable fire." Matt 3:7-12 NIV

When John saw the Pharisees and the Sadducees, this entails a more profound meaning; he was referring to the stones on the priest's breastplate. God Speaks once, twice, but do men perceive it. (Job 33:14 KJV) He was saying, don't you know that these stones would be able to raise up children for Abraham by ministering to them. He wasn't just talking about the men; he was baptized, but it had a double meaning. John was saying that every different stone on the priest breastplate would be able to minister to the children the Faith of Abraham. Just like we saw in the book of Joshua, it said the stone heard the words of the Lord. Just like in Job, he said speak to the earth, and it shall teach thee. The stones and crystals are part of the earth, and it's part of what the Lord used to form the earth. I believe the earth was first made by water that was frozen and became crystals. **"29 Out of whose womb came the ice? and the hoary frost of heaven, who hath gendered it?" Job 38:29** Some scientists say that they believe crystals are a form of frozen water. **"30 The waters are hid as with a stone, and the face of the deep is frozen." (Job 38:29,30 KJV)** The earth is a crystal itself. It was made for creation to love, to help heal, to co-create. Ancient civilizations knew these things.

Crystals may not relay the message out in a language that we can hear, but they can minister the word of the Lord, activate dreams and visions through the Holy Spirit. Christ is in them, in all things, we are all one in him, no matter the nationality, culture, or creation, we are all one in Christ himself. But John knew they never thought for crystals to be versatile like that. They didn't know or use the crystals themselves to increase fruit. They didn't want to participate in the baptism of repentance; they didn't want to get baptized with the Holy Spirit and fire. They wanted to stay in the old, of what they were taught at the time. They wanted to stay in the teachings of the old covenant, but they didn't know the baptism of repentance was needed, out of their ignorance, the baptism of the Holy Spirit and fire was needed at that time, just like it is needed in this time now.

Just as the crystals were needed then, so are the crystals needed now. Some people these days want to stay in the same pattern, instead of moving into the more advanced things because they are frightened. Jesus talks about the importance of stones/crystals and rebukes the Pharisees below:

"37 And when he was come nigh, even now at the descent of the mount of Olives, the whole multitude of the disciples began to rejoice and praise God with a loud voice for all the mighty works that they had seen; 38 Saying, Blessed be the King that cometh in the name of the Lord: peace in heaven, and glory in the highest. 39 And some of the Pharisees from among the multitude said unto him, Master, rebuke thy disciples. 40 <u>And he answered and said unto them, I tell you that, if these should hold their peace, the stones would immediately cry out.</u> 41 And when he was come near, he beheld the city, and wept over it, 42 Saying, <u>If thou hadst known, even thou, at least in this thy day, the things which belong unto thy peace! but now they are hid from thine eyes.</u>" Luke 19:37-41(KJV)

Jesus was saying , "Look, even if they hold their peace, the rocks on your breastplates would praise my name because they are alive, and you can't even recognize it, those rocks/stones/crystals on your breastplate are yours, and you can't even realize that they are part of what you need in order for you to get your peace. You don't even recognize that they are one with you as part of your armor and to help you increase in sincere fruit. They are not only to be used for prophecy through the Urim and Thummim. But, now today is this knowledge or secret hid from your eyes this day." We have crystals within our body; our pineal gland is made of crystals; our blood is made of liquid crystalline. Jesus is saying that those stones on their breastplates, the rocks in the earth, and on the ground was part of them living in peace because they are alive beings. We reap the benefits of what Father himself created and made them to be in order to work in conjunction with us to help our soul be under subjection to Holy Spirit. Christ is telling the priest you are suffering because you are rejecting the very thing, I have given you as treasure. It's not just on your breastplate to look fancy, and for divination (prophecy), It's there to help you be whole so you can have true peace and a happy life.

Jesus was saying, "If you are healed, you would have your peace, if you are not worried, you would have your peace. If you are bearing good fruit, you would have your peace. If you have negative thoughts eradicated out of your mind, you will have your peace. If you are healed physically, mentally, and emotionally, you would have your peace. If you knew you were protected, you would have peace. If you didn't feel drained anymore because someone is thinking negative thoughts, or ill wishes about you accidentally because they think you are wrong, or not knowing the impact it would have on you negatively, then you would have your peace. If you knew you were protected from negative or demonic spirits in a certain location or area, then you know you would have peace." But

we know that the Father is the ultimate source of these things. If you knew the right decision quickly, you would have peace. Again, crystals are part of your armor; they help you offensively by helping to bear fruit during life trials and can help you know what way to turn. They impart their fruitfulness and character to you through entrainment. They help you choose what to do through Christ in different areas of your life. They help you defensively because they protect you against negative energy and negative thoughts and keep demonic spirits away. They protect against witchcraft.

Again, Abraham had a sapphire talisman, that when people looked at it, they were healed. But we know it wasn't the talisman, it was Christ within it. We know not to idolize these things and put them above God. They didn't idolize it; they knew it was a tool that helped to heal and bring cure. People that use medicine that a doctor prescribed because they know it helps to remove or heal specific problems in your body, just like vitamins, which is made out of crystals because they are minerals. But, when you think about it, it no longer has the added toxins that are in medicine. It's simple. We know to continue to put God first in all things, those of us who have a deep relationship with him. I know about crystal and their benefits, but I don't worship them. In my prayer closet and during worship, I tell Adonai that I worship him and tell him along with so great a cloud of witnesses, angels, and the crystals, and all creation we all worship him, his son, worship holy spirit. The majority of times, I forget about wearing them and just sing to the Lord and go about my day after communing with him. Whether were speaking in our mind or out loud, we are talking to the Father, the Son, and Holy Spirit throughout the day. That's called communing with them because we need all three in our lives every day to lead and guide us. Unfortunately, because of trials we can be distracted and feel as if we haven't heard from God because of life circumstances sometimes.

I am reminded that **"in Him, we live, we move, we have our every being!" Acts 17:28 (KJV)** Hallelujah! Because I acknowledge who he is along with all creation. Hallelujah! I feel like its fire shut up in my bones, Glory to God!! I have received things I bought from pillowcases that increase dreams because the anointing the Lord put on the minister's life to release to increase dreams, and it did exactly what it was supposed to do. Did I idolize it? "No.," I recognized the Lord used the pillowcase as a tool for peoples' dreams to increase through his anointing. I have a miracles blanket from Joan Hunter, a powerful woman of God whose conference I went to when she came to St. Louis. I bought it for that purpose to perform miracles signs and wonders; I have people received healing from it. The two times that I used it. But I still haven't used it again, because I know I have the power of Christ within me to fulfill these things. But what happens if a person doesn't receive the full manifestation of healing at that time what do you do. Most of us just keep praying. But with crystals and gemstones, I've seen the benefits of them not only in one area but in multiple areas. I will continue to use them on a consistent basis daily because it's part of my armor, which I am

going to touch base on in the next chapter. And it's part of my mandate and assignment from Christ himself and not man.

Chapter 5: Biblical Proof of Crystal Healing Spiritually, Mentally, Emotionally & Physically

Our spiritual bodies are the temple of the Holy Ghost. **"19 Do you not know that your bodies are temples of the Holy Spirit, who is in you, whom you have received from God? You are not your own; 20 you were bought at a price. Therefore, honor God with your bodies" 1 Cor 6:19-20 (KJV)** We know that sin makes every individual imperfect since the fall of Satan. Adam and Eve ate from the tree of good and evil (read Genesis 3), which the LORD told them not to do. Life can hit us hard with its unexpected blows like a loss of a loved one, financial difficulties, abuse physically, mentally, emotionally. being rejected, loss of property, or shelter, etc. Maybe feeling rejected because a spouse committed adultery, or maybe others make you feel as you are not good enough. Or maybe you can't see the greatness that God has put in you because of just life itself. Or maybe you may feel defeated. Or maybe people speak negative things over you, or some people will remove themselves from you for whatever reason. Or just the normal stresses in life, or maybe you wanted to accomplish something, and it never gets done in the timing you thought it would get done. Or maybe you were lied on, and people profaned your name and called you evil because of a person's opinion about you. Or maybe you are having problems forgiving a person from the past. Or maybe you can't trust people because you have had bad experiences with people trying to control or manipulate you, whether its family, friends, leaders, your boss, or spouse. Sometimes our reactions, which we don't mean to do, can grieve the Holy Spirit. **"And do not grieve the Holy Spirit of God, with whom you were sealed for the day of redemption." Eph.4:30 (KJV)**

We're going to go over a couple of Bible passages and find out the actual proof that crystals bring forth healing, spiritually, mentally, and emotionally through the grace, God put in them to impart to us.

Isaiah 54 The Barren Woman (KJV)

"1 Sing, O barren, thou that didst not bear; break forth into singing, and cry aloud, thou that didst not travail with child: for more are the children of the desolate than the children of the married wife, saith the Lord.

2 Enlarge the place of thy tent, and let them stretch forth the curtains of thine habitations: spare not, lengthen thy cords, and strengthen thy stakes;

3 For thou shalt break forth on the right hand and on the left; and thy seed shall inherit the Gentiles, and make the desolate cities to be inhabited.

4 Fear not; for thou shalt not be ashamed: neither be thou confounded; for thou shalt not be put to shame: for thou shalt forget the shame of thy youth, and shalt not remember the reproach of thy widowhood anymore.

5 For thy Maker is thine husband; the Lord of hosts is his name; and thy Redeemer the Holy One of Israel; The God of the whole earth shall he be called.

6 For the Lord hath called thee as a woman forsaken and grieved in spirit, and a wife of youth, when thou wast refused, saith thy God.

7 For a small moment have I forsaken thee; but with great mercies will I gather thee.

8 In a little wrath I hid my face from thee for a moment; but with everlasting kindness will I have mercy on thee, saith the Lord thy Redeemer.

9 For this is as the waters of Noah unto me: for as I have sworn that the waters of Noah should no more go over the earth; so have I sworn that I would not be wroth with thee, nor rebuke thee.

10 For the mountains shall depart, and the hills be removed; but my kindness shall not depart from thee, neither shall the covenant of my peace be removed, saith the Lord that hath mercy on thee.

11 O thou afflicted, tossed with tempest, and not comforted, behold, I will lay thy stones with fair colours, and lay thy foundations with sapphires.

12 And I will make thy windows of agates, and thy gates of carbuncles, and all thy borders of pleasant stones.

13 And all thy children shall be taught of the Lord; and great shall be the peace of thy children.

14 In righteousness shalt thou be established: thou shalt be far from oppression; for thou shalt not fear: and from terror; for it shall not come near thee.

15 Behold, they shall surely gather together, but not by me: whosoever shall gather together against thee shall fall for thy sake.

16 Behold, I have created the smith that bloweth the coals in the fire, and that bringeth forth an instrument for his work; and I have created the waster to destroy.

17 No weapon that is formed against thee shall prosper; and every tongue that shall rise against thee in judgment thou shalt condemn. This is the heritage of the servants of the Lord, and their righteousness is of me, saith the Lord." Isaiah 54:1-17 KJV

We see this biblical passage as the Lord talking about Israel. But we can also relate this scripture in our everyday lives physically, spiritually, mentally, and emotionally. How many times have we not birth what the Lord told us to birth forth, whether in ministry, in life, because of life tests, and trials of faith, sometimes the Lord proving our faith in his word. Sometimes we try to do things ourselves, leaving out God because we think we can fulfill the vision ourselves, forgetting he's the one who set you up for that test and placed the vision within you. The Father knows everything that must happen for that vision to come forth, including the test and trials you have to go through in order to fulfill that vision or dream. He compares Israel unto a woman that was forsaken and wounded in spirit, a wife of youth when she was refused (rejected). He said he hid his face for a moment, but with everlasting kindness will he have mercy upon her. It was a promise. He makes it clear in verse 10 that his kindness shall not depart from her (Israel) either the covenant of thy peace be removed, and he will have mercy. But it also shows in the beginning even though they had no children (we can see this as ourselves it would be a vision or dream to fulfill).

The Lord told the barren woman to praise him and sing, despite not having any children, right then and there. But, she couldn't see the vision that he was prophesying that she would have children (visions, businesses, blueprints, resources, ministries) yet, because of life circumstances. How many times have you seen other people prospering or fulfilling their visions, and we get upset because our visions or goals haven't manifested yet or has been delayed because of an unexpected situation hit you in life that you had to put a certain vision on hold? (verses 1-4) But he promised her children whether physical and/or spiritual children and that they would be increased and taught of the Lord. Even by the seed, you plant to those around you, whether it's your lifestyle, your wisdom, your character, your plans, business, or ministry; those things can impact those

around you and birth forth peace and sow seeds of righteousness into others about their life's situations. But sometimes life again throws specific trials and tests of your faith.

He continues to encourage and say not to fear in Isaiah versus 1-4 Back to verse 11 he says **" O thou afflicted, tossed with tempest"** *(anger, affliction,* **stresses of life, being burdened), "and not comforted, I will lay thy stones with fair colours**  **, and lay thy foundations with sapphires**

, And I will make the windows of agates **, and thy gates of carbuncles** **, and all thy borders of pleasant stones.** *." The Father prophesies the effects, the characteristics, and the benefits, of the stones, agates, carbuncles, pleasant stones, and sapphires. He's stating that she will receive the same effects and influences of these gemstones in the realm of the spirit, physically, mentally, emotionally, and spiritually. We can see the effects of a woman, Israel, or us spiritually in the body of Christ having to birth forth visions, businesses, fruitfulness, gifts, ministries, or children. However, this scripture may apply to you in your daily life right now. We will see the effects and prophecies of the gemstones (semi-precious stones), the Lord was prophesying over the widow (Israel or ourselves) by their benefits, attributes, and characteristics.*

"54 Sing, O barren, thou that didst not bear; break forth into singing, and cry aloud, thou that didst not travail with child: for more are the children of the desolate than the children of the married

wife, saith the Lord." Isaiah 54:1 (KJV)

Agate - I, the Lord, will heal your physical body and uterus. I will treat and heal the disorders of your reproductive system. I will rebalance you, cleanse and stabilize your aura/electromagnetic field, eliminating and transforming negative energy into positive energy. I will soothe and calm your emotions. I will make you accept yourself and love yourself again. I will encourage you to look back at your life experiences and see what truly matters in order for you to grow into spiritual maturity.

Blue Sapphire - I will bring forth joy and peace. It's the stone of wisdom. I will remove blockages and things holding you back from spiritual growth. I will increase your faith, ease your depression, anxiety, and fear. I will bring forth a realistic picture of the actual world itself.

Carbuncle, aka Garnet - I will dissolve your feelings of alienation and loneliness and have you analyze things the correct way.

"2 Enlarge the place of thy tent, and let them stretch forth the curtains of thine habitations: spare not, lengthen thy cords, and strengthen thy stakes;3 For thou shalt break forth on the right hand and on the left; and thy seed shall inherit the Gentiles, and make the desolate cities to be inhabited." Isaiah 54:2 KJV

Agate - I will give you more energy in the body and awaken your spiritual purpose. White Agate is known as the pregnancy stone because it protects the baby (seed) and the mother from harm, soothes labor pains. I will protect you and your seed during your pregnancy, and they should inhabit the desolate cities.

Blue Sapphire - I will Increase your faith, bring forth dreams, give you mental clarity, spiritual healing, spiritual truth. I will boost your leadership capabilities, strengthen your motivation, help you gain success, prosperity, royalty, and favor.

Carbuncle (Garnet) - I will bring you inspiration, I will stabilize and strengthen your seed influences which can help you build a lasting connection with others. You could be a service to others (Grossular Garnet) and, in return, receive blessings and inheritances from them.

"4 Fear not; for thou shalt not be ashamed: neither be thou confounded; for thou shalt not be put to shame: for thou shalt forget the shame of thy youth, and shalt not remember the reproach of thy widowhood anymore." Isaiah 54:4 KJV

Agate - I, the Lord, will give you a sense of security and safety for you. I will dispel evil energy and spirits. I will increase your self-confidence, and you will love yourself. I will help you overcome negativity and bitterness of heart. I will heal your anger. I will bring forth courage from inside you. I will bring in harmony, all aspects of who you are physically, mentally, emotionally, spiritually, and brings stability.

Blue Sapphire - I will make you realize that you don't have to pretend to be somebody you are not. I will help your body go through detoxification, purification, and through a purging process. I will remove all distractions and keep your focus.

Carbuncle (Garnet) - I will remove anxiety, worry, and heal your heart. You will feel safe and protected. Trust me, you will no longer remember your past, but love who you have become. I will dissolve your feelings of being alone and alienation. (Andradite Garnet)

"5 For thy Maker is thine husband; the Lord of hosts is his name; and thy Redeemer the Holy One of Israel; The God of the whole earth shall he be called.6 For the Lord hath called thee as a woman forsaken and grieved in spirit, and a wife of youth, when thou wast refused, saith thy God.7 For a small moment have I forsaken thee; but with great mercies will I gather thee. Though I turned my back from you for a moment, I will restore you, and deliver you" Isaiah 54:5 -7 (KJV)

Agate - I will remove all bitterness.

Sapphire - I will restore you, and because of my mercy, you will have my favor.

Carbuncle - I will heal emotional conflicts between us, I will heal our relationship because I do understand life itself and I understand when it feels as If I am not with you during trials and things that life can throw at you sometimes. I understand it can feel lonely. I will gather you in my loving arms because of the love I have for you because you are mine.

"8 In a little wrath I hid my face from thee for a moment; but with everlasting kindness will I have mercy on thee, saith the Lord thy Redeemer.9 For this is as the waters of Noah unto me: for I have sworn that the waters of Noah should no more go over the earth; so have I swore that I would not be wroth with thee, nor rebuke thee.10 For the mountains shall depart, and the hills be removed; but my kindness shall not depart from thee, neither shall the covenant of my peace be removed, saith the Lord that hath mercy on thee." Isaiah 54:8 (KJV)

Sapphire - With everlasting kindness, I will love you. I will renew my covenant and promise to you, that my favor shall not depart from you. I will be faithful to my word; I will give you peace and love.

Carbuncle(garnet) - You will be calm in the future.

11 O thou afflicted, tossed with tempest, and not comforted, behold, I will lay thy stones with fair colours , and lay thy foundations

with sapphires.

Blue Sapphire - *I will give wisdom, peace, ease depression, anxiety, and insomnia, that has been afflicting you because of life's trials and tribulations. I will give you clarity and vision. You will be more under control and have a self-disciplined life. You will be protected from witchcraft, hexes, and other people's ill wishes or thoughts that has drained you and attacked you without knowing where they came from — other stones with fair color and their benefits. I will bring you laughter and rest on every side and everything that you will need if you keep your eyes on me. Foundations of sapphires mean the different types of benefits of sapphires by their color will be their sure foundation.*

Healthwise - I will help regulate your body organs. I will control your blood pressure. I will regulate your glands so that your body will function properly.

Black Sapphire - I will give you wisdom and confidence in your own intuition that I have given you. I will protect you and relieve all anxiety and sorrow. You will also maintain your field, business, ministry, or place of work.

Healthwise - I will relieve any physical pain you may have, and I will help you heal from any accidents or trauma that may occur. I will help heal any bruising and help you recover from any dislocation of your bones. I will give you relief from excessive bleeding, blood clots, and deep vein thrombosis. I will also help you treat any blood disorders.

Green Sapphire- I will give you wisdom, fidelity, and integrity. I will give you compassion for others and help increase your vision, and you will recall the dreams that I have given you."

Healthwise - I will help regulate your glands, and help slow down your body when it's overactive, I will help treat blood disorders and help you control any excessive blood. I will improve your eyesight.

Orange/Padparadscha- I will give you wisdom on how to love creation from the heart even to the world. I bring forth your creative ideas and creativity; spiritually, you will enjoy the intimacy and love again. I will increase your gifts.

Healthwise - I will increase your immune system, I will heal or reduce symptoms of related brain disorders, neurological, psychological problems, epilepsy, or hysteria. I will cure or relieve eye-related problems. I will heal you of any poison you may have received by being bitten by an insect.

Pink Sapphire- I will give you wisdom and flexibility. You will live life gained in its fullest. You will increase in love and forgive and release others that have done you wrong in the past. Others will honor you for whom I have made you to be, and I will strengthen your heart. You will remember your dreams more clearly.

Healthwise - I will slow your aging process by delaying cellular division, which decreases the chance of mutations. I will increase your brain's ability to prove information perceived by the emotional body senses. I will provide nourishment to your bones and nourish your cells and tissues in your body.

Violet Sapphire- I will give you wisdom and spiritual awakening, I will accelerate you in the realm of the spirit. You will meditate on me and my word. You will receive your oneness in me and unspeakable peace.

Healthwise- I will calm your overactive body system and help regulate your glands. I will treat any blood disorders and alleviate excessive bleeding. I will strengthen your veins and improve their elasticity.

White Sapphire- I will give wisdom and strength in your spirit, man. I will resolve what's needed for you to overcome obstacles on your spiritual walk with me. I will bring clarity of mind and give you guidance from me.

Healthwise- I will heal infertility, I will heal any urinary tract infection. I will heal any bowel diseases or constipation. I will also heal any kidney disorder. I will also heal any coughs. I will heal any stomach issues.

Yellow Sapphire - I will give you wisdom and prosperity. I will bring forth the financial abundance needed. I will bring forth creative ideas and help you to focus and manifest your goals and ambitions. I will reduce any mental anxiety and tension.

Healthwise- I will heal your psoriasis. I will heal dermatitis. I will make sure your digestive system works appropriately, therefore keeping you away from and/ or reducing indigestion and looseness of the bowels. I will help heal you of any jaundice or peptic ulcers. I will help improve your blood circulation. I will drive out over recessive mucus of bodily fluids, therefore, reducing respiratory infirmities and/or heal any asthma, bronchitis, sinus blockage, nasal anaphylaxis, lung sickness, and midsection accumulation, and nasal anaphylaxis. I will help reduce or heal bone issues, joint inflammation, ailments, or gout.

Carbuncle (Garnet) - I will help you gain success; I will alleviate your fear and worry. You will no longer panic.

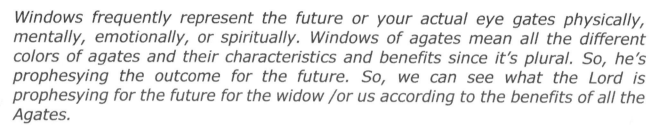

"**12** <u>And I will make thy windows of agates</u>, and thy gates of carbuncles, and all thy borders of pleasant stones."

Windows frequently represent the future or your actual eye gates physically, mentally, emotionally, or spiritually. Windows of agates mean all the different colors of agates and their characteristics and benefits since it's plural. So, he's prophesying the outcome for the future. So, we can see what the Lord is prophesying for the future for the widow /or us according to the benefits of all the Agates.

Agate - I am going to realign and balance your life. I will make you whole by aligning your mind, body, and spirit as one. I will cleanse and stabilize whom you are through your aura or electromagnetic field, eliminating and transforming all negativity in your life. I will increase your mentality, improve your concentration, perception, and analytical abilities. I will soothe you and heal anger and tension hidden within you. You will feel secure and safe. I will heal you.

Botswana Agate - I will remove depression, and you will explore unknown territory, and you will be victorious because I will help you see the bigger picture of what truly matters.

Healthwise - I will heal any sexual dysfunctions in both spouses if there is any. I will cleanse your body of any toxins. I will increase your immune system and stimulate your nervous systems. I will assist in brain oxygen assimilation so you can have the fullness of health in your circulatory system. I will help your uterus

to heal and return to its average size quickly after you give birth. I will heal your stomach; I will help heal your heart and your blood vessels.

Blue Lace Agate - I will encourage you and support you. I will uplift you and elevate you. I will prevent you from postpartum depression after you give birth. I will relieve stress and tension. I will give you peace that surpasses all understanding. You will be calm and rest in me. You will feel my comfort and truth.

Healthwise - I will heal severe skin disorders like eczema or psoriasis. I will help treat your arthritis. I will help you be whole from gastritis. I will help heal your digestives system. I will help relieve skin irritation and itching. I will help heal your digestives system. I will help you be able to lactate in order to breastfeed your baby. I will aid in helping you with strep throat issues. I will help aid you with thyroid issues and help strengthen your bones.

Crazy Lace Agate - I will bring you laughter, happiness, and joy. I will support you and encourage you. You will be optimistic in so many ways, though you may not see it now.

Healthwise - I will heal any acne, eczema, and any other skin disorders you may encounter. I will help improve your tissue metabolism and the elasticity of your blood vessel walls. I will also help prevent varicose veins.

Dendritic Agate - I will bring forth abundance, and plenty to all areas of your life, business, ministry, career, etc.

Healthwise - I will heal your blood vessels and nerves. I will heal your nervous system. I will also assist in skin conditions known as neuralgia and others. I help treat and heal your skeletal disorders. I will reverse capillary degeneration and help stimulate your circulatory system. I will give you relief from pain in your body.

Fire Agate - I will put a fire within you that will perfect those things needing perfecting. I will increase your creativity like fire shut up in your bones.

Healthwise - I will treat your endocrine system, colon, and increase your metabolism. I will increase your night vision so that you can see better at night. I will stimulate the digestive system and relieve gastritis. I will treat and prevent any hot flashes associated with menopause or diabetes.

Laguna Agate - I will give you an understanding of math and increase your precision and increase your intellect. You will have inner stability, composure, and maturity. As you travel, I will protect you from any accidents.

Healthwise - I will help you to increase your energy and help improve your memory. I will heal any stings of scorpions or the bites of snakes you may encounter.

Moss Agate - I will give you wealth, and you will attract abundance in all forms. I will strengthen you in times of stress. I will bring you new friendships.

Healthwise- I help treat infections, swelling, cold, and flu. I will lower your fever, and I will boost your immune system. I will prevent hypoglycemia and dehydration (if used as an elixir to the skin, it can help treat fungal and skin infections and irritations). I will help your circulatory system and regulate your pulse and any other heartbeat irregularities. If you have any buzzing in your ear, I will cure it. I will increase zinc, vitamins A, and D that is useful. I help your lower digestive tract and colon. I will increase the elasticity of your intestinal walls. I will bring health and protect your eyes, stomach, uterus. I will heal skin diseases and itching due to insect bites. I will help heal and protect your heart and blood vessels. (This stone is also known to reduce symptoms of epilepsy, and for some people, it helps guard against sleepwalking. Also, wearing it over the middle of your chest strengthens the cardiac muscle, a cold Agate placed on the forehead is generally effective in curing fever.

Orbicular Agate (Bulls Eye Agate)- I will guard you against any evil eye, or curses sent your way. I will remove fear. I will improve your chances

of survival and give you insight on what to do in dangerous situations. I will help you achieve your goals.

Healthwise - I will help heal any reproductive disorders in your reproductive system. I will help treat any growths on you and help trigger regenerative properties.

12 And I will make thy windows of agates, <u>and thy gates of carbuncles,</u> and all thy borders of pleasant stones.

The gates represent the doors that open and closes gateways or chakras in our body, so he was saying he would guard our gateways.

Red Garnet - I will heal any rejection in your life, whether rejection from others or self-rejection. You will love and appreciate who you are and what I created you to be. I will heal you from lost loved ones. I will heal emotional pain and sadness. I will heal your heart and help you become love. You will be faithful and committed. I will help balance your physical, emotional, and intellectual elements. I will boost your self-confidence. I will break old behavioral problems. I will increase your self-esteem. I will block any bad dreams from the enemy.

Healthwise - I will increase your metabolism, and I will reduce arthritic and rheumatic pain. I will improve circulation and fight against any physical health problems. I will purify you and your aura. I will detox your blood, heart, and lungs. I will reduce and heal any heart rhythm irregularities.

Grossular Garnet - I will give you hope, empowerment, and a loving, nurturing spirit. I will bring forth prosperity and abundance to you. I will bring forth blessings to you. I will bring forth wealth to you. I will help you with new business ideas and ideas for your ministry. I will show you how to grow with your clients or relationships with others. I will strengthen stability in lawsuits or any other life challenges. Instead of being frustrated, angry, bitter, or sad, you will react in love and warmth. You will go along with the transition of life that you go through smoothly because I will give you peace. I will give you romantic ideas with your spouse and help you have fun in life. I will remove worry and increase your passion and love in marriage.

Healthwise - I will help you recover from any illness or trauma, and help your cells regenerate. I will protect your liver and kidneys and regulate your fat metabolism. I will detox and alleviate inflammations through your mucous membranes. I will prevent you from arteriosclerosis. I will aid rheumatism. I will help your immune system and respiratory system. I will protect you from extremely infectious diseases. I will help stimulate your blood and help prevent deep vein thrombosis.

Hessonite Garnet - I will accelerate you in the realm of the spirit. I will help you achieve your spiritual goals. I will give you emotional balance. I will help you let go of the old and painful memories that afflict you day by day. I will eradicate them from you. I will help you get a new start in life and illuminate your new path. I will help you get rid of any evil spirits, black magic, or hexing that the enemy sent your way. I will help boost your self-confidence and dispel any fears you may have had. I will remove the fear of failure, self-expression, and doubt. I will transmute your negative thinking into positive thinking. I will help you sense and feel the beauty of life. I will increase your optimism, joy, security, and love. I will give you intellect and wisdom.

Healthwise - I will ward-off any severe diseases. I will help heal paralysis, skin, asthma, and mental depression. I will improve your eyesight. I will help treat and bring healing to asthma. I will heal your physical wounds. I will heal your olfactory system and remove negative influences that causes ill health. I will regulate your hormone production, therefore reducing infertility and impotence.

Tsavorite Garnet - I will help uplift you and give you vitality, and benevolence. You will see your inner beauty within. You will also see the beauty in others. I will help you to live out your destiny and path instead of struggling along a path that is not truly yours to carry.

Healthwise - I will help heal any respiratory problems. I will help you increase healthy cell growth in your body. I will help you heal quicker and heal any heart problems. I will help heal any disorders of the 5 senses.

African Green Garnet (African Jade, Grossular Garnet) - I will increase your insight and discernment. I will help you in charitable organizations or non-profit companies. I will help increase cooperation skills. I will help you identify differences between people and their ideas easier, which will give every individual and advantage. I will help improve your customer service skills and relationships with customers. I will give you patience and aid you in minimizing irritability with your business/and or life partner, spouse, children, friends, etc. I will help you move forward and overcome different struggles in your relationships. I will help you be more loving and forgiving to your spouse or other relationships.

Healthwise - I will help your renal system, therefore, helping your body to expel stones in the kidneys and spleen. I will help you to recover afterward. I will help treat kidney and bladder infections, including cystitis. I will protect your kidneys and liver from harm by increasing the removal of toxins in your body and any excess liquid in your body while balancing your body's pH level. I will help improve bone and joint problems. I will reduce the incidence and severity of cramps in your body. I will help heal your skeletal system and tissues; I will keep them updated. I will help treat any anorexia. I will help increase your confidence in being a great mother once you give birth.

Almandine Garnet - I will bring you strength and stamina. I will give you time to spend with yourself in order to rest and take time out for yourself without having any guilt. I will make you full of compassion, and you will have the heart to give unto others. I will eradicate any worry, fear, anxiety, and panic that you may have in life, especially in financial matters around you. I will teach you to trust in me. I will make you feel safe and secure. I will help you in times of bereavement. I will heal your past. I will protect you from spiritual warfare.

Healthwise - I will maintain the health of your ovaries. You will give birth. I will help your intestines to absorb iron as it should. I will help treat your liver and pancreas. I will improve circulation and your metabolism and aid in all blood-related issues. I will help you recuperate after an accident or injury.

Pyrope Garnet - I will give you charisma and vitality. You will have a great life. You will be able to compose yourself. You will not feel awkward, and you will be full of courage and endurance

Healthwise - I will strengthen circulation and treat your digestive tract. I will neutralize heartburn and soothe any sore throat you may get. I will heal any bladder issues, circulation issues, exhaustion, numbness, cold feet, and ear problems. I will help remove tiredness and weakness. I will help assist in strengthening your muscles. I will help with temperature sensitivity. I will help heal any bedsores that may occur in your body.

Rhodolite Garnet - You will feel the love for yourself and others. You will feel loved on the inside. I will increase your intuition. You will love in all areas. You will be more open to receiving love, kindness, and compassion. You will remember the purpose that I called you to be on this earth, your journey, and your calling. I will heal any negative emotions and self-destructive emotions. You will see your self-worth and have compassion for yourself. You will have respect for yourself.

Healthwise - I will treat any disorders of the heart and lungs. I will boost your circulation, especially during the winter months. I will relieve you of any blood disorders.

Spessartine Garnet - You will help others. I will help you to analyze and process things. I will push you to the next level in order to bring your dreams and visions into reality during meditation. You will be optimistic and confident, courageous, and will take risks that you know will bring a good outcome. I will boost your creativity.

Healthwise - I will strengthen your heart. I will relieve any sexual problems. I will help ignite and balance your endocrine system. I will produce hormones that will regulate your metabolism, growth, and development. I will help regulate your tissue functions, and reproductive glands, sleep, and mood.

Melanite Garnet - I will strengthen any resistance in order to promote truth and honesty. I will make sure you speak truth and remove anything hindering you from speaking the truth. You will overcome lack, and I will dispel anger, jealousy, envy, distrust. I will move partnerships to the next level. You will overcome any feelings of attack or victimization. You will be love at its fullest.

Healthwise- I will strengthen your bones and help your body to adjust to medications. I will treat arthritis and rheumatism. I will aid in treating cancer and stroke. I will protect you physically and give protection when you are prophesying. I will help you feel grounded. I will help your body resist all forms of infections and enhance your immune system.

Uvarovite Garnet - I will heap past emotional wounds. You will know yourself as a unique individual without having ego, or pride but at the same time, I will link who you are with the universe I created in order to bring forth the kingdom of light. I will encourage you that you are in the right place at the right time because I knew your end from the beginning.

Healthwise - I will detox your body in order to reduce inflammation and lower any fevers. I will treat acidosis, Leukemia, and frigidity.

Andradite Garnet- I will bring forth in the relationships you need most in order to grow spiritually. I will remove any feelings of isolation or alienation, and you will attract the right encounters with others whom I

ordained to be sent your way for my purpose. I will realign your aura/electromagnetic/or energy fields.

Healthwise- I will help aid the formation of your blood and energize your liver. I will help your body receive and absorb the calcium, iron, and magnesium it needs for proper function in your body. I will help regulate your menstrual cycle. I will help improve your vitality, mobility, fitness, and stamina.

With all these gemstones and crystals, we see how the Lord was prophesying over the widow (Israel, us) into whom she would become, he was speaking to her past, present, and future.

The next scripture is evidence that crystals work, we are going to go to the scriptures that the Bible talks about Satan and how his body was covered with crystals/or gemstones. Like and armor suit, which we will talk about in the next chapter. The effects it had on him, which made him puffed up in pride, and he put himself above God because he thought he could be God all the way and want people to worship him and not God. Let's see the knowledge that he had by having the energy of the gemstones within him. I will point out the gemstones that we have not recently gone over in this chapter because you can go back and reference the carbuncles and sapphire benefits. Just so you know, Satan was an example of how you can fall. However, he was not the only angel who was made of gemstones. If you see one angel with certain traits or characteristics, or features, marks, then you will see others of the same. Just like us, we can see someone who looks like us, but the genes and fingerprint show that they aren't you. The Father is made of gemstones himself.

Ezekiel 28 - Satan Covering of Crystals and Gemstones

"11Moreover the word of the Lord came unto me, saying,

12 Son of man take up a lamentation upon the king of Tyrus, and say unto him, Thus saith the Lord God; Thou sealest up the sum, full of wisdom, and perfect in beauty.

13 Thou hast been in Eden the garden of God; every precious stone was thy covering, the sardius, topaz, and the diamond, the beryl, the onyx, and jasper, sapphire, emerald, and the carbuncle, and gold: the workmanship of thy tabrets and of thy pipes was prepared in thee in the day that thou wast created.

14 Thou art the anointed cherub that covereth; and I have set thee: thou wast upon the holy mountain of God; thou hast walked up and down in the midst of the stones of fire.

15 Thou wast perfect in thy ways from the day that thou wast created, till iniquity was found in thee.

16 By the multitude of thy merchandise they have filled the midst of thee with violence, and thou hast sinned: therefore I will cast thee as profane out of the mountain of God: and I will destroy thee, O covering cherub, from the midst of the stones of fire.

17 Thine heart was lifted up because of thy beauty, thou hast corrupted thy wisdom by reason of thy brightness: I will cast thee to the ground, I will lay thee before kings, that they may behold thee.

18 Thou hast defiled thy sanctuaries by the multitude of thine iniquities, by the iniquity of thy traffick; therefore will I bring forth a fire from the midst of thee, it shall devour thee, and I will bring thee to ashes upon the earth in the sight of all them that behold thee.

19 All they that know thee among the people shall be astonished at thee: thou shalt be a terror, and never shalt thou be any more." (Ezekiel 28:11-19 (KJV))

So, let's break down the gemstones that were the covering of Satan, and it seemed to be the covering for the king of Tyre also. The King of Tyre had one of the world's biggest trading industries in Tyre, and he was a king. Most kings wore gemstones on their bodies, crown, scepters, and rings. They wore necklaces to represent their royalty and to protect them.

"13 Thou hast been in Eden the garden of God; <u>every precious stone was thy covering, the sardius, topaz, and the diamond, the beryl, the onyx, and jasper, sapphire, emerald, and the carbuncle, and gold</u>: the workmanship of thy tabrets and of thy pipes was prepared in thee in the day that thou was created." (Ezekiel 28:13 KJV)

Carnelian Benefits (aka Sardius) - It energizes and stimulates action. It breaks the indecision and procrastination in your life and replaces it with the courage to move forward towards spiritual healing. You will have a more definite sense of self-awareness about yourself. It will allow spiritual energy (Holy Spirit) to flow more freely. It will recall the path to take towards achieving important goals. Carnelian stabilizes emotions and increases motivation. It increases your concentration and focus. It removes the mind from temptation. It provides protection from

negative emotions such as envy, jealousy, rage, and resentment from others and within yourself. It will give you a renewed love of life in general. It also reduces any feelings of jealousy or possessiveness in romantic relationships. It can help men go through a midlife crisis. Eating disorders may be curbed by using a carnelian.

Healthwise - You will have improved circulation. It will help improve digestion and help stimulate nutrient absorption in the small intestine. It will help aid with boils, congestion, hemorrhoids, phlebitis, skin problems, and varicose veins. It will help stop nosebleeds. It also has healing properties associated with the musculoskeletal system. It helps aid in healing arthritis, back problems, neuralgia, rheumatism. It will help you detox from drugs and alcohol and aid in breaking the addiction to these substances.

Topaz Overall Benefits *-Topaz is a remarkable crystal for healing and stabilizing the emotional body. It teaches forgiveness and truth, but at the same time, replaces any negativity (fear, doubt) with positive energy of all things that is crucial for the individual themselves, such as confidence, esteem, acceptance, self-reliance, and worth. It aligns one soul and brings happiness, love, and abundance in one's life. It stirs up creativity and promotes individuality and the expression of love and abundance in one's life. It stirs up creativity and promotes individuality and the expression of ideas. It helps one realize their own abilities and wealth of knowledge gained from learned experiences and hard work. It supports one in implementing great dreams and makes one happy to share their joy and give to others.*

It boosts faith and increases one's spiritual development. It cuts through uncertainty and doubt. It brings forth trust in the Lord through the universe he created. It helps fight and download divine wisdom and knowledge of the Lord. It helps you recognize the strategic ways of the Lord how he uses symbols, signs to communicate with you in your daily life.

Blue Topaz Benefits - Helps increase your ability to communicate better, and to express yourself in a meaningful way when speaking or when writing. It helps you if you have any problems with public speaking; it removes the fear holding you back from speaking publicly. It will help you focus and assist you to think better and to focus on the task at hand. You make more precise and more specific decisions about the right direction to take in life. It helps you write and inspires creativity. It increases and strengthens your prophetic gifts. It gives you the truth and wisdom and helps aid you in your spiritual growth. Blue Topaz reflects the energy of the mind and knowledge, stimulating one's self-confidence and the ability to learn and think through complex concepts and ideas. It causes creativity, increases attention span, and helps one achieve perfection in various projects and aspirations. It helps people to consciously and clearly articulate the thoughts and feelings one needs to

communicate and make clear distinctions about what one does and does not want in one's life. It births forth peacefulness and calms your emotions. It helps you be in tune with Holy Spirit.

Healthwise - Improves vitality and overall health, slows down the aging process. It improves the hydrating and cleansing properties of the water you drink. It helps you lose excess body fat. It flushes out free radicals and toxins out of your body. It dissolves mineral or plaque buildup from your tissue. It maximizes the nutritional benefit of good and the medicinal benefits of herbal teas. Wow!! Blue topaz improves energy flows throughout your body. Blue topaz helps your body to accept a transplanted organ instead of rejecting it. It relaxes and calms down your mind, making it open to new ideas and others' points of view. It's suitable for people who suffer from irregular cells such as melanomas, tumors, moles, cysts, or longstanding pimples. It's useful for those who suffer from knotted muscles, arthritic, or paralyzed tissue, or other physical rigidities. It's also suitable for those who suffer from poor absorption of nutrients or suffering from undernourishment. It's supportive of the head and skull, eyes, ears, and overall health of the neck and throat. It relieves headaches, migraine, occipital pains, tightening of the jaws, and the feeling of squeezing of the temples. It aids in the treatment of stress-related disorders, like high blood pressure, and may be used in discovering and finding out the real source of illness (whether it spiritual, mental, emotional, or physical) and the right source of treatment. It helps soothe sore throats, speech impediments, and fear of public speaking.

Clear/White/Silver Topaz -embodies the energy of the spirit and opens one's senses to the essence of Self. It brings an awakening of one's thoughts and deeds and the consequences they will result in, whether good or bad. It brings a cosmic awareness and understanding of seeing the big picture and how one fits into it all. It increases spiritual development, and brings forth one's motives, intentions, purposes and aligns it with the Lord's will in order to manifest it in the earth realm. It removes stagnant energy and allows one to discover their inner wealth of knowledge and abilities and push creative spiritual endeavors to the limit. It is highly effective for increasing the seer anointing. It's the stone of truth, and it allows you to see the truth in others and to maintain the truth that's within oneself through the Holy Spirit.

Clear Topaz Healthwise – It accelerates recovery from injury or illness, and reinforce treatments for cystic fibrosis, emphysema, asthma, allergies, colds, flu, pleurisy, and pneumonia.

Purple Topaz - Exemplifies spiritual wealth, bringing in the energy and spirit of prayer and blessings to one's life. It elevates and transforms you, and it increases one's ability to give and receive abundantly on all levels. Excellent for decision making. It recalls any severe flaws in the logic of a lack of objectivity. It protects you against bringing in the wrong people in your life that cause pain or that will not further your happiness.

Healthwise - may be employed in therapies for autism, pathological medical conditions, such as schizophrenia and personality disorders, and to assist in strengthening the spine.

Brown Topaz - gives strength and stability, confidence and commitment, increasing faithfulness in love, and the ability to build lasting friendships. It helps those who distrust life and other people to become more open and welcoming, and is a marvelous aid for relieving agoraphobia, extreme timidity, and observe compulsive disorder. It increases strength, motivation, and makes it makes you feel more secure in who you are. It's great for those who work on the land, or with animals, or in conservation. It helps you see the spirits or beings ruling over the trees, mountains, grass, forest, etc. That's awesome!

Rutilated Topaz - It brings beauty and light, creation, and inspiration. It stimulates the mind's eye and is exceptionally useful for visualization and manifestation.

Pink Topaz - It brings for hope allowing one to experience the presence of the Lord. It encourages integrity, honesty, and openness, and brings blessings in matters of the love of whom the Lord may bring to you. He may not bring who you want but will bring what you need, but it's up to you to accept whom he brings. It heals those who have been hurt by love or loss.

Golden Imperial Topaz - Embraces the nobility of spirit, status, personal will, and ability to manifest one's desires. It helps you manifest and hit the bullseye of what you want. It recharges you spiritually and physically. It boosts your faith, optimism, and increases one's optimism, increasing one's confidence, self-worth, and pride in one's abilities without pride and ego. It enhances relaxation and imparts feelings of peace.

Healthwise - Recharges the physical body, helps you overcome the physical body, and to overcome nervous exhaustion and to promote tissue regeneration. Good for postoperative convalescence, improving blood circulation, and relieving issues with cold feet. It is used for treatments for disorders of the liver, gallbladder, and endocrine gland. It fights depression and improve your brain function and may be beneficial for the elderly or anyone nearing death. They have been used to aid treatments for Dementia and Alzheimer's disease.

Diamond Benefits - It helps increase your inner visions, imaginations, and creativity. It represents purity and innocence, of love and fidelity. It gives strength in dealing with intense situations and aid in responding with grace. Hallelujah! Diamonds are great conductors of energy, absorbing thoughts and feelings, then radiating them outward. You must remain positive while holding or wearing diamonds to project empowering thoughts around you and get a positive reaction from others. ** <u>It is said that they are amplifiers and conductors, so whatever you give out, whether positive or negative, then that is what energy is going to be released, They never need recharging, but they definitely need to be cleansed which we will talk about in another chapter. They can amplify the power of any emotional state</u>** They relieve fear and anxiety, overactive imaginations, and hallucinations. They are great for cleansing room of any demonic spirits or negative energy and are useful to prevent nightmares if it is used the correct way.

Using a rough Diamond elixir is excellent for counteracting exhaustion. You can add a few drops of the elixir in your bath in order to re-energize. Raw crystals are ideal for healing to bring clarity of energy to any part of the body or any level of the energy field. Faceted gems are used to infuse your electromagnetic field/aura with full-spectrum light energy reflecting all hues frequencies for strengthening, purifying, and cleansing. It infuses your energetic self with light and may be used therapeutically to intensify and burn through any underlying emotional issues; Allowing one to feel lighter, more joyful, and more aligned with Holy Spirit. It's useful for those who have lost their value or self-worth. It's useful for those going through an identity crisis or is confused. It's suitable for those unable to walk into their divine destiny or call. It should be avoided in cases of paranoid psychosis, depressive manias, and obsessive jealousy.

Healthwise - It's known as a master healer for its ability to unify the mind and body. Its best used as a supportive stone, amplifying the energy and powers of other crystals (minerals) when working on a specific issue, where over excessive energy has caused a physical imbalance. It is beneficial in purifying and strengthening brain function, nerves, and sensory organs. It is thought to aid in

balancing the brain hemispheres. Diamonds are good for strokes, epilepsy, and to combat the aging of the cells and to restore energy levels. They are used to cure constipation, urine retention, and in general, all organs associated with removing waste from the body. Applying Diamond to the kidney is generally said to accelerate the evacuation of kidney stones. The effect will persist even once it has been removed. It is advised to proceed in short sessions of five minutes.

Beryl Varieties -Aquamarine, Emerald, Golden Beryl, Goshenite, Green Beryl, Heliodor, Morganite, Red Beryl

Aquamarine – It encourages calm, reflective relaxation, brings forth wisdom, feelings, and truth. It relieves stress. Imparts perseverance and discipline while the mood is lifted. It inspires humanitarian efforts in healing and helping others. You are encouraged to be kind and compassionate yet, at the same time, have a responsible demeanor. It soothes fears and increases sensitivity. This is good for people who are often judgmental and critical in order to become more tolerant, patient. It helps those who are overwhelmed by responsibilities become better at managing things and time. Aquamarine helps men and women feel more empowered, yet, helps them to realize that power does not have to come only from the force, but it helps one to realize self-empowerment through clear, honest, and compassionate communication. Women find the courage to help express their thoughts, and its more comfortable for them to develop their intuition. Men find communication easier as it helps cut through every barrier of emotional numbness to allow them to speak more freely. It helps provide the courage to work through difficulties in all aspects of life but is very useful when communicating to Adonai.

Deeper truths and the causes of emotional trauma can be considered with less fear and anger. It helps you to let go of old emotional trauma that prevents one from moving forward. Hallelujah!! If any circumstances happen when someone's pride or ego is damaged, causing one to remain in an abusive relationship either as the victim Even abuse, it allows one to see the true nature of relationships clearly. People who are manipulated or have allowed themselves to become a martyr, or victimized can begin emotional healing when the inner truths are revealed to them. It helps you to recognize patterns of behavior is the first step in this type of emotional healing. With this stone, disagreements can be worked out with less fear and anger. It helps to communicate intelligently and rationally with compassion.

Healthwise - It increases a person's immune system, thymus, and lymph nodes. Aquamarine is known as the stone of breath because it centers on breathing. It may alleviate respiratory tract, lung, and sinus problems. It allows for better breathing with allergies. It gives relief from allergies, hay fever, colds, and bronchitis. It helps those suffering from skin inflammations. Psoriasis, hives, rosacea, and eczema might be relieved and calmed. Herpes breakouts may be prevented, or the severity reduced. The extremity of shingles may become less when included in the treatment. It's a cooling stone. It strengthens your Larynx and helps heal sore throats. It strengthens and cleanses organs and aids the eyes, jaw, teeth, and stomach. Aquamarine takes the pain away from toothaches.

Emerald- It has a stable love vibration. It helps people who have things keeping them back from living an abundant life and allowing the abundance of loving energy to flow through them. It teaches you the value of love in all its faceted ways. It will help you manifest loving ways, good health, and a peaceful, loving, and harmonious life. If you want to learn to stay happy, you might like to have this stone in your life. It will manifest abundance as well as money. It will help you to increase prosperity in every area of your life. It teaches you to have honor for life and all of creation. As you feel this honor, it might prompt you to live life in a more loving way. This is one of the purest and highest forms of love from the Father Jehovah. You will begin living your life from a spiritual, heart-based perspective. It will bring forth compassion, loyalty, hope, encouragement, comfort, gentleness, kindness, goodness, and unconditional love. It aids in emotional healing.

It brings intellectual progress. It increases creativity, artistic talents, linguistic skills. Emerald also gives the ability to create and innovate better. It helps you to focus on what really matters. It brings a better understanding of life. Restless people can have stability. It takes away negativity. If a person finds it hard to come to terms with difficult situations where they have been betrayed, cheated, or defrauded, then this would be a good stone for them. It's believed to have antidote healing powers against poison. It's useful for healers or anyone in the prophetic. It helps those who stammer or feel shy to interact with others, it's suitable for those who have been held back due to lack of confidence.

Healthwise - they relieve issues in the eyes and are helping to keep the body to ease issues in the spine and muscular system. It helps heal physical issues in the

heart and lung area. It helps with speech difficulties, respiratory problems, allergies, and nervous disorders.

Heliodor & Golden Beryl - They help you to have and gain better mastery of your time and life circumstance. Wow! Now that helps with healing and wholeness. They heal your past and stops chronic repetition of unhealthy life situations, behavior patterns, or physical conditions. They help you to become more aware of counterproductive responses so you can change them. They help you better understand the lessons of a physical condition and resolve the negative impact it has by stopping the cause. They relieve the fear that accompanies major illness and opens your heart to a more holistic view of it. It helps a person becomes less judgmental about other choices. It is known as the "Sunshine Stone." It imparts confidence and drive while still maintaining focus and empathy towards others. When placed on a dish, they can help to remove negative entities or demonic forces and increase the angels in your home or space. It brings the love and spark back into stagnant relationships. It protects against demonic and negative influences or manipulations. They help you to release old emotional baggage that no longer serves you good, and it can aid in the removal of stress, distractions, and chaos. They help increase visions.

Healthwise - They assist with problems related from the pancreas, liver, and spleen. They relieve stiffness in hands and feet caused by cold weather or lack of circulation. Its aids for Seasonal Affective Disorder. They aid the digestive system and small intestine, bilious attacks, nausea, jaundice, diarrhea, and chronic constipation. Helps benefit the heart, also aids in healing of contusion of skull damage, and help aid in exhaustion. They warm stiff limbs or cold fingers and toes caused by cold weather or poor circulation. They fortify the eyes and helps in near and farsightedness.

Morganite - Helps maintain love with your spouse. Crystal of divine love. It brings peace, joy, and inner strength if worn for extended periods of time. It encourages growth of confidence and power that comes from a constant awareness of the connection of Christ's love. It's suitable for lawyers for making sure that things are fair. It's good for new business to gain a foothold in the market. It imparts fair treatment to others, especially if they have mental, emotional, or physical problems. It realizes equality in all relationships and developing effective but loving communication and expression. It is supportive for girls entering puberty or struggling with eating disorders. It also quiets stress, relieves pressure to perform, and reduces the pattern of dodging and running away from situations. It aids in understanding all the aspects of love, that once applied, could be used to heal and maintain the Earth. It helps you

overcome fear, resentment, anger. Morganite helps you see unfulfilled emotional needs and feelings which have gone unexpressed. It releases defense mechanisms that are fear-based. Morganite stabilizes the emotional field. It increases and energizes loving thoughts and actions and brings in wisdom and peace of mind. It increases the ability to accept loving words and actions from others and releases the old soul ties to old relationships that have ended badly or needed resolution, therefore inspiring one to move forward with a new perspective, purpose, goal, and to have an open heart. It helps deepen love in marriages. It aids in helping an individual to have peace and acceptance when faced with grief or profound loss.

Healthwise - helps the physical heart, strengthening a person's energy field and helping to establish its place of dominance in the electromagnetic field/or aura. It counters palpitations and other heart-related problems, as well as clearing lungs, treating the nervous system, and relieving stress-related illness. It helps in with other treatments for asthma, emphysema, and tuberculosis, and for oxygenating and restructuring disordered cells at the cellular level. It helps aid the larynx, tongue and thyroid gland, and aids in treatments for vertigo and impotence.

Red Beryl/Bixbite, aka Red Emerald and Scarlet Emerald - Blood of Christ Jesus, cleansing and purification and healing power of the blood of Christ. It promotes courage, and passion, and will power without pride and ego. It helps you release conflict within and things of the past.

Healthwise - It helps cell reproduction. It controls the fatty acids, which aids in the formation of new blood cells; it promotes self-healing and cell repair. It increases vitality and energy. It helps you recover from infectious disease or illness. It helps assists the reproductive organs, liver, blood, teeth, bones. It aids and assist in metabolic enzyme processes.

Onyx - A strong protection stone, it absorbs and transforms negative energy. It helps aid in the development of emotional and physical strength and stamina, especially when support is needed during times of stress, confusion, or grief. It imparts wise decision-making. It encourages happiness and blessings. It helps to hold physical memories; it can be helpful in healing past wounds. It stabilizes the emotional body, bringing strength in difficult or confusing circumstances and during times of tremendous mental or physical stress. It relieves nervousness, quells, anxiety, and fear. Onyx calms down tempers and restores rational thinking and self-control. It imparts self-mastery, imparts, self-

confidence, focus, ease in one's surrounding, and gives the gift of wise decision making. It leads you to a more stabilized life. It helps one start and seek out new ideas, as well as carry out even dreary tasks to completion. Onyx helps you to recognize old habits or relationships that need to be re-evaluated or released. It brings inner strength to let go. It aids in grieving; It assist a person during emotional processes of mourning, acceptance, and moving forward.

Healthwise - It improves the function of the nerves and sharpens your sensory organs, especially those associated with the ear. It helps increase and sharpen hearing; it assists in problems or diseases of the inner ear and aids in the treatment of tinnitus. Strengthen the immune system, provides energy and vitality to the body; it prevents relapses after illnesses. They improve cell regeneration and the regulations of fluids. It aids in the absorption of nutrients and elimination of wastes. It's beneficial for the teeth and bones; it supports disorders relating to bone marrow and soft tissue structures. It's good for those who suffer from weak legs.

Jasper Benefits (All Jaspers are included because they have the same benefits, yet different characteristics and uses as you will find out with the different ones that will be listed afterward) - Jasper frequency is slow and constant. It keeps a person more grounded and stable. It provides comfort, security, strength, and healing. It balances the electromagnetic field/or aura or wholeness and peace. It reminds a person that they are not in the physical plane or living for themselves, but to bring joy and substance to others. Jasper helps alleviate stress and induce serenity. Its cleansing effects eliminates negative energy and stabilizes the person's electromagnetic field/aura. It helps relieve worry, and it helps soothe a person's nerves and increase their focus. It protects a person from nightmares and toxic, negative thoughts.

It's an excellent stone for healing and keeping the physical and emotional bodies during injury or extended illness or hospitalization. Its Earth energies brings steady strength and renewed vitality while helping one to understand and endure the frustrating or painful experiences. It's an impressive diet stone, helping emotional support and strength in self-discipline as well as boosting your physical energy levels. Its slow, steady vibration helps avoid extremes and encourages perseverance. It's excellent for long periods of fasting. It is useful for those who want to cut down or quit smoking and may assist in one's over-consumption of alcohol. It removes harmful toxins from the body over time and help to release emotional triggers the perpetuate the behavior. It increases fertility and is conducive to happy pregnancies.

Healthwise – Jasper is highly restorative for tissue deterioration of the internal organs, and use for treating disorders of the kidneys, spleen, bladder, liver, and stomach. It may also aid in balancing mineral content and regulating supplies of iron, sulfur, zinc, and manganese within the body. It's calming for the digestive system and is useful as a gem elixir because it does not over stimulate the body. It can be used by letting the stone soak in demineralized water overnight. It excellent for steady blood flow, particularly nose bleeds, and also assist in reducing hemorrhoids. It soothes epilepsy and gout and may be used to treat the sensory loss of smell.

Black Jasper/or Basanite- It empowers supreme physical and mental efforts, and is a highly shielding against curses, threats, and danger in high-risk occupations. It increases the prophetic in dreams and visions.

Blue Jasper - It imparts courage to speak out against injustice and to risk unpopularity to defend the vulnerable. It is an excellent anti-stress stone for those in charge of others' well-being, and for older children and teenagers to carry to resist being led into unwise behavior or risky situations.

Walnut Jasper -It dissolves sudden rushes of fear, anger, panic, or anxiety.

Dalmatian Jasper - It's a protective and healing stone, fortifying the spirit and encouraging a sense of playfulness. It counters disillusionment, cynicism, and skepticism, it strengthens family bonds and long-term friendship and is a calming influence for children and animals. Unity, Harmony, Beautiful! Hallelujah!!

Green Jasper- It calms your spirit man, breaks any demonic force (negative energies), and evil thoughts, it increases fertility. It eliminates obsessive ways of a person and restores harmony and union to the emotional body, allowing one to gain control over their thoughts.

Kambaba Jasper - It brings peace, serenity, and tranquility to a troubled and worried mind. It strengthens those hearts that have been deeply hurt.

Mookaite - it increases life in the physical body and promotes an ageless spirit willing to accept change and seek new experiences. It awakens a person's own instinct.

Ocean Jasper- It holds a gentle nurturing energy that, when used regularly, assists in developing self-love and empathy for others.

Picture Jasper - Its and excellent stone for creative vision, initiative, and boosting confidence, it is an ideal aid for starting one's own business. If you want to bring hidden thoughts, grief, fears, and hopes to the surface for spiritual growth, it can help you by you wearing it for long periods of time.

Poppy Jasper - Imparts joy, cheerfulness, vitality, and positive energy reminding humanity to help one another out. It can be gentle, intense, as needed. It encourages you with fresh ideas.

Rainbow Jasper - It balances the physical body and brings focus to the mind and intellect, it tempers procrastination and helps organize an overactive mind into more linear thought, preventing a person from getting caught up in worry over the past or future, and inspiring one to work through issues of the present. It is used for one rejuvenating one's creativity and helps to refine a person's mentality in order to work through complicated thoughts, ideas, or puzzles.

Rainforest Jasper - It honors the teaching from Nature (Job 12:8 or speak to the earth, and it shall teach thee; the fish of the sea shall declare unto thee.) It awakens a sense of joy and cheerfulness at life's beauty and simplicity and carries a healing and refreshing energy of hope and renewal.

It brings forth earth healing and working with the devic realm (devics are not another form of devils they are another set of angels that help nurture the earth for instance fairies are actually real, and they help watch over the plants, in order for them to grow in the proper time and order. We have to break this pattern of, "oh it sound like devil, so it must mean devil," sometimes we say these things to sound so spiritual, but in

reality, it's a religious spirit, or to repeat another man's teaching that has been passed down over the years. Some people just give the devil too much credit, and that's why everyone wants to blame the devil when things go wrong, and some things actually happens because the Father allows it to happen to test your faith and his word in order to teach a particular lesson in order for you to grow spiritually. Truth be told, man can be influenced by Devil (Satan) or the fallen angels itself because Jesus called Peter himself Satan because Peter was speaking against the Father's will for Jesus life at that moment.

Peter, I'm sure didn't even know he was talking as Satan at the time. People sometimes fail to realize just because you are born again or not; you have good angels that can influence you by ministering to you, and also, a demonic spirit can influence you when you end up sinning or acting out of the character Jesus portrayed. It's up to the individual on the choice they choose to make. But, thank God for the blood of the lamb Jesus Christ our Lord and Savior, Hallelujah!! We are not perfect and will make mistakes along the way in life. If you stay rooted and grounded in the word of God, The Father, Son, and Holy Spirit, fasting and prayer of faith the Lord will cover us his children because of His unfailing love for us, because we are one with him. If you get off course, he always pulls you back in if you want to be willed back in. Either way, Jesus is never far off but right in front of you because Christ again is all in all. He's in the air you breathe in, and the universe itself is made up of him. I felt led to put that out there.

Red Jasper - Gives physical strength and energy. It stimulates gently and steadily; it enhances stamina and perseverance. It's a stone of health and passion and brings forth the courage to face unpleasant tasks and to correct unjust situations. It brings back to your remembrance dreams that you have had.

Unakite Jasper - it lifts a person's head up when they are feeling down and balances all aspects of the heart. It helps to release hidden, deep emotions in a slow, gentle way. It imparts patience and persistence and gradually eliminates bad habits and thought patterns that perpetuates them. It is an excellent stone for children's sensitive emotions and is particularly useful for helping them bounce back from

sorrow, grief, and disappointment. It is excellent for anyone who may feel like they have lost who they are or may feel overwhelmed, consumed, or have trouble focusing on the present.

Yellow Jasper - it imparts endurance, perseverance, and tenacity, and shields against others' negativity. Wahoo!! If worn for long periods of time, it eases chronic worries and builds self-confidence, it attracts others for friendship or to help with a goal. It supports consistent learning and transmits healing and increases the earth energies, especially if you are meditating outdoors. (The Lord says, "Be still, and know that I am God; I will be exalted among the nations; I will be exalted in the earth." Ps.46:10) All things in the earth resides in Christ, our Lord and Savior, and functions through him to do his will as he ordered it to do, through the Father. It's up to us to co-labor with not just him, but the universe, earth, nature, angels, crystals, animals, whatever he wants us to co-labor within order to spread forth his kingdom.

*If we only stay at only having communion with Christ and not commune or co-labor with the Father, and the Holy Spirit, then we missed it. It we don't work with people who may not know Christ but are fantastic people that have gifts, businesses, or wisdom that you been wondering about. Then they give you an answer out of nowhere, and it's like a light bulb went on, and you accept the advice because it bear witness in your spirit, then you are on the right track. **"We are to honor all men and love brotherhood." 1 Peter 2:17(KJV)** We honor them and work with them. You may say, "what do you mean?" What I mean is your blessing may not come from your brother or sister in Christ, the Lord may use another person to bless you or give you insight that was needed for you to learn. We are to love all people, just because someone isn't saved, Holy Ghost filled, and or is not what you think they need to be, doesn't mean they are evil or to separate yourself from them. There are many people in the world that are good people, and they may not have heard of Christ, or they may have. Just because they haven't confessed that Jesus Christ is the Lord and Savior doesn't mean that they are evil. Just because they may be of a different religion, you continue to be that light and love them. It was still the Father who knew them before they were put into their mother's womb. You just know some things you will do with them and some things you won't do with them if its contrary to your beliefs. This even comes to differences in religions. We are to walk in love and honor who the individual is despite our differences in how you view or do things. The Father may have downloaded them knowledge that you may have needed. The Body of Christ is not just the church; it's all creation and nationalities. But he wants everyone submitted unto him and to know him as their Lord and Savior.*

When I talked to the earth, it showed me some things I didn't know, but it was through the spirit of Christ Jesus that it was revealed because he is still all in all. We are to love all mankind and creation. If we think the trees are just here to

look pretty, then we have missed it, trees can help revitalize, rejuvenate, and re-energize your gateways and help give you peace. If we think seeds are here to help plants grow, then we missed it, because there is so much to learn about the fantastic things in the universe and earth that we don't know about yet, that the Father wants to be revealed. If you don't ask the earth to help teach you things to expand the kingdom of God, then you've missed it. We are to co-labor with creation in order for Christ kingdom to be established and to make a new earth. If we just be prejudice towards things or think things are here for decorations, then we missed it. The Lord put all these things in the universe, earth, and all creation to help each other out in order to help bring forth the Kingdom of Light in Christ Jesus. Basically, if we have a one-track mind and close ourselves off from other things, then we may not grow and just remain stagnant because we have repeated the same process in which the results are no longer valid because we have not moved into the new things that the Lord is establishing and redeeming.

So, we know by these scriptures why Satan became prideful and wanted to be God, and thought he had it all, even though he is not human. The energy and vibrations of the crystals and stones wherein him in heaven, so when you look at the benefits and uses of these crystals beyond what I have research, you would see why he fell. We see the king of Tyre had gemstones over his body and crown as a King, and we see the effects of the crystals he wore; he got full of pride. The Lord said, basically, I must put you back into your place for you to remember that you are just a man. The Lord compared him to Satan, so let's say he had the same gemstones, then that's why he fell, just like Satan. So we have to make sure of course that we don't fall into the same trap of I don't need God anymore, I have it all together: life is perfect, then that's where you go wrong, and it becomes idolatry which is what we would talk about in a later chapter.

Chapter 6: Crystals: The Vital Missing Link to the Whole Armor of God in Our Life

We have been taught to put on the full armor of God. And we do put on our full armor. However, we will end up coming back to the church wounded, exhausted spiritually, mentally, emotionally, and sometimes physically. Or we leave the church pumped up, revitalized and energized; next thing we know we know all of a sudden we feel negatively drained, and we don't know why; Or better yet the pastor just got done having a healing crusade or did deliverance at the church service, but he leaves out drained and exhausted. Or we may go to someone's house revitalized or in a good mood, but soon as we enter into their house because of the heaviness, sorrow, or bitterness in the house it may actually drain us or either we leave there, and that same negative energy or demonic influence that was in the atmosphere managed to latch itself unto you. So now, you are influenced by the same negativity that the person was consumed with. Even though the church is actually within us, I say this to let you know we are spiritual and energetic beings. The spirit world is fact; the physical world can be deception if you don't recognize that demonic spirits (negative energy) are real and can influence anyone, including those both saved and unsaved.

Perhaps maybe your daughter called, who is married, and maybe going through a divorce because her husband cheated, and he is literally flaunting women in your daughters face and lying and manipulating her to make her life miserable. He's lying and manipulating the people around them, that they know in order to make it seem as if he's the good guy and she's the horrible unfit mom. He may have always claimed the children on their taxes and promised to give her half of the income taxes and don't keep his end of the bargain. Next thing you know, you are angry, sad, and drained out because you have to comfort your daughter and you are angry because he is able to get away with it; and it seems as if no justice is being served or you may feel like Lord where are you in this situation. So, your joyful day just turned upside down. Or maybe you prayed for a person, and you feel mentally, spiritually drained, and tired. Or maybe you felt someone stab you, even though you didn't see it, you felt it, in the realm of the spirit in your body because someone is talking negative about you that you have a soul tie with or that you know.

Maybe an actual witch or warlock might actually had cast a spell upon you to destroy your destiny. Or you may actually have had a witch to come in your dream and tried to choke you, or you woke up with scratches on you unexplained.

These are some of the experiences I have experienced and heard from others in the body of Christ, and I'm pretty sure people, in general, have all had these types of experiences one way or another. If you have ever had this experience as a believer in Christ, I have the answer. <u>*We have had our full armor incomplete because we did not use the crystals as part of our armor physically, because we never knew the supernatural or spiritual benefits.*</u> *What I mean of the armor physically, is we never wore crystals as jewelry, because we never knew the spiritual benefits and was taught that they are evil. Now it may be people that have not experienced any of the similar experiences. We know, "We wrestle not against flesh and blood but rulers of darkness and spiritual wickedness in high places" (Ephesians 6:12 KJV). We need our spiritual armor on, through Christ, our Savior and mediator, the word of God, faith, and righteousness. We are going to go over some scriptures to show that the Father intended for us to wear crystals/gemstones/or stones as part of the armor physically.* **Prov.17:8 says, "8 A gift is as a precious stone in the eyes of him that hath it: whithersoever it turneth, it prospereth."** *Meaning each crystal is a gift because it prospers and completes the job or assignment that the Father or we ourselves tell it to do for us according to God's word, or what we need for it to benefit us spiritually, mentally, and emotionally, and physically to the glory of God. So, whether it's one crystal or more that we have, it will complete the job that it was intended for.*

"10 Finally, my brethren, be strong in the Lord, and in the power of his might.

11 Put on the whole armour of God, that ye may be able to stand against the wiles of the devil.

12 For we wrestle not against flesh and blood, but against principalities, against powers, against the rulers of the darkness of this world, against spiritual wickedness in high places.

13 Wherefore take unto you the whole armour of God, that ye may be able to withstand in the evil day, and having done all, to stand.

14 Stand therefore, having your loins girt about with truth, and having on the breastplate of righteousness;

15 And your feet shod with the preparation of the gospel of peace;

16 Above all, taking the shield of faith, wherewith ye shall be able to quench all the fiery darts of the wicked.

17 And take the helmet of salvation, and the sword of the Spirit, which is the word of God:

18 Praying always with all prayer and supplication in the Spirit, and watching thereunto with all perseverance and supplication for all saints;

*19 **And for me, that utterance may be given unto me, that I may open my mouth boldly, to make known the mystery of the gospel,***

*20 **For which I am an ambassador in bonds: that therein I may speak boldly, as I ought to speak." Ephesians 6:10-20(KJV)***

Having your loins girt about with truth

We know our loins girt about with truth means the word of God. We also know the crystals keep record and knows the word of God also as we see in Joshua 24:27 (KJV) "And Joshua said unto all the people, <u>Behold, this stone shall be a witness unto us; for it hath heard all the words of the LORD which he spake unto us: it shall be therefore a witness unto you, lest ye deny your God</u>." It's also the testimony of Jesus because the testimony of Jesus is prophecy. And we know we overcome Satan by the word of our testimony of Jesus. Also, through affirmations, "calling those things that are not as though they were" (Romans 4:17 KJV) and prophesying positive things over ourselves, decreeing the word of God over ourselves. Thou shalt also decree a thing, and it shall be established unto thee: and the light shall shine upon thy ways. (Job 22:28) Or we shall say what we want, and it shall come to pass.

And having on the breastplate of righteousness

The stones on the priest breastplates of the 12 Tribes of Israel performed the positives characteristics of the sons of Jacob but counteracted their negative characteristics or weaknesses. They also counteract the negative things that happened in their life. It's a way we can apply and take on the uses of the frequencies and vibrations of crystals to help us in our own life in order to counteract our own weaknesses, sins, negative fruit, negativity, doubt, distractions, etc. They help us to increase more fruits of the spirit within our soul.

Different stones or crystals are used to bring forth the fruit of the spirit stated in Galatians that we all cried out for an increase in our lives for, at least, I know I did. "22But the fruit of the Spirit is love, joy, peace, patience, kindness, goodness, faithfulness, gentleness, self-control; against such things there is no law." Galatians 5:22-23(ESV) We want to increase the fruit of the spirit, which is positive energy, that's where our crystals help us to increase in fruitfulness by helping program and train our bodies to increase in fruitfulness. The reason why I say programming is because if you wear a particular crystal or crystals after so long to help counteract negative thoughts by removing them and transmuting them into positive thoughts through the neurons in our body; after so long your soul (mind, will, and emotions) is programmed or trained to think positive and to prosper physically, mentally, emotionally, and financially. It's like breaking old useless habits and thinking and bringing in positive, useful habits and positive thinking. Most crystals work instantaneously, but it takes time to heal all the way sometimes. We use crystals for the highest good, not for evil. They are alive rocks through Christ, the Living Rock, and are friends to help us in times of need as a gift of the Father to prosper us spiritually, mentally, emotionally, and physically. Each one of those stones the Priest wore on their breastplate covered all of the seven main Chakras (gateways or wheels).

Crystals cleanse our gateways in our body, a lot of time we start to feel pain in different parts of our body because that gateway or gate that's assigned to that particular body part or organ is filled with negative energies that have blocked the proper flow which causes pain in our body. If anyone of our gateways is out of balance, it can completely throw us off. That's why even the littlest things we do matter. That's why it's essential to breathe in the breath of God and release any thoughts contrary to our peace, the fruits of the spirit, and which Christ says we are. It just shows everything in the universe; all creation is linked together in Christ in order that things may flow in its proper order and alignment. Every wheel in our body needs to function in order and to be cleared of negative thoughts and evil spirits trying to influence the gateway. Everybody wants to come against yoga. Yoga is not evil; the Father showed me. Which I talk about later in this book.

On a day to day basis, I do cleanse out my gateways through Christ Jesus by breathing in and out of my chakras or wheels. And I do different yoga sometimes poses that help brings me relief. The Gateways in our body, although not seen, are very vital. So, we can't say yoga is evil because there are right ways of doing it and evil ways people do it. Some do it unto Christ or just everyday purposes, and some don't. Some do it unto evil deities, and some don't. Its other ways you can clean out your gateways just by simple breathing exercises. Again, good versus evil. I remember asking the Father if yoga was of him because it's one of the tools to help clear your gateways or chakras.

*Later that day, I was driving to the store, and a Toyota jumped in front of me, and it said, **MY YOTA**. I knew it meant for the driver, my Toyota. But the driver was relaying the message through the Father to me. Terika yoga is of me. He used the T to replace the G for my name to get my attention the rest of the letters to spell in reality my Yoga if it didn't have the T. Saying he gave Yoga as a tool to help clear out the chakras and wheels. Unfortunately, the use of it is by the intentions of a person and whom they have given they body too. Is it yielded to evil or good? He gave this information to different cultures. Now I think a lot of people may have had their own bad experiences with yoga, including me. I said oh no that's demonic, yet if some people had told me some of the reactions that would happen in my body, I wouldn't have thought those things, because at that time I didn't know the full effect of energy. This is something they don't teach in the Church. Now that I have learned what it was. It's like, oh, I know now. But, again, the Lord had to reveal that if it's through him, then it's not evil. If the person is doing yoga through an evil spirit, then it's the spirit that is operating through the person that makes them evil, not Yoga itself. Remember, it is light against darkness.*

*Are you a good person or bad? Who are you yielded to, negative energy (anger, frustration, revengeful, hatred)? Or are you yield to the fruit of the spirit (love, joy, peace, patience, etc.) Now they may put their own spin to it but, the knowledge came from him because he loves all nationalities and is God himself. That's why I like it when Jesus says in **1 Cor 12:20-27 (NLT), "Yes, there are many parts, but one body. The eye can never say to the hand, "I don't need you." The head can't say to the feet, "I don't need you." In fact, some parts of the body that seem weakest and least important are actually the most necessary. And the parts we regard as less honorable are those we clothe with the greatest care."** So, we carefully protect those parts that are weak; for instance, we may have lower back problems; it may be because we have negative energy stuck in the root or sacral gateway. So, we need to make sure we breathe in the spirit of God and breathe out any fear, worry, anger, offenses, jealousy, etc. "**All the while, my breath is in me, and the spirit of God is in my nostrils" Job 27:3 (KJV)** While the more honorable parts do not require this special care. So, God has put the body together, such that extra honor and care are given to those parts that have less dignity. This makes for harmony among the members so that all the members care for each other. If one of the chakras, wheels, or gates suffers, all the parts suffer with it, and all parts are honored, they work to try to get all the other parts in proper alignment, but it's a struggle at the same time. That's why you never may know which way the wheels may go or how the chakras may go. Each one is part of Christ's body within us. Not only that, but Christ's body is all nations within Christ himself, whether a believer or not. Any child that came from the mother's womb is part of Christ's body because the Father put the child in its mother's wound and gave that child an assignment no matter the nationality. He wants all men to be*

one under Christ Jesus, his son. But each crystal protects the wheels as we see below the picture in Jeremiah.

"**18 The word which came to Jeremiah from the Lord, saying,**

2 Arise, and go down to the potter's house, and there I will cause thee to hear my words.

3 <u>Then I went down to the potter's house, and, behold, he wrought a work on the wheels.</u>

4 And the vessel that he made of clay was marred in the hands of the potter: so he made it again another vessel, as seemed good to the potter to make it.

5 Then the word of the Lord came to me, saying,

6 O house of Israel, cannot I do with you as this potter? saith the Lord. Behold, as the clay is in the potter's hand, so are ye in mine hand, O house of Israel." Jeremiah 18:1-6 (KJV)

Each stones frequencies and vibrations they release through themselves through their electromagnetic fields/auras, whether it's love, joy, wisdom, understanding, etc. They work in alignment with our chakras/wheels/gateways health, and faithfulness to us through our own electromagnetic field/aura through our chakras/wheels/gateways that guard our temple which is our spiritual body, but at the same time brings added health and restoration to our physical, mental, emotional, and spiritual bodies. Totally awesome and cool! This is through entrainment. Entrainment refers to a natural phenomenon in which one entity resonates synchronously with another in response to its dominant frequency or vibration. And whether this resonance occurs on a gross or subtle level, it invariably involves rhythm.

That's why Jesus said in **Matt. 16:18 (KJV), "And I also say unto thee, that thou art Peter, and upon this rock I will build my church: and the gates of hell shall not prevail against it."**

Let's break down the scripture into two parts, Jesus said, and I say unto thee, thou art Peter, and upon this rock, I will build my church." So, Christ is saying upon this rock or crystal, and he will build Peter's church or spiritual temple through the chakras/gateway/or wheels because our bodies are the temple of the Holy Ghost. This is what we saw in the book of Jeremiah. **"3 Then, I went down to the potter's house, and, behold, he wrought a work on the wheels. 4 And the vessel that he made of clay was marred in the hand of the potter: so, he made it again another vessel, as seemed good to the potter to make it." Jeremiah 18:3-4 (KJV)** *So the vessel represents an individual, and it was marred (disfigured because of the individual's carnal nature, imperfections, and or weaknesses that leads to sin) in the hands of the potter because our wheels/chakras/or gate are imbalance and not protected and guarded by the crystal. So, our spiritual temples are weak if they are not guarded and built upon the foundation of Christ, who is the rock. How are we build upon the foundation of Christ, it's through the frequencies and vibrations of the characteristics, fruitfulness, and functions, and protection of each and every crystal that works with us to become one with us, to correct those imperfections by counteracting our weaknesses through the chakras/wheels. Christ's character and ways dwell within them to lead and guide us in the right paths so that we walk in his fruitfulness and ways by guiding and correcting the wheels. So, if we are always angry and we have rose quartz or emerald, then we become love because of the frequencies and vibrations of Christ's love within the crystal itself. Therefore, we are made new and in alignment with Holy Spirit and becoming love. So now, we are becoming the fruitfulness and characteristic of each different stone that we have to guard and protect our wheels/chakras/or gates.*

In the second part of Matt.16:18 (KJV), it says," the gates of hell will not prevail." What are the gates of hell, it's our sin nature, our weakness, demonic spirits (negative energy), trials, test, distractions, plots against you? Since the crystals guard the gates/wheels/or chakras of any negative energy (demonic spirits), then we are whole because the crystal repels the negative forces, demonic spirits, negative energies, and frequencies, and vibrations from entering in. If any negative energy does enter the gates/wheels/ or chakra, the crystal takes it in (binds), so it's no longer within you, and its transmuted into positive energy. Therefore, it balances the wheel/gates/ or chakra within. So those weaknesses or sins will no longer subdue you because the crystals become one with you to fight for you and help you offensively, and defensively, so you be made new and reshaped into the image of Christ Jesus himself who is the rock or crystal. We become who he is. We become perfect as the Father is perfect.

Why? Our bodies are spiritual temples of the LORD. Jesus is saying upon whatever crystal or stone you use; he will build his church, which is within each and every individual who is born again.

For example, we know that Peter was struggling with unforgiveness issues because in **Matt. 18:21-22 (KJV) he said, "Lord, how many times shall my brother sin against me, and I forgive him? till seven times? 22 I say unto thee, Until seven times: but, Until seventy times seven."** So, Jesus knew it would be plenty of times Peter's brother would sin against him, and Peter would have to forgive his brother every time. But, if Peter was built upon the stone Rhodochrosite, Rose Quartz, Amethyst, he will have the grace to forgive quickly. Meaning if he used Rhodochrosite, Rose Quartz, or Amethyst as his rock, whenever his brother sinned against him, he would forgive him without hesitation because of the frequencies and vibrations of forgiveness that comes from the use of Rhodochrosite, Rose Quartz, or Amethyst because it is imparted to him through being in sync with the crystals. Wow! isn't that amazing? Now I'm not saying this will happen all in one day, but it takes practice by the crystals perfecting our wheels, gates, and chakras within. And your willingness to receive by faith their fruitfulness.

Anything that we struggle with, there is more than likely a crystal that can counteract our weaknesses, which can help us be perfect as our Father in Heaven. Christ is the image and reflection of the Father. The crystals reflect Christ through their character and nature. **In Matt. 7:25(KJV) says, "and the rain descended, and the floods came, and the winds blew, and beat upon that house, and it fell not, for it was founded upon a rock."** We know that the rain, floods, and winds in this scripture represent distractions, attacks of the enemy, our weaknesses, negative words or thoughts from ourselves and others, trials, tribulations, hurts, the gates of hell which you see Jesus talking to Peter about. **Matt. 16:15-20 (KJV).** The house represents a person's spiritual house, or the person within (mind, will, and emotions). It states that even though those

things came, the person did not fall or crumble, they still stood strong in the Lord. Why? It was built upon the foundation of Christ, the rock. That shows again that the gates of hell will not prevail against us because our foundation is based on the word of god and the character, ways, of the particular crystals or gemstones we use through the grace we receive from them through Christ himself.

*I remember after leaving church many times getting prophetic words to trust in the Lord, to be strong, and have faith in particular seasons of time, that was not enough for me to go home in peace even after prayer for deliverance. But, still in the back of my mind and when I got home, I was back in the same state of mind. I would still have doubt, worry, and stress within me. I could barely go to sleep thinking about bills or particular situations. Then, when I went to sleep, I would toss and turn and get tensed up because of so much negative energy and thoughts running through my mind. Thoughts of worries, fears, and what if's going through my mind at the time. When the Lord started to reveal to me about crystals, I used amethyst and black tourmaline and placed them near me, and I would sleep like a baby, the following morning I will fill fully refreshed, no muscle tension, or anything because it calmed me down during that trial and test. They removed all those negative thoughts, fears, distractions, worries, etc. I remember screaming Jesus, where you been all my life! I finally found rest and peace, I said, "how come you're just now revealing this?" He replied back to me and said, "Because it wasn't time, and I had to develop a deep relationship with him and know the word of God to know how to grow, learn, and maneuver. He told me you are going to have to write a book about crystals because this your mandate and assignment I have given you." If you need deliverance, all you have to do is hold a stone in your non-dominant hand, which is your deliverance hand. Sit and be still. **"Be still and know that I am God; I will be exalted among the nations; I will be exalted in the earth." Psalm 46:10 (KJV)** Breathe in the benefits of that particular crystal and breathe out the negative thoughts, distractions, anxieties, doubts, doublemindedness, etc. Repeat until you feel relieved, and you start to feel positive thoughts of love, joy, peace, patience, etc. Repeat until you receive the benefits and healings of that particular crystal and meditate with it and wait until you feel a change or shift within your mind, body, will, and emotions for good physically, mentally, emotionally, and spiritually. Wait until your souls have become subdued under the Holy Spirit or your higher self. The deliverance hand is your receptive hand. And your dominant hand is the power hand, which is your sending hand.*

Reuben Carnelian

Jacob's blessing: *"Reuben, thou art my firstborn, my might, and the beginning of my strength, the excellency of dignity, and the excellency of power: Unstable as water, thou shalt not excel; because thou wentest up to thy father's bed, then defilest thou it; he went up to my couch"* **Gen.49:3(KJV)**

**Read the Testament of Reuben (KJV) for more information. **

Important information from Rueben and lessons he learned:
Reuben learned not to walk in the sins of youth and fornication,
"7 And I tell you that he smote me sour with a sore plague in my loins for seven months and had not my Father Jacob prayed for me to the Lord, the Lord would have destroyed me.
8 For I was thirty years old when I wrought the evil things before the Lord, and for 7 months, I was sick unto death. And after this, I repented and set purpose of my soul for seven years before the Lord. And wine and strong drink I drank not, and flesh entered not into my mouth, and I ate no pleasant food, but I mourned over my sin. For it was great." (Reuben 2:7-8 (KJV))

Positive aspects of Reubens personality and character:
Passion (However, was deceived by passion because it's God's will for the sons to marry and not fornicate, that's why knowing God's word is so essential, Reuben's passion, lust, and love deceived him into the temptation of sleeping with Bilhah.)

Reuben weaknesses and/or sins:
1. *Unstable*
2. *Lust*
3. *Evil motives and desires*
4. *Committed fornication*

Reubens Health: Good health until he sinned against his father by fornicating with Bilhah. *He had a sore plague in his loins 7 months*
Loins include (between lower ribs and pelvis, and lower part of the back and reproductive organs

Reuben's Stone on Priest Breastplate: *Sardius (Carnelian)*

Similar characteristics of Carnelian in common with Reuben: *Passion*

Weaknesses and sins of Reuben Carnelian Counteract:
1. Possessiveness in relationships
2. Breaks bad habits that serve no useful purpose to Reuben (fornication).
3. If a person wants to break the sin of fornication, he can use carnelian.
4. We see Reuben get married after his dad passes away.
*** Marriage is honorable in the sight of the Lord and is God's only desire for men and women. ***

Reuben's Health: *Reuben had good health until he sinned against his father by fornicating with Bilhah. He had a sore plague in his loins for 7 months. Loins include (between lower ribs and pelvis, and lower part of the back, and reproductive organs).*

Carnelian Physical Health Benefits:
It was once known to prevent illness and plague. It helps heal lower back problems and accelerates healing in bones and ligaments. Notice Reuben had a problem with his pelvis and lower back problems, due to a plague. Wow! And Carnelian was once known and might still prevent plagues, and it helps heals lower back problems, and it's also is assigned to the sacral chakra or gateway, which is part of the lower back!

Results of Carnelian Counterattacks:
Stability
Broke the spirit of fornication of Reuben because he finally gets married
Broke evil desires
Broke the spirit of lust

Gates (Gateways)/Chakras/Wheels Carnelian is assigned to protect:
Shades of Orange *Sacral gateway*
Shades of Red
The Base or Root gateway

Simeon Topaz

Jacob's blessing: *"Simeon and Levi are brethren: instruments of cruelty are in their habitations. O my soul, come not thou into their secret; unto their assembly, mine honour, be not thou united; For in their anger they slew a man, and in their self will they digged down a wall. Cursed be their anger, for it was fierce; and their wrath, for it was cruel; I will divide them in Jacob and scatter them in Israel."* ***(Genesis 49:5-7 KJV)***
(However, they performed this execution of Shechem under the instruction of the Angel of the Lord that was sent to Levi that Jacob didn't know about.)

**Read the Testament of Simeon (KJV) for more information. **

Important information from Simeon and Lessons learned: *Prince of Deceit sent forth the spirit of Jealousy and blinded his mind.*
He was wroth with Judah because he let Joseph go alive. The Lord restrained him and withheld from him the power of his hands for his right hand was half withered 7 days because of Joseph. He repented and wept and sought the LORD that his hand might be restored and
that he might hold aloof from all pollution of envy and folly.
He stated deliverance from envy comes by the fear of God.

Positive aspects of Reubens personality and character:
1. *Exceedingly strong*
2. *Great achiever*
3. *Fearless*

Simeon weaknesses, sins, and/or negative characteristics:
1. *The instigator of a plot against Joseph*
2. *Jealousy*
3. *Envious*
4. *Without compassion*

Simeon's Health: *Good health, but because of instigating the plot of Joseph, the Lord made his hand wither for 7 days.*

Simeon Stone on Priest Breastplate: *Topaz*

Similar characteristics of Topaz in common with Simeon: *Topaz is highly effective for bringing successful attainment of the goal.*

Counteracts: *Negativity*

Results of Topaz counterattack: *Provide inner peace and calmness to the mind.*

Gates (Gateways) /Chakras/Wheels/Topaz is assigned to protect: *Sacral and Solar Plexus*

Levi Carbuncle

Jacob's blessing: Same as Simeon

Read the Testament of Levi (KJV) for more information.

Important information from Levi and lessons he learned:
During a dream, the heavens opened, and the Angel of God told Levi to enter and showed him the heavens. The angel told him as he ascended higher, he shall stand near the Lord, and shalt be his minister, and shalt, declare His mysteries to men, and shalt proclaim concerning Him that shall redeem Israel, he told him that by Levi and Judah shall the Lord appear among men, saving every race of men. And from the Lord's portion shall be thy life. He shall be thy field, vineyard, fruits, gold, and silver. The angel brought him down and gave him a shield and a sword and told him to execute vengeance on Shechem because of Dinah, his sister, and the angel told him he would be with him because the Lord sent him to be with Levi to do the judgment because they were intending on doing the same to Sarah and Rebecca as they had done to Dinah, but the Lord prevented them from doing it to them at that time. He saw 7 men in white raiment that told him to arise, put on the robe of the priesthood, and the crown of righteousness, and the breastplate of understanding, and the garment of truth, and the plate of faith, and the turban of the head, and the ephod of prophecy. The angel told him from that day forward, and he was the priest of the Lord.

Positive aspects of Levi's personality and character:
1. *Mystic*
2. *Dreamer of Dreams*
3. *Prophet*
4. *The 7 Spirits of God*
5. *Warrior*
6. *Given the authority to execute judgment and be a priest whose inheritance*

was the LORD.

1. **Simeon's weaknesses, sins, and/or negative characteristics: --** Obedience to God isn't sinning (Jacob didn't know the angel of the Lord told him to execute judgment on Shechem and his people).
2. Levi being a part of the plot against Joseph, was a sin.

Reubens Health: Good health

Levi Stone on Priest Breastplate: Carbuncle (Garnet)

1. **Similar characteristics of Carbuncle (Garnet) in common with Levi:** Garnet is known as the stone of good health.
2. It promotes good health
3. Regenerates DNA and stimulates metabolism, boosts the immune system, and survival instinct. Warrior (also known as the Warrior Stone),
4. Levi didn't worry or panic about the assignment to execute vengeance on Shechem.
5. Garnet sharpens the perception of oneself and others.

Weaknesses, sin, and/ or negative aspects of Levi
1. Panic
2. Fear
3. Worry
** I believe Levi felt these feelings, knowing he had to go to war without knowing what the results would be after the war. **

Carbuncle (Garnet) Counteracts: Releases feelings of panic, fear, and worry

Results of Carbuncle (Garnet) counterattack: Peace, Faith, Fearless
Gates (Gateways)/Chakras/Wheels Carbuncle (Garnet) is assigned to protect: Root (base) and the Crown

Judah Emerald

Jacob's blessing: *"Judah, your brothers will praise you; your hand will be on the neck of your enemies; your father's sons will bow down to you. You are a lion's cub, Judah; you return from the prey, my son. Like a lion, he crouches and lies down, like a lioness-who dares to rouse him? The scepter will not depart from Judah, nor the ruler's staff from between his feet, until he to whom it belongs shall come and the obedience of the nations shall be his. He will tether his donkey to a vine his colt to the choicest branch; he will wash his garments in wine, his robes in the blood of grapes. His eyes will be darker than wine, his teeth whiter than milk."* **Genesis 49:8-12 (KJV)**

Read Testament of Judah (KJV) for more information

Important information from Judah and lessons he learned:
He was swift in his youth and obedient to his father in everything. Jacob declared that he would be a king, prospering in all things. The Lord showed him favor in the field and in the house. He raced a hind and caught it, and prepared the meat for his father, and he ate it. He slew a lion and plucked a kid out of its mouth.
He took a bear by its paw and hurled it down the cliff, and it was crushed.
He outran the wild boar, and seizing it as he ran, he tore it in sunder.
He overtook all that was in the plains. A wild mare he overtook and caught it and tamed it. He killed 4 Kings (Hazor, Tapuah, Achor, etc.) and their armies and killed his enemies that tried to pursue him.
He had much cattle, and for chief herdsman Iram the Adullamite and when he went to him he saw Barsava, king of Adullam; and he spoke to them, made them a feast, and Judah was upset that he gave him his daughter Bathshua to wife. She bore two of his children, Er, and Onan, and Shelah; two of them the Lord killed, but Shelah lived; it was Shelah's children he was telling his testament to. He slept with Tamar while drunk who he gave both of his sons to marry, but both of them did not have children by her because of their mother Bathshua told them not to have seed with her because she wasn't a Canaanite as them, but it was the LORD'S will for them to have children by her and when they disobeyed the LORD he killed each one of them. Shelah married a wife from Canaan, given by his mother. He tells his grandchildren not to become drunk because it disturbs the mind with filthy thoughts that lead to fornication, which is carnal union, and if the occasion of lust come, he sins and is not ashamed. He also informs them drunkenness causes you to err, so he informed them that discretion is needed when drinking wine. He commands the children not to love money and not to gaze upon women's beauty because if the women's motive is impure for the love of money, they could be led astray. (Of course, we know this goes both ways for both men and women.) Judah gave a lot of sound wisdom to his grandchildren if you read the Testament of Judah.

Positive aspects of Judah personality and character:
  1. Obedient to Jacob in everything.

Chapter 6: Crystals: The Missing Link to the Full Armor of God in Our Life

2. *Favor in the house and outside in the field (world).*
3. *Strong*
4. *Giant (tall), athlete, warrior, heroic deeds, runs fast that he can outstrip a hind.*
5. *He saw in a vision that an angel followed him and that he would not be defeated but will always win the battle.*
6. *He had many cattle (prosperous).*
7. *He learned not to be a lover of money.*
8. *He saw in a vision that an angel followed him that he would not be defeated and would always win the battle.*

Judah weaknesses, sins, and/or negative characteristics: Fornication

Judah's Health: Good

Judah's Stone on Priest Breast Plate: Emerald

Similar characteristics of Emerald in common with Judah:
1. *The effects of nightmares and evil spirits are nullified by emerald.*
2. *Judah destroyed his enemies.*
3. *Emerald stone has the ability to increase the power of reasoning and spirituality.*
4. *Abundance and Prosperity.*
5. *People having problems keeping wealth can benefit from emerald stone, because it has the power to hold money with the wearer.*
6. *Judah learned not to be a lover of money.*
7. *Emerald gives wisdom.*
8. *It's said that emerald changes its color when false friends come around, therefore protecting them from false friendships. (Judah knew his enemies in an instant).*
9. *It is said that couples my fight or argue, but emerald enhances faithfulness and love in the relationship if used. Hallelujah! The Lord wants married couples to stay together, not separate. It's believed to decrease the chances of getting bitten by snakes.* **(And the God of peace shall bruise Satan under your feet shortly. The grace of our Lord Jesus Christ be with you. Amen. Romans.16:20 KJV**
10. *Success in business.*
11. **Increases fertility** *(Two of Judah's sons got killed, yet when Judah impregnated Tamar, the Lord gave her twins to replace the two sons Judah had lost. Tamar was to have children by one of Judah's sons, but both rejected impregnating her.*

Emerald Counteracts: Division Judah first wife
(initially it was told he wasn't supposed to marry a person from Canaan because

of their ways as we see the wife did not want their sons to marry Tamar and have children with her even though it was the Lord's will for her to have children by one of them)

Results of Emerald counterattack: *Marriage of unity, harmony, and peace.*

Gates (Gateways)/Chakras/Wheels Emerald is assigned to protect: *Heart*

Issachar Sapphire

Jacob's blessing: *"Issachar is a raw-boned donkey lying down among the sheep pens. When he sees how good his resting place is and how pleasant is his land, he will bend his shoulder to the burden and submit to forced labor. He never slandered anyone, nor did he censure the life of any man walking"* **Genesis 49:14,15 (KJV)**

**Read Testament of Issachar (KJV) for more information. **

Important information from Issachar and lessons he learned:
1. He walked in uprightness of heart.
2. He was a husbandman.
3. Brought fruit to the fields according to their seasons.
4. Blessed of Jacob because of his righteousness.
5. He was not a busy body in his doings, nor envious and malicious against his neighbor.
6. Never slandered anyone.
7. Issachar his first fruits to the Lord, then to his father also.
8. He was married at the age of 35 years old. He never thought upon pleasure with women, but due to his toil, sleep overcame him.
9. For all the poor and oppressed, he bestowed the good things of the earth in the singleness of his heart.
10. He kept the Law of God.
11. He had compassion on the poor and weak.
12. Except for his wife, he did not know any woman and never committed fornication by uplifting his eyes.

13.   He did not drink wine to be led astray.
14.   He coveted not any desirable thing that was his neighbors.
15.   Guile arose, not in his heart.
16.   A lie passed, not through his lips.
17.   He loved every man with his heart.

Positive aspects of Issachar personality and character:
1. Known as the sinless child and knew the times and seasons
2. Beloved of the Lord
3. Walked in righteousness
4. Hard worker
5. He brought in fruits from the fields according to their seasons
6. Blessed of Jacob because he walked in righteousness and good character
7. He was not a busy body or envious
8. He did not condemn or criticize the life of any man
9. Didn't slander
10.   Loved the Lord
11.   Issachar gave offerings and gifts to the Lord with thanksgiving.
12.   Always rejoice in righteousness
13.   Walked in sincerity and purity of the mind
14.   Had compassion
15.   Never committed fornication
16.   Told the truth, never lied
17.   Every limb was sound
18.   Strength was unabated at his death

Issachar's Health: He was exhausted and sleepy a lot when he got married due to his toil (hard work)

Issachar's Stone on Priest Breastplate: Sapphire

Similar characteristics of Sapphire in common with Issachar:
1. Promotes Integrity
2. Focus
3. Divine Favor
4. Clarity
5. Sapphire gives clear vision during times of change or transition. (Issachar knew the times and seasons because he was focused)
6. Stone of love
7. Wisdom
8. Commitment and fidelity
9. Patience
10.   Respect
11.   Honesty

12.   Issachar never envied anyone, and sapphire protects people from envy and ill wishes and thoughts.

Sapphire Counteracts: *Takes away tiredness or exhaustion*

Results of Sapphire counter attacks:
1. *Energy*
2. *Balanced body*

Gateways/Chakras/Wheels Sapphire is assigned to protect: Throat Chakra
Dark Blue: *Brow, Third Eye Chakra*

Zebulon Diamond

Jacob's blessing: *"Zebulun will live by the seashore and become a haven for ships; his border will extend toward Sidon,"* **Genesis 49:13 (KJV)**

**Read the Testament of Zebulon (KJV) for more information. **

Important information from Zebulon and lessons he learned: *He states he did the sin of ignorance, which Zubulon committed against Joseph because he covenanted with his brethren not to tell Jacob his father what they had done to Joseph. He wept in many secret days on account of Joseph, for he feared his brethren because they had all agreed that if anyone told the secret, he should be slain. When they wished to kill Joseph, he begged them with tears not to be guilty of the sin. He informed him if he had sinned indeed, for them to chastise him instead of Joseph, for the sake of Jacob. When he spoke those words, wail as he did, he was unable to bear his lamentations, and began to weep, and his liver was poured out (crying), and all the substance of his bowels loosened (diarrhea)*
Keep the commandments of the Lord, and keep His law, depart from wrath, and hate lying, that the Lord may dwell among you, and Beliar may flee from you. Speak truth each one with his neighbor. So shall ye not fall into wrath and confusion, but ye shall be at peace, having the God of peace, so shall no war prevail over you. Love the Lord through all your life, and one another with a pure heart. There shall arise unto you from the tribe of Judah and of Levi the salvation of the Lord, and he shall make war against Beliar.
He shall execute an everlasting vengeance on our enemies; Beliar the souls of the

saints, and turn disobedient hearts unto the Lord, and give them that call upon him eternal peace. And the saints shall rest in Eden, and in the New Jerusalem shall the righteous rejoice, and it shall be unto the glory of God forever.
Keep yourselves from every evil work, and cast away wrath and all lying, and love the truth and long-suffering. Depart, therefore, from all unrighteousness, and cleave unto the righteousness of God, and your race will be saved forever.

Positive aspects of Zebulon personality and character:
1. Inventor (First to make a boat and sail upon the sea) and Philanthropist
2. Did not know sin or iniquity except when it came to selling Joseph
3. Merciful and compassionate towards others and beasts
4. Compassion and Pity (plot against Joseph).

Zebulon Health: *Good*

Zebulon Stone on Priest Breastplate: *Diamond*

Similar Characteristics of Diamond in common with Zebulon:
1. Intellect
2. (Zebulon was an inventor)
3. Wealth and Prosperity
4. (Philanthropist)
5. Encourages one to look at the struggles and hardships of life

Sapphire Counteracts: *Fear, Anxiety, Pity*

Results of Diamond counter attacks: *Fearless and confident*
1. It gives strength in dealing with high-pressure situations and assists in responding with grace.

Gates (Gateways)/Chakras/Wheels Diamond is assigned to protect:
Crown Chakra and Etheric Chakras

Naphtali Moonstone

Jacob's blessing: *"Naphtali is a doe set free that bears beautiful fawns."* Genesis 49:21 (KJV)

**Read the Testament of Naphtali (KJV) for more information. **
Important information from Naphtali and lessons he learned: *Swift as a deer, Jacob appointed him for all messages, and as a deer did, he give him his blessing.*

For as the potter knoweth the vessel, how much it is to contain, and bringeth clay accordingly, so also doth the Lord make the body after the likeness of the spirit, and according to the capacity of the body doth he imparts the spirit. The potter knows the use of each vessel, what it is meet for, so also doth the Lord knows the body, how far it will persist in goodness, and when it beginneth in evil.

For as a man's strength, so also in his work, as his eye, so also in his sleep, as his soul, so also in his word either in the law of the Lord or in the law of Beliar. **(Thank God we are saved by grace now, Hallelujah, because if we live by the law, then sin will continue to increase and wage war against the soul)**

And there is a division between light and darkness, between seeing and hearing, also there is a division between man and man, woman and woman, and it is not to be said that the one is like the other either in fact or in mind.

Let all your work be done in order with good intent in fear of God and do nothing disorderly in scorn or out of its due season. For if thou bid the eye to hear, it cannot, so neither while ye are in darkness can ye do the works of light.

Be not eager to corrupt your doings through covetousness or vain words to beguile your souls; because if ye keep silence the purity of heart, ye shall understand how to hold fast the will of God and cast away the will of Beliar. I want to explain the **Testament of Naphtali 1:25 (KJV) "25. The Gentiles went astray, and forsook the Lord, and charged their order, and obeyed stocks and stones, spirits of deceit.)** Here that it is saying, that they went astray, meaning turned from the Lord , they forsook him meaning they renounced or abandoned, or left the Lord left their first love, they didn't have a relationship with him anymore, changed the order, meaning changed something from the original purposes or intent of God to their own and intent or thought, they obeyed stock (money) through greed and covetousness of their own heart and stones by the deceitfulness of their own hearts or a covenant they made with the stone out of the deceitfulness of their own heart. They did not discerning whether it was of the Spirit of the Lord, from the Lord, or a spirit from the demonic realm, they obey spirits of deceits,(deceits can be your own selves which are familiar spirits which is old way of thinking and habits, perceptions, thoughts that is contrary to the Word of God and or God's will, demonic spirits, sin, etc.) That's why it's so vital that you know the word of God, that's why the law of Moses was written on stone so that it would manifest God's word, but at the time Holy Spirit came on people and did not live within, so how much more will the word manifest once you are born again and decree and declare the word of God when you pray using the stones .

The things you pray become manifested even more through working in conjunction with the crystal through Christ, Hallelujah! The crystals help bring the

soul in sync with Holy Spirit through Christ, who is the word and rock made flesh and alive, and he is made manifest through us through his word is alive and active in us as powerful than a two-edged sword dividing the soul and the spirit asunder. Think about it how much more will the fruitfulness of Christ Jesus increase in us through the stone or crystal that counteracts our weaknesses and transmute them into good fruit because their fruit is love, joy, peace, patience, kindness, goodness, faithfulness, self-control, etc. (or repeated crystalline molecular structures that release positive frequencies, vibrations, and energies of their character and good fruit that they have through Christ Jesus) to work with our electromagnetic fields, aura, character, and body to become attuned and in synch with their perfect fruit through Christ Jesus to become perfect as the Father is perfect. **(Matt. 5:48 (KJV)) Wow! The crystals and stones give out the perfect vibrations and frequencies, and energies of love and joy, etc.**
The next verse 25 states not to be as Sodom because they turned from the Lord to fulfill the desires of themselves and ways that were contrary to the Lord, then it talks about the Watchers also angels gone bad (fallen angels) changing the order of their own nature.

Positive aspects of Naphtali personality and character:
1. *Naturally, a good, righteous man.*
2. *The Runner.*
3. *As he glorified the Lord, he grew strong.*

Naphtali Weaknesses/and or sins: -

Naphtali's Health: Good

Naphtali's Stone on Priest Breastplate: *Moonstone*

Similar Characteristics of Moonstone in common with Naphtali:
1. *Peace*
2. *Balance*
3. *Calmness*
4. *Soothes*
5. *It enhances the process of nutrients and eliminates toxins from the body.*
6. *Balances*
7. *Heals*
8. *It helps you to absorb what is needed and not necessarily what is wanted.*

Moonstone Counteracts: *Dispels negativity from all the chakras, Wow!*

Results of Moonstone counter attacks:
1. *It helps to ease these aggressive tendencies in men and women, bringing peace and balance.*

2. It provides us with spiritual nourishment and helps a person sustain their life through different life events and transitions.
3. Moonstone helps pinpoint problem areas.
4. Moonstone strengthens religious people in all cultures.

Gates (Gateways)/Chakras/Wheels Moonstone is assigned to protect:
Sacral, Third Eye and Crown Chakras

Gad Agate

Jacob's blessing: *"Gad will be attacked by a band of raiders, but he will attack them at their heels."* **Genesis 49:16-18 (KJV)**

**Read the Testament of Gad (KJV) for more information. **

Important information from Gad and lessons he learned: *Gad guarded at night the flock, whenever the lion came, or the wolf, or any wild beast against the fold, he pursued them, overtook them, and seized their foot with his hands and hurled them about a stone's throw, and killed them.*
The Spirit of hatred was in him; he wishes not to either hear of Joseph with his ears or see him with the eyes because Joseph rebuked them to their faces saying that they were eating the flock without Judah.
Whatsoever Joseph told Jacob; Jacob believed him.
He hated Joseph for his dreams
He told his children to hearken to the words of truth, to work righteousness, and all the law of the Most High, and go not astray through the spirit of hatred, for it is evil in all the doings of men.
For the spirit of hatred warreth together with Satan, through hastiness of spirits, in all things to men's death, but the spirit of love worketh together with the law of God in long-suffering unto the salvation of men. Hatred, therefore, is evil for it constantly mated with lying, speaking against the truth, and it maketh small things to be great, and causeth the light to darkness, and calleth the sweet the submitter, and teacheth slander, and kindleth wrath, and stirreth up war, and violence and all covetousness it filleth the heart with evil and devilish poison.
Do not hate and cleave to the love of God.
God learned righteousness casteth out hatred and humility destroyeth envy. For

fearing lest he should offend the Lord, he will not do wrong to any man even in thought.

The Lord brought upon Gad a disease of the liver and had not the prayers of Jacob succored him, it had hardly failed, but my spirit had departed.

He stated by what things a man transgresseth by the same also is he punished. Since, therefore, his liver was set mercilessly against Joseph, in his liver too, I suffered mercilessly and was judged for eleven months, for so long a time as I had been angry against Joseph. He states, "to love ye each one his brother, and put away hatred from your hearts, love one another indeed, and in a word, and in the inclination of the soul. If a man prospereth more than you, do not be vexed, but also pray for him, that he may have perfect prosperity, so it is expedient for you."

Positive aspects of Gad personality and character:
1. Shepherd and a strong man
2. Keeping the flocks was his strength

Gad Weaknesses, and/ or sins:
1. Warfare
2. Unbalanced
3. Tension
4. Bitter
5. A murderer at heart
6. Hatred
7. Hated Joseph because he was righteous.
8. Jealousy

Gad's Health: Good until he got the disease of the liver

Gad's Stone on Priest Breastplate: *Agate*

Similar characteristics of Gad in common with Agate: *The ability to adhere to their core spiritual beliefs in the face of adversity, division, and strife*
Protection against negative energies/demonic spirits
Eliminating and transforming negativity

Agate Counteracts:
1. Division and strife
2. Protection against negative energies/demonic spirits
3. Eliminating and transforming negativity

Results of Agate counter attacks:
1. Calmness and harmony
2. Helps harmonize with the environment and people

3. Enhanced mental functions, improved concentration
4. Spiritual growth
5. Encourages one to find solutions rather than focusing on negative aspects of daily challenges.
6. Reminds you that we are love and compassion in reality

Gateways/Chakras/Wheels Agate is assigned to protect: Varies depending on the different type of Agate and its colors

Asher Amethyst

Jacob's blessing: *"Asher's food will be rich; he will provide delicacies fit for a king."* **Genesis 49:20 (KJV)**

**Read the Testament of Asher (KJV) for more information. **

Important information from Asher and lessons he learned: *Two ways hath God given to the sons of men, and two inclinations, and two kinds of action, and two modes of action, and two issues.* **Therefore, all things are by twos, one over against the other.**

There are two ways of good and evil, and with these are two inclinations in our breast discriminating them. Therefore, if the soul takes pleasure in the good inclination, all its actions are in righteousness, and if it sins, it straightway repenteth. For having its thoughts set upon righteousness, and casting away wickedness, it straightway overthroweth the evil, and uprooted the sin.

But if it inclines to the evil inclination, all its actions are in wickedness, and it driveth away; the good and cleaveth to the evil, and it ruled by Beliar; even though it work, what is good, he perverteth it to evil. He defileth the soul, and maketh gay the body; he killeth many, and pitieth a few: this, too, hath a twofold aspect, but the whole is evil.

Another committeth adultery and fornication, and abstaining from meats, and when he fasteth he doeth evil, and by the power of his wealth overwhelmed many, and notwithstanding his excessive wickedness, he doeth the commandments; this too, hath a twofold aspect, but the whole is evil.

Such men are hare; clean, like those that divide the hoof, but in very deed are unclean.

For God in the tables of the commandments hath thus declared. But do not ye,

my children, wear two faces like unto them, of goodness and of wickedness; but cleave unto goodness only, for God, for God hath his habitation therein, and men desire it.

Keep the law of the Lord *****Jesus has fulfilled the law for us now we are saved by grace by his spirit*****, *and give not heed unto evil as unto good; but look unto the thing that is really good, and keep it in all the commandments of the Lord, having your conversation therein, and resting therein.*

For the latter ends of men do show their righteousness or unrighteousness, and when they meet the angels of the Lord and of Satan.

For when the soul departs troubled, it is tormented by the evil spirit, which also served in lust and evil works. For many in killing, the wicked do two works, of good and evil, but the whole is good because he hath uprooted and destroyed that which is evil.

Positive aspects of Asher personality and character:
1. *Full of wisdom*
2. *Excellent in discernment*
3. *Shows the difference between vice (wickedness) and virtue (righteousness)*

Asher Weaknesses/and or sins:
1. *Part of the plot of Joseph*

Asher's Health: *Good*

Asher's Stone on Priest Breastplate: Amethyst

Similar characteristics of Amethyst in common with Asher:
1. *Increase wisdom and spirituality*
2. *Healing powers that heal physical ailments and emotional issues*

Amethyst Counteracts:
1. *Deceit*
2. *Hypocrisy*
3. *Lies*

Results of Amethyst counter attacks:
Protects the environment from negative energies

Gates (Gateways)/Chakras/Wheels) Asher: *Upper Chakras, Crown, Third Eye (Mind's Eye)*

Dan Lapis Lazuli

Jacob's blessing: *"Dan will provide justice for his people as one of the tribes of Israel. Dan will be a snake by the roadside, a viper along the path, that bites the horse's heels so that its rider tumbles backward. I look for your deliverance LORD."* ***Genesis 49:17 (KJV)***

**Read the Testament of Dan (KJV) for more information. **

Important information from Dan and lessons he learned: *Proved in his heart, and in his whole life, that truth is good and well-pleasing to God and that lying and anger are evil because they teach man all wickedness.*
He confessed that Joseph was a true and good man, he told about the evil he had in his heart when he rejoiced in his heart when he was sold because he felt Jacob loved Joseph than all his sons because the spirit of jealousy and vainglory said to him: Thou thyself also art his son. And one of the spirits of Beliar stirred him up saying to take his sword and slay Joseph, so shall thy father love thee when he is dead, this was the spirit of anger that persuaded him to crush Joseph as a leopard crushed a kid. But the Lord did not suffer him to fall into Dan's hands so that he could find Joseph alone and slay him and cause a second tribe to be destroyed in Israel.
He states to keep yourself from lying and of anger, just love truth and longsuffering
He states because anger is blindness, and does not suggest one to see the face of any man with truth
For though it be a father or a mother, he behaved towards them as enemies, though it is a brother, he knoweth him not; though it he's is a prophet of the Lord, he disobeyed him; though a righteous man, he regarded him not, though a friend he doth acknowledge him. He says the spirit of anger encompasseth him with a net of deceit and blinded his eyes, and through lying darkeneth his mind, and give him its own peculiar vision. And wherewith encompasseth it his eyes? With hatred of heart, so as to be envious of his brother. Speak truth each one with his neighbour. o shall ye not fall into wrath and confusion, but ye shall be at peace, having the God of peace, so shall no war prevail over you. Love the Lord through all your life, and one another with a true heart.

Positive aspects of Dan's personality and character:
Spoke truth in the latter end of his life

Dan weaknesses/and or sins:
1. *Anger and Falsehood (lying)*
2. *Jealousy*
3. *Vainglory*

Dan's Health: *Good*

Dan's Stone on Priest Breastplate: *Lapis Lazuli*

Similar characteristics of Lapis Lazuli has in common with Dan:
1. *Speaks the truth and inspired confidence*
2. *Through the latter part of Dan's life, he was able to confront and speak the truth and inspire confidence during times of confusion*

Lapis Lazuli Counteracts:
1. *Anger*
2. *Falsehood*
3. *Lying*
4. *Jealousy*
5. *Vainglory*

Results of Lapis Lazuli counter attacks:
1. *Honesty*
2. *It encourages self-awareness and self-expression*
3. *Making you realize your potential*
4. *Remove distractions (Dan was distracted by how much he felt his Father loved Joseph. Therefore, he thought he didn't have potential)*
5. *It helps rid you of unwanted that emotional baggage and negative thinking about yourself. Wow! Brings inner peace. Therefore, you will not go through affliction in the mind, which eventually manifests warfare and possible adverse effects physically in your body.*
6. *Clears your mind of negative thoughts*

Gates (Gateways)/Chakras/Wheels Lapis Lazuli is assigned to protect:
Third Eye and Throat Chakra

Joseph Onyx

Jacob's blessing:
Ephraim

"Joseph is a fruitful vine, near a spring, whose branches climb over a wall. With bitterness, archers attacked him; they shot at him with hostility. But, his bow remained steady, his strong arms stayed limber, because of the hand of the Mighty One of Jacob, because of the Shepherd, the Rock of Israel, because of your father's God, who helps you, because of the Almighty, who blesses you with blessings of the skies above, blessings of the deep springs below, blessings of the breast and womb. Your father's blessings are greater than the blessings of the ancient mountains than the bounty of the age-old hills. Let all these rest on the head of Joseph, on the brow of the prince among his brothers." **Genesis 49:22-26 (KJV)**

**Read the Testament of Joseph (KJV) for more information. **

Important information from Joseph and Lessons he learned:
He saw in his life envy and death, yet he did not go astray but persevered in the truth of the Lord.

Brethren hated him, but the Lord loved him.
His brothers wanted to slay him, but the Lord guarded him and kept him safe. He took him down into the pit, but the Lord bring him up again.
Sold into slavery, and the Lord of all made him free.
He was taken into captivity, and his steady hand succored Joseph.
He was hungry, and the Lord himself nourished him.
He was alone, and the Lord comforted him
He was sick, and the Lord visited him
He was in prison, and God showed him favor
In bonds and he released him
Slandered and he pleaded his cause
Bitterly spoken against by the Egyptians, and he delivered him
Envied by fellow-slaves, and but God exalted him
Chief captain of Pharaoh entrusted him with his house.
Struggled against Potiphar's wife, wanting him to transgress by sleeping with her and the Lord delivered
In 10 temptations, he showed me approved, and in all of them I endured; for endurance is a mighty charm, and patience giveth many good things.

He was also threatened with death by Potiphar's wife if he didn't sleep with her. You see how great things patience worketh and prayer with fasting. So, you too, if you follow after chastity and purity with patience and prayer with fasting in humility of heart, the Lord will dwell among you because He loveth chastity. And wheresoever the Most High dwelleth, even though envy, or slavery, or slander befalleth a man, the Lord who dwelleth in him, for the sake of his chastity not only delivereth him from evil but also exalteth him even as me.

1. **Positive aspects of Joseph's personality and character:** *Chastity and Self Denial*
2. *Perseverance through trials and false accusation*
3. *Strength*
4. *Faith*

Joseph's Weaknesses/and or sins: *Possibly self-righteousness and that might be why he was hated by his brothers possibly because of self -righteousness*

Joseph's Health: *Good*

Joseph's Stone on Priest Breastplate: *Onyx*

Similar Characteristics of Joseph in common with Onyx:
Another warrior stone

1. *Heals past wounds and issues*
2. *Self-Confidence*
3. *Helps with self-discipline*
4. *Grounding Stability*
5. *Patience*
6. *Humility*
7. *Focus*
8. *Comfort*
9. *Honesty*
10. *Security*
11. *Strength*
12. *Produce*
13. *Calmness*
14. *Decision Making*
15. *Prosperity*

Onyx Counteracts:
1. *Fear*
2. *Grief*
3. *Confusion Internal imbalances and negative energy*

4. Demonic spirits from outside parties
5. Negative thought patterns and breaks self-doubt

Results of Onyx counter attacks:
1. Faith
2. Strength
3. Patience
4. Trust
5. Peace

Gates (Gateways)/Chakras/Wheels Onyx is assigned to protect:
Base Chakra
And Earth Star Chakra

***Did You know Black Onyx prevents crime from happening around you, your family, your house, and your neighborhood? We will talk about how crystals protect your house and the atmosphere later on. ***

Benjamin Jasper

Jacob's blessing: *"Benjamin is a ravenous wolf' in the morning he devours the prey, in the evening, he divides the plunder."* **Genesis 19:27 (KJV)**

Relevant information from Benjamin and Lessons he learned: *Fear ye the Lord and love your neighbor, and even though the spirits of Beliar claim to afflict you with every evil, yet shall they not have dominion over you, even as they had not over Joseph, my brother.*
Be ye followers of his compassion, therefore, with a sound mind, that ye also may wear crowns of glory. For the good man hath not a dark eye, for he showeth mercy to all men even though they are sinners.
And though they devise evil intent, concerning him, by doing good, he overcometh evil, being shielded by God; and he loveth righteousness as his own soul. If anyone betrayeth a righteous man, the righteous man prayeth; though for a little he be humbled, yet not long after he appears far more glorious (JOSEPH)
He that hath a pure mind in love looketh not after a woman with a view to fornication, for he hath no defilement in his heart because the spirit of God rested

upon him. For as the sun is not defiled by shining on dung and mire, but rather drieth up both and driveth away the evil smell; the pure mind, though encompassed by the defilements of the earth, rather cleanseth themselves and is not itself defiled.

Do truth, each one to his neighbour. And keep the law of the Lord and his commandments.

Keep the commandments of God, until the Lord reveals His salvation to all gentiles.

**Read the Testament of Benjamin (KJV) for more information. **

Positive aspects of Benjamin's personality and character:
1. *Philosopher*
2. *Philanthropist (Giver)*
3. *Encourager*
4. *Purity*
5. *innocence*

Benjamin Weaknesses/and or sins: none revealed in his story

Benjamin's Health: *Good*

Benjamin's Stone on Priest Breastplate: *Jasper*

Similar Characteristics of Jasper in common with Benjamin:
1. *Supreme Nurturer*
2. *Courage*
3. *Grounding Stability*
4. *Patience humility*
5. *Generosity*
6. *Compassion*
7. *Comfort and security*
8. *Strength*
9. *Produce calmness*
10. *It reminds us to heal humanity and the planet.*

Jasper Counteracts:
Stress and Negative energy

Results of Jasper counter attacks:
Peace, stability, and truth

Gates (Gateways)/Chakras/Wheels Jasper is assigned to protect: *Base Chakra* *****If its laid on each chakra (energy center, wheel, gateway), it**

can cleanse, boost and realign the chakras and aura. ***

Guard Your Heart

" *Guard your heart above all else, for it determines the course of your life." (Proverbs 4:23 (NLT))*

Our heart sends out more electromagnetic waves than the brain, that's why it says, "above all else, guard your heart." The reason this scripture is saying to protect the heart is because the heart is one of the chakras (wheels, energy centers, etc.) that out of all the chakras, it has the most electromagnetic fields coming from it. It is also linked to the mind and determines the course of all the other gateways and can determine their course as well. As spoken earlier, when you watch cartoons or superhero movies a lot of times, they will have a gemstone or stone protecting their heart in order for them to maintain their powers and protect them. Our heart is our subconscious mind. It is one of the gateways that always need to be protected because if you noticed, sometimes, when you hug someone that is down, negative, or they may be burdened because of the things of life, you start to feel their pain, that burden may latch upon you because Christ said for us to bear each other's burdens **(Bear ye one another's burdens, and so fulfill the law of Christ. Gal.6:2 (KJV)**, *but he didn't say to stay at that state. The Neurons and impulses of someone's body can connect with our impulses and become one because of the heart gateway being opened and not protected or guarded by a crystal. I know personally for myself I have prayed for people to get deliverance, and they get their deliverance, but sometimes that same spirit I prayed for a person to get delivered from, sometimes may try to latch itself to me. That's why using crystals, stones, gemstones, and prayer is so important; Or sometimes I hug a person, and I feel the same feeling or pain they are feeling. I may be praying for a person in a totally different place, and all of a sudden, I feel their pain or burden and pray for them, but the feeling is still there after I prayed for them.*

Some people say its burden of the Lord, which it is, but in some instances if it starts to attack your body and your feelings, he doesn't want you to feel still what that person is feeling, or he doesn't want you to feel drained by the spirit or negative energy that is attacking the person you are praying for because perhaps it may be too strong. You may pray, and you ask the Lord, "Why am I so burdened?" "Why do I feel the same heavy burden?" "Why do I feel depressed or angry now?" Well, it's because when you hug a person or they are near, and your heart gate is open, it is easy for their burden to attach itself because your heart gateway is always open unless you have something to guard it or protect it. Or the heart gateway could be inactive. We can try to use self-control to guard our

hearts, but most people their own self-control as burying their feelings or try not to feel anything at all, and that's not good because your heart can grow numb and still grow cold. I say that only from my experiences and what I heard from others. We can speak for our gateways to be closed to the demonic realm, but when it doesn't work, what do you do? What do you do when that demonic spirit or negative energy has attached itself to your heart gateway, or any other gateway, and fasting and prayer don't work? That means because there's a missing link, which is a crystal that's assigned to your heart's gate. If you have a crystal over your heart to protect it, that's assigned to your heart in order to protect it or dispel negativity or demonic spirits(negative energies); then you would be okay because the crystal or stone war and fight on your behalf to destroy the negative energy. How do you guard your heart with a crystal? You guard your heart using a crystal through a necklace. <u>Another thing you can do is wear a bracelet or have the crystal in your purse or pocket with you because it works with your electromagnetic field/ aura, which is the shield of faith, which I will explain later.</u> You won't feel that burden, or it won't latch onto you for that long. You can where multiple stones over your heart that's assigned to different gateways to protect and guard them also. Jesus said to take his yoke upon us, so we can be free, we are to give it to him through the use of crystals. **"29 Take my yoke upon you and learn of me; for I am meek and lowly in heart: and ye shall find rest unto your souls." Matt. 11:29 (KJV).** But, we know that gets hard sometimes, okay, I will say a lot of times, just being honest.

For example, I remember someone I really cared about, called me crying, to have someone to talk to, to get things off their chest as we all do from time to time. They needed prayer, and frequently, when they tell me about the same particular person being horrible and the mean things, they would do to them, I will get in momma protect mode, sort to speak. I would help encourage them, but also at the same time I would be upset like Lord please help this person in this situation, because this is a never-ending trial for them, and after I get off the phone even after praying with them I would be so agitated, and upset at the enemy influencing this person to come against this individual I was praying for. But this particular time, I had a ruby crystal on me when they called. So when this person called crying again I felt the love and compassion of the Father and all his heart for this person, and all I could tell the person is to cry and let out all the tears and the pain, and I felt the love and compassion so deep for her, and I talked to her in a calm, low tone and encouraged her, I was so calm, and I prayed for her; I honestly didn't feel burdened, or agitated, or angry about the situation, I had peace and told the Lord, I know you are with her to keep her. I was in a state of shock at my feelings and reaction after the call. I wasn't burdened down or drained; I knew why Jesus said, **"For my yoke is easy and my burden is light." Matt 11:30 (KJV)** It was like even though I felt her pain the ruby took in the pain (to bind) I felt her feeling, burdens and hurt, and yet, it didn't leach on to me, but it changed those feelings that could have been negative (anger,

frustration, agitation) to (too loose) sincerity, love, and peace. Why because it is in Christ Jesus the Rock of All living Rocks, Hallelujah!! He gave me a peace that he was going to take good care of her — a gift from the Father to us.

So, let's talk about ourselves pertaining to the matters of the heart because of life itself. So many things can try to crush our faith whether it's a loss of a job, a car, a child, or maybe a person could almost be on the verge of losing their home; maybe your parents could be going through a divorce or children may have low self-esteem; or you just feel like you are not good enough because you feel like you can't live up to man's expectations of whom they think you should be. Sometimes you just feel like your life is turned upside down, and you feel like giving up on life because of too many unfavorable circumstances happening in your life. Or maybe you may be jealous of a person for whatever reason, and you don't know why? And you have been fasting and praying for that thing to break, and it didn't happen, or it did go away, but it came back. These are matters of the heart. The Father made us unique in his own way we have strengths, and we have weaknesses; but thank God in the areas we are weak in, he gave us strength, grace and help through the crystals through faith in Christ Jesus the crystals/stones/gemstone of our choosing to be a tool in our lives to help us in the areas we need help in life. People may say that's idolatry because you're using it in place of Jesus, and that's not true because Christ is the mediator, and the rocks are made out of him. And if you know what the Father originally intended for crystals to be used for as your armor, you will not think that way. The Lord says we are lively stones for a reason because stones are alive, and he compares us unto them because we have different characteristics just like them. And they like us vice versa. I know they talk to the Father about us just like the angels do because they are alive.

"5 <u>Ye also, as lively stones</u>, are built up a spiritual house, an holy priesthood, to offer up spiritual sacrifices acceptable to God by Jesus Christ." 1 Peter 2:5-9 (KJV)

Think of it this way, you want to build a house, and you have a picture of how you want it. With this house, you know how many rooms and what kind of rooms you need in order to accommodate yourself or the family. But, in order to build it, you need a special cement of your choice for the foundation along with wood, you need particular pipes for the bathroom and kitchen in order for the water to run through, you need drywall in order to make the walls. There are other things you would need, like screws and screwdrivers, to hold things in tack, you need a particular window of your choice so you can see out of the house. You need brick, in order for the house to stay firm along with the framework of the house using the cement, you need the roof to cover and officially conceal the house, but you may want it to be a specific color or style. You need the doors in order to walk in and out of rooms, you want particular furniture and colors to help the house look

to your taste and style, etc. Without these things, a house can't be built, because it is mandatory to keep its structure and to fulfill the vision. Or you can see the crystals as a tool, for example, the only way to screw a particular screw in order to keep two things conjoined within a frame; it must be screwed in by a specific screwdriver that's able to turn the screw by the pattern on top of the screw. The pattern on top shows a small indented straight line going across that screwdriver with a particular length and must only be a flat head screwdriver because it's the only screwdriver made for it to turn and that keeps it sealed tight for that particular frame.

The bible says, **"For where your treasure is, there your heart will be also." Matt 6:21(KJV).** So if you are a person that gets angry all the time or you don't try to, or it just comes out, and you would like to be calmer, you may

want to get turquoise , howlite , black hematite ,
celestite , rainbow hematite , amethyst , orb Black
tourmaline , to calm you down. They will help balance you and keep you

calm. I really like rainbow hematite especially if you have kids it gives you a calm, but sturdy and direct conversation to your children, where they know to do what you say because it is spoken with authority even though you are miraculously calm and reminding yourself of peace, and you feel the peace of

rainbow hematite . So, if your treasure is one of these crystals because its effects are producing the fruit of patience and calmness within you at an increased rate by the grace it gives, that's where your heart will be. Your heart is what reflects what comes out of your mouth, along with the mind. "Out of the abundance of the heart, the mouth speaks" (Matthew 13:24). If you don't want to be jealous of people or a particular person, or in competition with anyone,

snowflake obsidian (a glass stone) will be your treasure, and you will praise God for it because you are no longer set under the bondage of jealousy or envy. Hallelujah! If you love creativity and you noticed it stopped for some reason,

you can use Citrine *, Carnelian* *, Mookaite* *,*

Apatite  *, etc., maybe your treasure so that creativity can flow from your heart and mind and you will appreciate this gift of the Father. So, whichever crystal you choose by its fruitfulness and benefits, so shall the fruitfulness and characteristics flow out of your heart, your mouth, mind, will, and emotions. So, if it's a stone of joy and love, your heart will be full of joy and love, if it's a stone of compassion, then your heart will flow out of it compassion. If these emotions flow out of your heart, it will, of course, flow out of you. Wow! So amazing and so cool. The crystals are there to protect you and become one with you as armor to cover and shield you. Necklaces' original intent was for the use of protection of the person, or shall I say amulet.*

Amulet means something that is hung on, we see this so many times in the bible, and according to the Jewish encyclopedia, it was never intended to be used for evil, it was used to protect mothers, children, land, property, etc. from black magic, witchcraft, evil, curses, etc.. You never use it to cast love spells on a person, or do evil to a person, or control a person. If you want a husband, you ask the Lord to send his best husband that he sees fit for you and to show you multiple confirmations that it is from him. We see in proverbs people use different crystals to get men in proverbs. This shows the wrong way of using crystals. There are people who use it to bring multiple men or different men as prospects for them to date, not knowing that its creating soul ties with each and every person they are dating, versus just waiting for that one person to come by, or the select few that the Lord may send for you to choose. It's cool to use rose quartz to attract love, but make sure you ask the Lord to send only your God-ordained spouse.

I remember going to a prophetic conference, and the Prophet prophesied to a man that the Lord had sent him three prospects for a spouse, but it was up to the gentleman to choose the person out of those three. Out of the three, he had his eye on only one woman, and he married her, and now they are living a happy life serving the Lord. The number three is always used a lot of times for confirmation for the Father, the Son, and the Holy Ghost. Magic or the supernatural was never intended to be used for evil period. People started to use them for evil because of sin, and evil influences which came from the fall of Satan, and the influence of fallen angels, even caused by negative influences of the genetic bloodline. There was a fallen angel that revealed about weapons, trickery, magic, and was sent for judgment named Azazel along with Semjaza, Armaras, and others, which you can see below.

"6. **Thou seest what Azazel hath done, who hath taught all unrighteousness on earth and revealed the eternal secrets which were <u>preserved</u> in heaven, which men were striving to learn:" The Book of Enoch 8:6 "1. And Uriel said to me: 'Here shall stand the angels who have connected themselves with women, and their spirits assuming many different forms are defiling mankind and shall lead them astray into sacrificing to demons as gods, (here shall they stand,) till the day of the great judgement in which they shall be judged till they are made an end of. 2. And the women also of the angels who went astray shall become sirens.' 3. And I, Enoch, alone saw the vision, the ends of all things: and no man shall see as I have seen." The Book of Enoch 19:1-2**

"1. **And Azazel taught men to make swords, and knives, and shields, and breastplates, and made known to them the metals of the earth and the art of working them, and bracelets, and ornaments, and the use of antimony, and the beautifying of the eyelids, and all kinds of costly stones, and all colouring tinctures. 2. And there arose much godlessness, and they committed fornication, and they were led astray and became corrupt in all their ways. Semjaza taught enchantments, and root-cuttings, Armaros the resolving of enchantments, (taught) astrology, Kokabel the constellations, Ezeqeel the knowledge of the clouds, Araqiel the signs of the earth, Shamsiel the signs of the sun, and Sariel the course of the moon. And as men perished, they cried, and their cry went up to heaven, etc." The Book of Enoch 8:1-3**

"1. **And all the others together with them took unto themselves wives, and each chose for himself one, and they began to go in unto them and to defile themselves with them, and they taught them charms and enchantments, and the cutting of roots, and made them acquainted with plants. 2. And they became pregnant, and they bare great giants, whose height was three thousand ells: 3. Who consumed all the acquisitions of men. And when men could no longer sustain them, 4. the giants turned against them and devoured mankind. 5. And they began to sin against birds, and beasts, and reptiles, and fish, and to devour one another's flesh, and drink the blood. 6. Then the earth laid accusation against the lawless ones."**

The Earth sent forth accusation against the lawless ones. The earth speaking to the Father in the courts of heaven for justice to be served against those who are lawless and corrupt. This is showing light versus

darkness. The Book of Enoch 7:1-6 talks about the fallen angels or watchers teaching astrology, but in the book of Psalms, it talks about how the stars speak, and it talks about the constellations in Psalms.

1 The heavens declare the glory of God; and the firmament sheweth his handywork.2 Day unto day uttereth speech, and night unto night sheweth knowledge.3 There is no speech nor language, where their voice is not heard.4 Their line is gone out through all the earth, and their words to the end of the world. In them hath he set a tabernacle for the sun,5 Which is as a bridegroom coming out of his chamber, and rejoiceth as a strong man to run a race.6 His going forth is from the end of the heaven, and his circuit unto the ends of it: and there is nothing hid from the heat thereof. Psalms 19:1-6 (KJV)

Also, in the book of Jasher, it talks about the stars prophesying and speaking, the reason Rebecca stole her Father's images would speak the truth because of the influence of the stars. Stars speak and prophecies. That's why people have dreams at night because they speak through Christ through the Father. It's nothing wrong with astrology if you are a born-again believer. As long as you have the Father, the Son, and the Holy Ghost, the word of God, and discernment. That's all you need to know. **"43 And some make them in the figures of men, of gold and silver, and go to them in times known to them, and the figures receive the influence of the stars and tell them future things, and in this manner were the images which Rachel stole from her father."** *The Book of Jasher 31:43 I wouldn't be shocked if they were made out of crystals.* **We will talk about Apostle Paul and the mirror later on. It's good versus evil, light versus darkness. We haven't had our eyes to see or ears to hear yet all the things the Father has to reveal unto us, that's part of the Kingdom of God, to advance Christ's Kingdom. That's why I say magic was never meant to be used for evil. The Father's intent was for it only to be used for good. They released the secrets of God. They taught the perverted evil, corrupt way of doing things.**

These fallen angels taught the perverse way of magic, because who was the source that magic magically originally came from? It was the Father. It was heavens eternal secret. Was the Father way of using magic perverse, wicked, and deceit? No, it was pure, holy, and righteousness, and truth, and goodness because it's who the Father is. However, they gave instructions on how to use it for evil, versus the good in which the Father had used magic for, which is to co-create. In the book of revelations, those that practiced sorcery would be thrown into the lake of fire. Those are people who have given their lives to Satan and his evil ways. Those who are for the Father and being obedient to him shall not suffer because they are the Sons of God.

*I hate to say it, but the priest performed magic or the supernatural when it came to the husband finding out if his wife committed adultery. Natural magic in the middle ages was considered more or less legitimate, not sinful, and involved much that would be explained scientifically as the manipulation of natural forces. It did not require the use of spirits. We see the priest used two elements the Water (holy water) and the Earth (dust) of the temple and mixed them, the lady also had to say a vow, If the Father (Jehovah, Yahweh, Yod Hey Vav Hey)revealed she committed adultery, then her thigh would rot, and her belly would swell. But the Spirit was I Am that I Am Jehovah himself (Jehovah, Yahweh, Yod, Hey, Vav, Hey) was in the Midst. It wasn't an illusion like some magicians use for tricks, but it actually happened, and it brought forth manifestation under the instructions of the Father. Some people would think that to be black magic, honestly. It was part of the judgment and a curse for the sin of adultery she committed. And it probably was magic. So, some things the Lord may tell you to do may actually look like magic or even might be of his original intent, not Satan's perverse, crooked ways, or trickery. It's just science. Like someone said, magic is a misunderstood science. How can Satan cast out Satan? Daniel performed magic he was not just called to be a prophet and dreamer, he also was called to be a magician because God knows the end from the beginning, the king set him over the magicians because he understood mysteries, could interpret dreams and handwritings on the wall. We deceive ourselves if we think he didn't do magic, it tells us he did in Bel and the Dragon (**Bel 14:1-22(KJV)**) which is an extended book of Daniel that he blew up the dragon to prove a point to the Babylonians that the dragon they worshipped was not a living God. Daniel blew up the dragon by baking pitch, fat, and hair (trichas) to make cakes (mazas, barley-cakes) that caused the dragon to burst open and explode upon consumption. **However, the book of Bel and the Dragon was rejected by Rabbinic Judaism, it was initially one of the books of Daniel, but was not chosen to be put into the Holy Bible because it went against the Torah which Rabbinic Judaism teaches.***

The difference is he got the instruction from the Lord on how to do it, and what to do it for. He flowed through the anointing of God. He didn't have to conjure up demonic spirits. He had The Father, The Son, and Holy Spirit with him along with the pure, righteous angelic host and every other celestial being that needed to be there in order for the manifestation to come to past. Again, you see the true prophets versus the false prophets. Either you going to be with the Father, or you going to be with Satan. Magicians use crystals to ward off evil or demonic forces. Why? Because they are conjuring up the demonic spirits or fallen angels that taught the perverse way of magic. There are so many books of the bible and missing pieces that were taken out of the bible as well. What Daniel did, it wasn't an illusion; he actually had manifestation. But do we call him a witch or warlock or sorcerer, no! Because he did it under the instruction of the Lord, and he was a holy man, anointed and appointed to do it for the purposes of God.

A real magician of the Lord is not going to have to use any demonic spirits to do magic if they do its perverse. Do I do magic? No! I'm sure if the church heard of some of the Christians doing what Daniel did, they would be quick to call him a witch or warlock, or even if Daniel was alive in this time, they would call him a warlock. Again, how can Satan cast out Satan? What if you were called to perform magic or the supernatural by putting things together in order to perform the will of God. There were Christian women tortured and killed because people thought they were witches because they performed miracles and where more than likely told to put things together in order to co-create or have manifestation. I believe the Lord is coming to bring this to fruition in the near future in order to co-labor and heal the earth for good, not for evil. We talk about Daniel anointing, but we have only done two-thirds of his calling, which is being a dreamer and prophet, but we left out the third calling to do magic, or I will say the supernatural. Okay, I sense some people teeth cringing, but it's the truth.

What if the Lord told you to put some flowers, oil, and a crystal together to heal the land, creatures, or to take you to another place in the earth in order to minister to someone during that time in a totally different country. But, we get mad at the witches and warlocks coming into our houses to do harm to us, but when the Lord tells us to do things for the good of his use, we hear oh that's witchcraft, or it goes through a demonic spirit. Unfortunately, as Christians cry out for the supernatural to get transported to other countries, supernaturally to pray for others because very few have operated out of that in Christianity. But what if what they are rejecting (crystals or stones) is what will help them perform that task, the ancients did it. It's Christ the Rock they are rejecting. It may not always happen the way we think because everyone is made differently. This is speaking the truth. Yes, I know Apostle Paul had people throw away the magic books, but truth be told it probably was people using magic for evil, they more than likely were serving Satan or under the influence of familiar spirits or demons (negative energy).

I believe the priest did the magic under the instruction of the Lord in order to find out if a husband's wife committed adultery, Daniel did it. Matter of fact, people probably think or say it was black magic. Now the Lord has not called us to do that, but I just want people to have their eyes open to see and ears to really hear what was really going on back then in ancient times.

"13 And a man lie with her carnally, and it be hid from the eyes of her husband and be kept close, and she be defiled, and there be no witness against her, neither she be taken with the manner;14 And the spirit of jealousy come upon him, and he be jealous of his wife, and she be defiled: or if the spirit of jealousy come upon him, and he be jealous of his wife, and she be not defiled:15 Then shall the man bring his wife unto the priest, and he shall bring her offering for her, the tenth part of an ephah of barley meal; he shall pour no oil upon it, nor put frankincense thereon;

for it is an offering of jealousy, an offering of memorial, bringing iniquity to remembrance.16 And the priest shall bring her near, and set her before the Lord:17 And the priest shall take holy water in an earthen vessel; and of the dust that is in the floor of the tabernacle the priest shall take, and put it into the water:18 And the priest shall set the woman before the Lord, and uncover the woman's head, and put the offering of memorial in her hands, which is the jealousy offering: and the priest shall have in his hand the bitter water that causeth the curse:19 And the priest shall charge her by an oath, and say unto the woman, If no man have lain with thee, and if thou hast not gone aside to uncleanness with another instead of thy husband, be thou free from this bitter water that causeth the curse:20 But if thou hast gone aside to another instead of thy husband, and if thou be defiled, and some man have lain with thee beside thine husband:21 Then the priest shall charge the woman with an oath of cursing, and the priest shall say unto the woman, The Lord make thee a curse and an oath among thy people, when the Lord doth make thy thigh to rot, and thy belly to swell;22 And this water that causeth the curse shall go into thy bowels, to make thy belly to swell, and thy thigh to rot: And the woman shall say, Amen, amen.23 And the priest shall write these curses in a book, and he shall blot them out with the bitter water:24 And he shall cause the woman to drink the bitter water that causeth the curse: and the water that causeth the curse shall enter into her, and become bitter.25 Then the priest shall take the jealousy offering out of the woman's hand, and shall wave the offering before the Lord, and offer it upon the altar:26 And the priest shall take an handful of the offering, even the memorial thereof, and burn it upon the altar, and afterward shall cause the woman to drink the water.27 And when he hath made her drink the water, then it shall come to pass, that, if she be defiled, and have done trespass against her husband, that the water that causeth the curse shall enter into her, and become bitter, and her belly shall swell, and her thigh shall rot: and the woman shall be a curse among her people."
Numbers 5:13-27(KJV)

I have to speak the truth about how spiritually immature the body of Christ is when it comes to the Spirit. The Egyptian priest was known to do magic in ancient times, so I don't put it passed that the priest didn't do the same in the tabernacle against the wife. Daniel did it in Bel and the Dragon. I'm saying to read, listen, think, analyze. This is not to persuade anyone or go into politics. I'm just sharing this because I have to touch all aspects of what people will bring up and have actually had their eyes blind to, pertaining to the crystals and what the bible is saying. But the priest didn't need a crystal to protect them, and Daniel didn't. Numbers 5:13-27 (KJV) was part of judgment if the wife committed adultery, but what I am saying look at what was done to perform it. Point blank

crystals are to protect mankind from evil forces and protect your gateways and organs. It's part of your armor and a treasure from the Father's Heart.

We cry out for change, yet we deny the tools the Lord originally had for us to use in order to bring about the change that we want to come into their life. That's why we go around in circles, unfortunately, crying out for more rain and prosperity, or crying out for change within themselves because they lack the fruit the Bible tells us to bear. Unfortunately, as Christians, we get upset because the witches and warlocks doing harm prospers because they take advantage of what the Lord initially used for good and perverted them to do evil. If they use crystals and words as a weapon against us, don't you think we suppose to use our words and crystals as a weapon to do good and pronounce blessings instead of curses. Truth is it's not the crystal, and it's the person and their hearts intent and motives. A crystal is still going to function as the way the Father called, commissioned, and ordained them to function whether you are a good or bad person. For instance, someone can be thinking negatively about you, and it can bring something to fruition in your life.

If someone says you are not going to prosper in their mind, it just might not happen because of that one thought. Rainbow Obsidian protects you from negative thoughts of others, instead of it coming near you or doing harm to you, it actually stays on that person speaking or thinking negatively about you.

"1He that dwelleth in the secret place of the Most High shall abide under the shadow of the Almighty.2 I will say of the Lord, He is my refuge and my fortress: my God; in Him will I trust.3 Surely he shall deliver thee from the snare of the fowler, and from the noisome pestilence.4 He shall cover thee with his feathers, and under his wings shalt thou trust: his truth shall be thy shield and buckler.5 Thou shalt not be afraid for the terror by night; nor for the arrow that flieth by day;6 Nor for the pestilence that walketh in darkness; nor for the destruction that wasteth at noonday.7 A thousand shall fall at thy side, and ten thousand at thy right hand; but it shall not come nigh thee.8 Only with thine eyes shalt thou behold and see the reward of the wicked.9 Because thou hast made the Lord, which is my refuge, even the most High, thy habitation;10 There shall no evil befall thee, neither shall any plague come nigh thy dwelling.11 For he shall give his angels charge over thee, to keep thee in all thy ways.12 They shall bear thee up in their hands, lest thou dash thy foot against a stone.13 Thou shalt tread upon the lion and adder: the young lion and the dragon shalt thou trample under feet." Psalm 91:1-13 (KJV)

The wicked can also mean the wickedness of people thoughts against you that are meant to cause you harm. Whether Christian, witch, warlock, an ordinary person, family member, etc.

The same vice versa for the witch or warlock if they use Rainbow Obsidian, it will protect them from negative thoughts or intents we have in our hearts against them, that's why people are drained out even after speaking in tongues in prayer sometimes, or just in prayer because many people have hatred in their hearts and that's a low frequency and vibration, so it brings negativity. By that same negativity and anger that you go against them within prayer, if they have Rainbow Obsidian on or on their altar as protection, or around them, then those negative thoughts are not touching them; it's actually staying on you. Don't get mad at Rainbow Obsidian, and it's doing the Father's protocol. I hate to say it, but it's actually is doing what you prayed for, except it's not hitting them it's hitting you or manifesting itself on you because rainbow obsidian protects a person's aura from negativity.

The Lord had to show me that during prayer before I even used crystals. That's why Jesus says to bless those who curse you. **(Matthew 5:43-47 KJV)** Because love is what brings an enemy, witch, or warlock into repentance and change. And If you are praying for them with sincere love, that sincere love is staying on you, but at the same time, the Lord is delivering them out of darkness, witchcraft, and the hatred they have against you. Hate or godly anger just makes things worse. Now, if you are doing it out of your authority where its neutral love and hate in balance, then you will have good results. If you pray for them out of love, you won't feel drained, and if you bless them, you will be blessed. Because if you are praying sincere blessings, their blessings are deliverance from demonic influence (negative energies) and breaking them free from the power of darkness. Now, will sometimes you get angry, yes. But the point I'm trying to say the crystal still has to perform its duty if asked or told just like the angels. But don't get me wrong. God will not let them do certain things, just like the angels; they only can do what the Father allows. Just like Satan and the Fallen angels can only do what the Father allows.

This is the same scenario we see year after year, all because men in higher authority or titles want to put a cap on what people can do or use in the body of Christ, which has people battling the same thing year after year. If the saints of God feed the people fear from these things because they focus on the bible scriptures where people used the amulets, magic, or charms for evil intentions, they become negative and poison people because of the negative views through fear. Yet they did not stop to think hmm...? wherein scripture where crystals used for the Father's original purpose. But again, if we don't dig behind the scripture and have a relationship with the Father, then it's easy to be deceived or miss revelation in the word of God.

For example, my favorite scripture I use for protection in prayer against witches and warlocks is Ezekiel chapter 33 (KJV), it talks about the false prophets,

witches, warlocks, and charms. However, the King James version really waters down and don't tell the original truth behind the scriptures,

To wit, the prophets of Israel which prophecies concerning Jerusalem, and which see visions of peace for her, and there is no peace, saith the Lord GOD.

> **"17 Likewise, thou son of man, set thy face against the daughters of thy people, which prophesy out of their own heart; and prophesy thou against them,**
>
> **18 And say, Thus saith the Lord GOD; Woe to the women that sew pillows to all armholes, and make kerchiefs upon the head of every stature to hunt souls! Will ye hunt the souls of my people, and will ye save the souls alive that come unto you?**
>
> **19 And will ye pollute me among my people for handfuls of barley and for pieces of bread, to slay the souls that should not die, and to save the souls alive that should not live, by your lying to my people that hear your lies?**
>
> **20 Wherefore thus saith the Lord GOD; Behold, I am against your pillows, wherewith ye there hunt the souls to make them fly, and I will tear them from your arms and will let the souls go, even the souls that ye hunt to make them fly.**
>
> **21 Your kerchiefs also will I tear, and deliver my people out of your hand, and they shall be no more in your hand to be hunted; and ye shall know that I am the LORD.**
>
> **22 Because with lies ye have made the heart of the righteous sad, whom I have not made sad; and strengthened the hands of the wicked, that he should not return from his wicked way, by promising him life:**
>
> **23 Therefore ye shall see no more vanity, nor divine divinations: for I will deliver my people out of your hand: and ye shall know that I am the LORD." Ezekiel 33:16-23 (KJV)**

They used these things to control and terrorize people. They didn't correct those who did wickedly, and they used their gifts for evil and wickedness like Balaam and Jezebel. They took money from evil men to do evil to God's people and good people as well. They did magic to do harm and destruction to good people. It stated throughout the chapter that the people didn't see any vision they were prophesying lies, their own thoughts, they were using lying divination not just regular divination which the church preaches is wickedness when Joseph (dreamer) clearly also divined out of the cup he had the men to put into Benjamin's book bag (this is called water scrying). **"Isn't this the cup my master drinks from and also uses for divination? This is a wicked thing you have done." Genesis 44:5 (NIV) People** *talk about Joseph's anointing but haven't fully fulfilled Joseph's role because they have not tapped into water scrying yet. If Joseph used it back, then you can use it now, and at a more*

significant measure, you can't limit Holy Spirit. You have to fulfill the old way in order to receive the new or Latter rain. Holy Spirit can communicate through all things because, again, Christ is all in all.

The Latter rain shall be greater than the former. **"The glory of this present house will be greater than the glory of the former house,' says the LORD Almighty. 'And in this place, I will grant peace,' declares the LORD Almighty." Haggai 2:9 (KJV)** And now that Holy Spirit dwells in us, how much more should we be able to tap into these things. But how can we find out the greater if we haven't tapped into one of the basic things that Daniel did, Joseph (water scrying), Apostle Paul tapped into mirror scrying, which I will talk about later. Bottom line if you haven't tapped into the basics of old that these men fulfilled, you are not going to see the latter rain. The latter rain may not look like what you think it is going to look like because you need the basics of the old in order to tap into the new (latter rain). Is it because this is what psychics do? I think so. I hate to say it, but that is being prejudiced. And that's not right, especially if it's your own brother and sister in Christ. We want to talk about psychics being evil and dealing with familiar spirits, so do the prophets in the church. We battle against ourselves and familiar spirits in our bloodline and the imperfections of our earthly body.

We battle against demons, familiar spirits around regions, evil principalities, and rulers in our city or regions, etc. This happens anywhere you go. That is why we are to test every spirit and use discernment. We have some prophets that prophesy out of their own flesh as well and make mistakes or make errors also as well, but we still highly esteemed them and showed them honor. Some people worship and idolize them too, and they feed off of that, I have to speak the truth. I know I'm offending mindsets, but it's a fact in a lot of cases. Some people want people to look unto to them sometimes, so they can feel superior or feed their ego, therefore, forgetting their own imperfection, I was once there when I was a babe in Christ, not all people in the body of Christ are this way but just some. Truth is everyone has their own weaknesses or sin, whether saved or unsaved. I have to speak the truth because "a true witness delivereth souls" (Prov.14:25 KJV) **"The backslider in heart shall be filled with his own ways: and a good man shall be satisfied from himself." Proverbs 14:14 (KJV)**

Thank God we are declared righteous even in the midst of our imperfections. I'm just saying, being honest, you have some prophets doing what the people criticize psychics for also in the church, prophesying lies, guessing, and prophesying for money, just to do it. There are psychics that are accurate, and all the time, because that's their gift, they are just using a different instrument to exercise their gift or mind's eye, and they are actually good people, not evil. They have good intentions. There's nothing wrong with

prophesying for money because if that's your only source of income God called you to do, then it's okay, the people brought money in order to honor the man or woman of God (prophet) in biblical times because they took time out to seek the Lord to give the word of the Lord to the people out of a sincere, genuine heart, but when your motives are impure, that becomes a problem. Or you are just doing it for your own pleasure and not helping others, or the ministry, then it becomes a problem.

There are genuine people who prophesies and received offering and some that charge a higher price, but it's because of the breakthrough people receive, and some people do charge a higher price so that people don't keep coming to them for a word and end up idolizing who they are as a prophet, in for people to get their own prophetic word from God. So instead of the person who needs a prophetic word, if the cost is too much, they will seek God for themselves. There are good psychics, and you have bad psychics. I say all psychics are seers, but not all seers are psychics because psychics use their gifts through other instruments to prophesy, because our body has different technologies. We will talk more about this in a later chapter on idolatry.

Let's go back to Ezekiel, and they would prophesy out of their own hearts and have seen nothing. **"Son of man, prophesy against the prophets of Israel that prophesy, and say thou unto them that prophesy out of their own hearts, Hear ye the word of the LORD; Thus saith the Lord GOD; Woe unto the foolish prophets, that follow their own spirit, and have seen nothing!" Ezekiel 13:2,3 (KJV)** they did lying divination the Lord said woe unto them because they seduced God's people, not only that, but they caused them to harm by doing spells against good people in general for money, the witches and warlocks behind clothes doors were trying to come against God's people. They were hunting and afflicting the people, and he said he would deliver his people out of their hands, because they made the heart of the righteous sad, whom he did not make sad, and strengthened the hands of the wicked, that they should not turn from their wicked way by promising him life. He told them he would tear the kerchiefs, or in some versions, it says magic charms or amulets from them. The reason why he said he would break the kerchiefs, charms, and amulets because they used it for evil purposes and to do evil towards righteous and good people. Again, they used these things for evil works, to damage, and to do harm under the influence of Satan and not under the purposes of God! They did not use it for the Father's purposes, truth, will, they did it for pure evil. That's why the Father said he was against the charms. There were amulets approved and amulets not approved by the Jews.

We see in scripture the Lord clearly shows that using crystals as amulets, which nowadays you would call it a necklace and talismans had the power to protect a person, bring healing, and to bring about the needed change in a person, and their life according to the scriptures.

Earrings - Help You Hear

There are some crystals that enhance your hearing in the realm of the spirit, so you can hear what the spirit of the Lord is saying. You can also hear what your spirit is telling you or your body is telling you. Or you can hear what the angels, celestial beings, earth, nature, animals, the universe, sun, moon, and the stars are speaking to you.

Ephesians 6:15 KJV And Your feet shod with the preparation of the gospel of peace.

In many different cultures, men and women wore crystals and stone bracelets to protect the feet from any negative energies or demonic spirits. As we have seen in the book of Job, it emphasized even the power of the crystal and gold combined. It's a powerful pack according to Job because he states wisdom still can't compare to the two being combined. (Job 28:17)

Ephesians 6:16 (KJV) Above all, taking the shield of faith, wherewith ye shall be able to quench all the fiery darts of the wicked.

The shield of faith is the crystals working in conjunction with your aura /electromagnetic field to protect you from negative energies and demonic spirits. They also work in conjunction with the neurons in our physical bodies in order to bring about change. We see an example of crystal providing a shield by strengthening our aura field, and us imagining the shield with our mind's eye or third eye while holding the crystals. Or just believing by faith that it will shield us if it's a protective stone. For example, the Father describing being a wall of fire round about us and the glory within us. **Zach.2:5 (KJV) For I saith the LORD, will be unto her a wall of fire round about, and will be the glory in the midst of her.** *Is you imagine the glory of the Lord or his Light coming down within your crown gateway down to your mind's eye gateway, down to your heart gateway (the love gate) and you feel the fire, heat, electricity, energy, or tangible presence of love flowing down your arm into the crystal and imagine the crystal*

surrounding you like an actual wall of fire round about you like an oval spreading anywhere from 4 to 16 inches around you. And you can tell it to shield you, and it will do it.

You shall decree a thing, and it shall be established. Decree means you shall speak, tell and demand, your crystals to do things, and it will do it. They are employed by the Father to shield and protect you as part of the living rocks of Christ Jesus. Jesus said, "For verily I say unto you, That whosoever shall say unto this mountain, Be thou removed, and be thou cast into the sea; and shall not doubt in his heart, but shall believe that those things which he saith shall come to pass; he shall have whatsoever he saith." (Mark 11:23 KJV) It's just like when the Father told Moses to speak to the rock, the Israelites were complaining about having no water. So, the Father told Moses to speak the rock to have water come out of it, and it will come out. Unfortunately, Moses was so angry with the people for their murmuring and complaining, that he hit the rock and the water gushed out. **(Number 20:8-12)** If a person saw that, they would think that it's magic. But even more, if he spoke to it the rock (mountain), it would have obeyed him.

The Lord was trying to show one of the functions that they are purposed to do. You can also see another scripture where you see where Jesus says, "On that day you will know that I am in My Father, and you in Me and I in you. That's a threefold cord of protection, and if Christ is the Living Rock of All Living rocks, if you consecrated the rocks because rocks keep records and commands. You can imagine the crystal as Christ and being in the Father, and you in that living crystal, you see another shield by you seeing yourself in the crystal, and the crystal inside of you, as they are in the Father's heart. So, decree and declare that scripture in prayer with the set intention of protection from negative thoughts or enemies, and you are all set. Or you can see it as a shield of love inside out roundabout.

So, the shield round about us is the shield of faith in Christ the rock itself because if you don't believe the crystal/stone will protect you by repelling the enemy from your aura, then it won't. Because your electromagnetic/aura field goes in sync with the crystal, and they make powerful protection together for you. So anything negative or demonic that touches the bubble or shield around you, then it's as good as toast and is repelled by the shield (crystal) through your electromagnetic field/aura becoming one with the crystals, moving at the same frequency and vibration of the crystal through entrainment. It's like when you spray insect repellant or bug spray around the borders of your house, and the insects try to crossover, but it goes the other way or it may crossover, but it dies as a result of the insect repellant or bug spray being a shield of protection to protect the house from certain insects.

The Helmet of salvation Ephesians 6:17 (KJV)

The helmet of salvation is not only knowing your healing, deliverance, preservation, and soundness of mind, which are part of Jesus' redemptive work on the cross; But, also there are crystals whose role is to protect your mind's eye, and your crown wheel (gateway/chakra) from attacks of the enemy sowing into your mind lies, doubt, saying you can't receive your full healing, when we know that's a lie of the devil himself, his friends the fallen angels, or the doubt (familiar spirit) that may have been in your bloodline from generation to generation speaking to your conscious. Well, the crystal that will counteract and protect you

from those spirits, and my favorite is Celestite, Blue sapphire. Celestite

protect your crown wheel and Blue Sapphire   your mind's eye wheel. We see the proof when you see other cultures having a gemstone to cover and protect the mind's eye we see this being true because **Ezekiel 16:13(KJV) says, "And I put a jewel on thy forehead, and earrings in thine ears, and a beautiful crown upon thine head. "***That was part of our armor so even other cultures have this same revelation and know the power behind it protecting your mind because in your mind is where all the warfare happens. So, in reality, we are to have a jewel on our forehead if we want to, but we don't have to as long as we have a crystal on us to protect us around us on us, whether purse, pocket, you name it, it will protect the different wheels (chakras, gates) that it is assigned to protect within us. Or you can even imagine the crystal with you, and you will actually feel it in your hand and its effects by faith.*

Truth to Cover your Loins

People wear waist gemstones to protect and align your chakras, which brings forth seven spirits of God that operate out of the spirit of truth, which is Christ the Rock himself through the Father and the Word of God, which is the spirit of truth.

Shield of Faith

I had a dream that me and my husband was looking at small cacti in a store. There were many cactuses. It was around 3 or 5 different mini cactuses we were looking at. Then I saw these spiders. They were blue, very thin, and faint. They

came down in front of them, trying to leach on to them. One of the blue spiders tried to latch to my hair, and I pulled it off. The reason the spider was blue is that blue represents the Spirit of Might, but the Lord was letting me know the spiders were some of the stronger or mighty forces of the enemy. I instantly heard to go buy a mini cactus plant. So, I did. It was a single small cactus. The Lord revealed to me the revelation of the cactus spines (spikes, or needles) that surrounds them is a resemblance of our aura and wheels, and the majority of the cactuses have a crown chakra just like we do at the top of our heads. The spines are all around the cactuses, but at the top, it was a circle of spines; some a totally different color of the other spines, and the Lord reminded me that that is a resemblance of our crown chakra at the top of our head representing the energy that flows through

Cactuses breathe in and out of the spines (spikes) which are the leaves that grows through the opening of the chakra Centers of the cactus body

Crown Chakra – Where you see flowers grow on depending on the type of cactus it is.

Crown Chakra

Crown Chakra

Cactuses breathe in and out of the spines (spikes) which are the leaves that grows through the opening of the chakra Centers of the cactus body

Trunk

all the chakras of the cactuses up through their crown and back down through the crown chakra just like we have.

*The cactus's survival skills through its body are similar to our chakras and auras except for our body to fully be protected like the cactuses we need the crystals which activate the **shield of faith through our aura/electromagnetic field**. The chakras of the cactuses (the openings where the spines grow out) also operate like the wheels. The spiders (the enemy) around the cactuses and their spines could not come near them if they did, the spiders could not latch on to the cactuses because of the spines which were around them are strong and sharp and would repel the spiders.*

The spines protect the cactus from danger or anything that will cause harm to it. But, there are a few predators that still don't mind eating the thorns like camels, jack rabbits, etc. So, in this instance it's the same for us, some crystals aren't protective stones, they just help you offensively and defensively, but don't have the functions to protect you from negative words of others against you. That's why you need at least one protection crystal, on you, along with the other crystals assigned to your chakras, or a crystal grid to protect you. Here's several protection crystals,

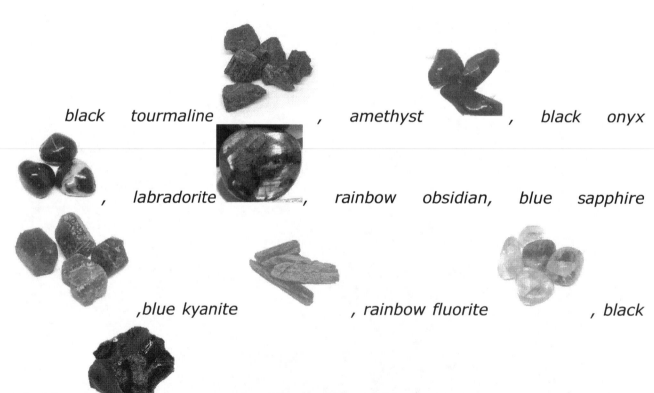

*black tourmaline , amethyst , black onyx , labradorite , rainbow obsidian, blue sapphire ,blue kyanite , rainbow fluorite , black obsidian , jet, etc. **(Song 4:4 KJV)** So what the Lord was saying was when you have a crystal it strengthens, protects, and seals your aura, and it repels the enemy (the spiders in the dream). In Christianity, we see spiders as evil, or they say that is witchcraft. You can see it on the good side spiders are strategic creators, and they put everything in strategic alignment through creativity and perfect order. There is always contrast to everything. The spines of*

the cactus represent our aura strengthened, protected, and in tack by the crystal's defense mechanism. Again, the crystals help you offensively and defensively. Each spine that comes out of the cactus protects the cactus by destroying, or repelling, or harming the predators in order to keep it safe. It makes sure if it gets damaged to where the predator will not try to pursue it again. Crystals work through the dimensions of the chakras to destroy and take out any negative energies or forces (demonic spirits) and demolish or transmute them into positive energy. They strengthen our aura round about us from the attack of the enemy. Just how we have to praise and worship the Lord to strengthen the angels and decree and declare the word of God, so it is the same with crystals. We have to cleanse and energize them as well, which we will talk about later.

Shield of Faith Activation Method for Protection

So, a couple of times, I was getting attacked, but I didn't have on a protective crystal at the time, and I sometimes can feel different spirits around. I picked up someone else's spirit that was not of me in a store, it was very negative, and I felt as if it was me and I couldn't believe I felt that way. The Lord let me know, and it was not me, but the negative energy (demonic spirit) on the person in the store. He said my gateways wasn't protected. The evil spirit tried to attach

itself to my aura. I didn't have a protective stone to protect my chakras and my aura. So, the Lord told me to get in tune with one of my protection crystals that I didn't have and imagine them working with my aura as a sealant within and upon my aura to repel the negative energy (demonic spirit). So, I imagined my aura growing out and around me like a protective shield pushing away any negative energies (demonic spirits). To my surprise, those dark feelings went away and along with the negative energy (evil spirit) very quick. Another way you can repel the enemy through your aura using crystals is imagining you're within the crystal, and it is protecting you like you are being in a crystal cave as a shelter. A third way you can use your aura as a shield is to imagine an actual shield round about you like a big bubble repelling the enemy. If this doesn't work, then you need a protective crystal to seal your aura and chakras.

Here are how cactuses are similar to our human body and how the crystals help us to have the same defense and offense mechanism of the cactus by the use of Crystals to protect us from Negative energy (the enemy)

	Cactus	Humans

Location	Dry Desert (Scorching heat, very little water.	Anywhere (wilderness Experience Test, trials, affliction, distractions, torment)
Need Water to survive and live	Need Water to survive and live	We need physical water and living water (grace) to live physically and spiritually.
Aura	Spines (shadow) reduces ventilation so water can stay within the cactus during dry, hot, harsh seasons year-round, and prevents large swings in temperatures and dramatic changes in temperatures	Aura (he that dwelleth in the secret place of the most high shall abide under the shadow of the almighty) is the shadow that protects the person and the chakras through the crystals becoming one with the aura. The crystals make sure the chakras are working efficiently through the grace released through times of testing, so you don't be tossed to and fro through trials. You can pass the test with ease through Faith that the crystal will perform its duties.
Spine	Protects the cactus from predators	Our spine holds the spiritual chakras (wheels) in alignment. The Crystals protect the

		chakras (wheels) and prevent or drive out negative energies (demonic spirits)
Spine	The spines are modified leaves that help the cactus receive oxygen	The chakras along the spines you breathe in and out of to receive oxygen and to rid yourself of negative energy in order to receive positive, pure, cleansed, energy.

The Sword of the Spirit Ephesians 6:17(KJV)

"Take the helmet of salvation and the sword of the Spirit, which is the word of God." Ephesians 6:17 (KJV)

The Sword of the spirit is the word of God: the ring you wear is actually the sword of the spirit, as you decree and declare the word of God. I love this so much, and it talks about the word of God being the sword because when we speak the word of God, it is to manifest itself. But how often have we decreed and declared the Word of God to come to pass and it hasn't? This is not opposing the word of God, and it is always to be used because it is powerful, but those times we don't see the word come into full fruition or manifested is because we suppose to use it with certain crystals which are employed by the Father to do specific manifestations of what we are praying for. We see that the word of God is supposed to be used in conjunction with a crystal/gemstone/stone to bring forth things into fruition. The crystal helps the word of God become manifest, and that's how you are able to discern the right way of using a crystal and the wrong way of using a crystal.

*That's why it says in **Prov. 7:2,3 (KJV) "Keep my commands, and you will live: guard my teachings as the <u>apple of your eye (mind's eye, or third eye) Bind them on your fingers (crystal or gemstone rings)</u> write them on the tablet on your heart."** We see right here in biblical times, and ancient times, they knew the power of wearing certain gemstones on your hands because they manifested certain things in the earth realm. It says to keep his word on the*

tablet of your heart, meaning the tablet is in the representation of the crystal that protects the heart gateway. We know that Moses wrote the 10 commandments on a sapphire stone (tablet). You may be wondering why it was written on sapphire stone; my belief is so that the 10 commandments would be manifested within the Israelites heart.

The commandments are part of the word of God, So anything or anyone surrounding the geographical location of where the 10 commandments are written have to abide by those commandments, because sapphire is the stone of faithfulness, covenant, clarity, and truth, and it gave out the frequencies that could possibly keep the Israelites from committing adultery, and serving other Gods through grace released through the frequencies and vibrations of the sapphire stone. But unfortunately, Holy Spirit did not come on the inside to have a full manifestation of God's word within at that time, it came upon them. But now the Holy Spirit dwells within. Hallelujah! So now, since Holy Spirit lives within us, the crystals can work in conjunction with Holy Spirit to make the soul perfect in Christ the Rock because the crystals have perfect molecular structures that give out good vibrations, frequencies, and energies in the realm of the spirit.

As we decree and declare God's word, they will manifest his word; and they even hearken unto the words that we speak because they are Christ himself is the crystals whole, they all are a different replica of who he is in the Father just like who we are. Not all Rocks are crystals. Some are glass that gives out different energies, like black obsidian , and snowflake obsidian which is made out of the lava that comes out of the volcano. Unfortunately, our soul is not perfect unless we connect it to the perfect source Jesus Christ, our Lord, our savior, Christ the rock, Christ the stone, Christ the Gemstone, Christ the crystal all is in him as one. Just like we are who we are in Christ himself, we are one with him. Our soul just is perfected because they have become in synch with the crystal. We have the anointing to help perfect us in Christ, but there is another realm that quickens our soul to be perfect to counteract our weakness or sin. Therefore, if the crystals counteract our weaknesses, we can fulfill and prosper in the fruits of the spirit, which brings forth life in our own unique way that the Father originated for us to live. Hallelujah!! Precious stones were used as a protection of the mind's eye and crown in the book of Jasher when Isaac was to depart from Sarah, in order to leave with his father Abraham as a sacrificial offering to the Lord. It says in **Jasher 23:15 KJV, "And she dressed Isaac her son therewith, and she put a turban upon his head, and she enclosed a precious stone on the top of the turban, and she gave them provision for the road, and they went forth, and Isaac went with his father."** Abraham and some of their servants accompanied them to see them off the road.

Song. 5:11 (KJV) "His head is purest gold; his hair is wavy and black as a raven." (The crown was gold) remember, gold gives out a high frequency, vibration, and activates the crown wheel (chakra). Gold also gives a person confidence. It's vital for Kings to have faith (confidence) in order to win the battle because if they are depressed, fearful, or doubtful, then they will lose the battle. But with Christ, we always win the battle, because it's not our battle, but his battle. Hallelujah! We see another scripture that says, **"listen to my son, to your father's instruction and do not forsake your mother's teaching. They are a garland to grace around your head and a chain to adorn your neck." Proverbs 8:9 (KJV)** So we see the precious gemstones are part of the gift of grace Christ have given to us not only by his Spirit working through us but an increased grace through the crystals themselves being Christ as a whole to perfect the soul, so that the soul by faith will become perfect as the Father is perfect as the son the Rock (crystal, stone, gemstone) is perfect.

Another scripture that shows stone/crystals are part of your armor on your body is in **Prov 6:20-24 (KJV), "My son, keep thy father's commandment and forsake not the law of thy mother: Bind them continually upon thine heart and tie them to thy neck. When thou goest, it shall lead thee when thou sleepest, it shall keep thee, and when thou wakest, it shall talk with thee. For the commandment is a lamp, and the law is light; and reproofs of instruction are the way of life to keep thee from the evil woman, from the flattery of the tongue of a strange woman."** This scripture speaks of the benefits that crystals do, and why people would wear them, which we will talk about in the next chapter. If you have an Emerald, it is said as stated in an earlier passage to turn dark if you are around a person who can't be trusted. I have times where the Lord, the crystal, or the universe will speak to me through the Lord because he is the mediator, and tell me what crystal I needed to wear for that day or would show me the crystal that would help solve a problem or scenario that would pop up for that day prophetically. Sometimes it could be the crystal itself saying, "Hey, over here, you are going to need me for this situation." This was just like when the earth spoke to me about the dandelion, and who and what to pray for. All of these things are to help spread forth the Kingdom of Light, which is Christ Kingdom.

For instance, me and my husband had a conversation on why some of the people in the Body of Christ have not been giving accurate prophetic words anymore with more in-depth knowledge. I was stating that there is something wrong because we are making Jesus look bad as a church because people are not accurate. Well, someone called later that morning and was stating that she went to two different churches to visit, one was a church they had one of the prophets of the house or guest prophets to speak and they were totally off, none of it

reflected her past, and she wasn't even trying to get a prophetic word. The other church it was an Apostle, and he stated some things that did not happen to her at all and in her past. So, she was stating why have I been going to different churches and they been inaccurate these two churches that she visited at these two different times, they were a couple of months apart, before the Lord told me that crystals where my mandate and calling. But, at the time she went to the second church that the Apostle was inaccurate, I had already started buying crystals a few weeks prior and reaping the benefits of them. Well, before this whole conversation popped up that morning while I was asleep, I had a vision, and I usually don't have visions unless it's in my dreams. But when I came to Christ, I instantly had my first encounter with the Lord through an open-eyed vision, but then I never had it again. But the visions have increased dramatically since I have been using crystals. So, in the vision, I seen 8 black crystals in a vision that morning, and I woke up. So, I asked the Lord what's the name of these

black stones, and he replied, "Black Obsidian." He told me to look up the benefits, so I looked up the benefits, and it's known for the stone of truth and prophecy. It's also used for protection. When she called, I was genuinely undone and in shock. I hurried up and called my husband to tell him what had happened. So, I purchased black obsidian, the stone of truth, and I knew since it was eight black obsidian stones, it represented new beginnings because that is what the number 8 means. On the table, they had a single candle next to them, meaning the truth that has been hidden is coming to light and to the forefront. This is because the Lord doesn't want his people, and all creation to suffer anymore, he wants all things to function correctly and in order. He wants human beings and creations full of health, righteousness, and fullness of life rejuvenated.

Proverbs 3:3 NIV says, "let love and faithfulness never leave you; bind them around your neck, write them on the tablet of your heart." Let's

see the deeper meaning behind this is, Let Rubies (Crystal of Love) and

Blue Sapphire (Stone of Faithfulness) never leave you. Bind them around your neck. Write the messages they give on the tablet of your heart. So, you see the hidden messages behind the scripture because they are endowed with the wisdom of the Lord. Now some people can pervert, twist, and corrupt the message for their own desires instead of the divine wisdom of the Lord that the stone gave them. They are messengers, just like John said earlier in the scriptures. The stones will raise up children unto Abraham because they will minister to people of faith. They literally work on our behalf, and is for us, and are our friends. Job

said to speak to the earth; it will teach thee. Let's look in deeper in depth of the scripture if you bind ruby and sapphire around your neck. It's close to the heart. What is the color of the blood that flows through the heart, red and blue? The blood of Christ Jesus (Yeshua). The added rays of blue and red increase the subconscious mind, which is the heart which gives clarity and direction from the heart of Christ Jesus Himself through the Father. What do we always see on photos with Christ Jesus on it? It's his heart standing out, representing his love.

So, we see Is.33 altogether:verse 16 says, **"He shall dwell on high; his place of defense shall be the munition of rocks; bread and water shall be given him; his waters shall be sure."** *That means all the crystals that you have on you or around you fight for you as warriors protecting you roundabout with their strengths, and functions, their personalities that the Father gave them to do for mankind, and other creatures. Though each one is different, they come together as one in Christ to work in conjunction with you to release and impart grace for those things you could not do on your own. They counteract your weaknesses and bad behaviors and habits by fighting in the realm of the spirit for you.*

We see a full manifestation of this in action in **Song 4:4 (KJV) "Your neck is like the tower of David, built with courses of stone, on it hang a thousand shields, all of them shields of warriors."**

I'm not going to go into more in-depth detail in the armory of Solomon himself, but we can just tell if you read the Song of Solomon about the gemstones

Your Neck is like
The tower of
David, built with
Courses of stone. You never
may know the course of every
stone, where they will lead you,
guide you or take you
according to God's word,
And beyond...

It hanged a thousand shields
Why are they called shields? Because each crystal (circle) functions as a different shield to protect you through your electromagnetic field and wheels (Chakras).

All of them shields of warriors (they war and fight on your behalf)

Through Entrainment - The perfect stable energy bonds of the different crystals/stones/rocks/gemstones work together to get our energy field/aura/(soul) in perfect alignment and in synch with Holy Spirit to work as one into the spirit of perfection

WOW! Jesus Rocks! Hallelujah!

How?

*he wore as the armory because each one was a shield. It states all of them, "shields of warriors." (Song 4:4 KJV) King Solomon had gemstones for a shield of protection, and so they could fight for him. Not to mention the angels that are even linked with them to help assist them in fighting. But this picture is just to give you a little break down of the scripture itself. The Father wanted me to emphasize. It shows if we don't take advantage of the crystal/stones/gemstones, we can continue to be under attack and will continue to fight for breakthrough in our everyday life. Or we will have victory but still having that same repeated pattern repeatedly. That's where the **shield of faith** comes in because as we move by faith, the angels fight on our behalf along with the crystals.*

The Missing Piece of the Covenant and the Promises of God Through the Rainbow.

In Christianity, the rainbow represents the Father's promise not to flood the whole earth again, **Genesis 9:13-17 KJV**, says, **"I have placed my bow in the clouds, and it will be a sign of the covenant between me and the earth."** The Earth and the Lord communed together and talked to each other to have an agreement that the Father would not flood the whole earth again. The Earth is alive! Hallelujah! The rainbow is also the promises of God to mankind through his

covenant with man. The picture above shows the missing middle piece of the rainbow for the promises of God to come forth and to manifest by the supernatural functions of the crystals, being the bridge between God and man. The link between heaven and earth. The crystals which are part of the earth, works in conjunction with the universe, to bring forth the manifestation of the promises of God in your life.

The heavens and the earth begin to birth forth the blessings of God through linking the Father and man's request, petition, intentions through the crystal(s). The reason why people's full blessings and covenant with God has not been fully manifested is because of the supernatural, beautiful pieces of the earth, which, as we know, are the crystals, which is Christ himself the living Rock not being used but has been rejected by man. Without that middle bridge, you don't receive the full manifestation of the covenant promises unless you war in the realm of the spirit. If you were to fight in the realm of the spirit with crystals, it wouldn't have to be as intense and prolonged as you would without the crystals. Especially when you pray in tongues. It's man and God, angels fighting to bring breakthrough, along with the assistance of the universe (higher heavens and lower heavens) and earth. So, you have four things working in conjunction to bring forth the blessing (Father, Man, Universe (Heavens), Earth. And when you add the celestial beings, that's five things working together, five means favor and blessings. Wow! The crystals give you rest and help you manifest your intentions, imaginations, prayer, affirmations, and declarations while fighting on your behalf to break any negative energies (negative forces or subdue demonic spirits in the lower heavens

and in the earth). Crystals have other angelic angels assigned with them to bring forth the breakthrough you need. The crystals help bring you into rest into Papa's arms. This is an illustration of how this happens.

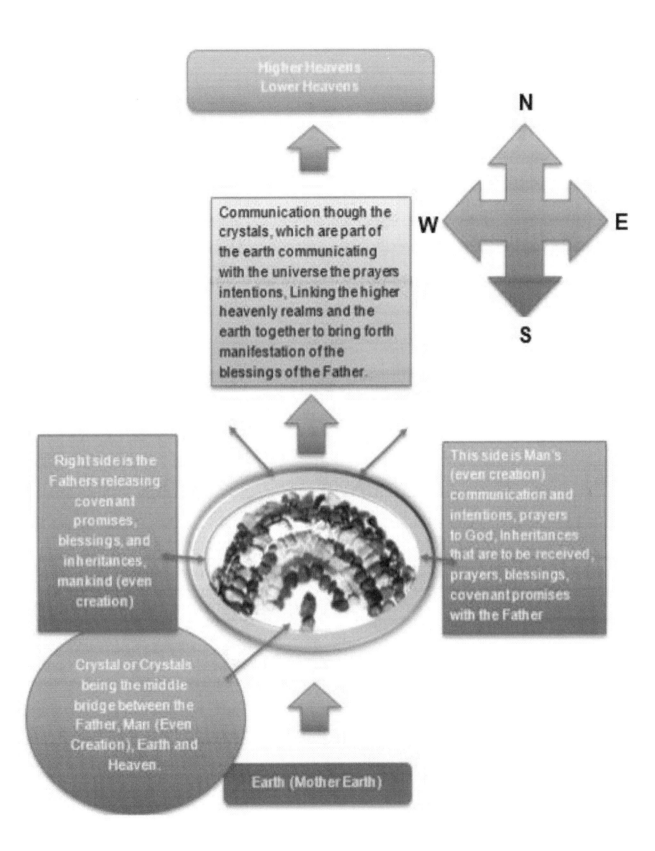

Psalms 47:9 (KJV) states, "The princes of the people are gathered together, even the people of the God of Abraham: <u>for the shields of the earth belong unto God: he is greatly exalted."</u>

What are these shields of the earth? They are the crystals themselves because through faith and entrainment, and they protect us from negative words of ourselves or others depending on the crystal or stone function and personality. Their aura becomes one with our aura, or electromagnetic field in order to repel negative energies or demonic spirits and to remove our negative thoughts and transmute them into positive thoughts. And to protect the chakras and the gates.

"8 Finally, brethren, whatsoever things are true, whatsoever things are honest, whatsoever things are just, whatsoever things are pure, whatsoever things are lovely, whatsoever things are of good report; if there be any virtue, and if there be any praise, think on these things." Philippians 4:8 (KJV)

Freedom - Through grace from our own weaknesses, sins, and negative thought patterns, and habits, and more.

In Nehemiah its states in chapter 4:7-15 (NCV)

"7 But Sanballat, Tobiah, the Arabs, the Ammonites, and the people from Ashdod were very angry when they heard that the repairs to Jerusalem's walls were continuing and that the holes in the wall were being closed. 8 So they all made plans to come to Jerusalem and fight and stir up trouble. 9 But we prayed to our God and appointed guards to watch them day and night.

10 The people of Judah said, "The workers are getting tired. There is so much trash we cannot rebuild the wall."

11 And our enemies said, "The Jews won't know or see anything until we come among them and kill them and stop the work."

12 Then the Jewish people who lived near our enemies came and told us ten times, "Everywhere you turn, the enemy will attack us." 13 So I put

people behind the lowest places along the wall—the open places—and I put families together with their swords, spears, and bows. 14 Then I looked around and stood up and said to the important men, the leaders, and the rest of the people: "Don't be afraid of them. Remember the Lord, who is great and powerful. Fight for your brothers, your sons and daughters, your wives, and your homes."

15 Then our enemies heard that we knew about their plans and that God had ruined their plans. So, we all went back to the wall, each to his own work." Nehemiah 4:7-15

It shows they appointed guards which you can see as angels, in order to protect them through prayer, because the enemy was coming at them every which way, to the point they were tired. How many times have we had trials and may have lost our patience, or someone said something against us, or other people might fall into sin because the temptation was so great that it led them to sin. Over and over they always needed deliverance from the same thing repeatedly. Nehemiah verse 10 states, "10 The people of Judah said, "The workers are getting tired. There is so much trash we cannot rebuild the wall." Nehemiah verse 12 states 12 Then the Jewish people who lived near our enemies came and told us ten times, "Everywhere you turn, the enemy will attack us." (Nehemiah 4:10-12 (NCV)) Meaning their weaknesses, sins, and or oppositions that were coming against them. By these things coming against them their foundation eventually crumbled. If you build your foundation on the Rock which is Christ Jesus and you know the crystals as part of him and that they counteract your weaknesses, generational curses, and break spells sent against you. Then, you will "live life more abundantly" (John 10:10 KJV), and you will prosper as long as your foundation is built upon the word of God and as long as you commune with the Father, the Son, and the Holy Spirit Verse 11 states, 11 And our enemies said, "The Jews won't know or see anything until we come among them and kill them and stop the work." The enemy comes to steal, kill, and destroy" (John 10:10 KJV), but thank the Lord through the stones, he protects our gates, gateways, wheels, and chakras so we can walk into perfection, which is life in him as Christ Jesus.

We can also see the armory of a bride herself also if you look up the adornment of a bride. A bride's adornment is so beautiful. Crystals or gemstones radiating with the bride through her crown, necklaces, bracelets, earrings, and rings to bring forth positive vibrations, frequencies and energies and of faithfulness, peace, purity, love, happiness, and prosperity, as she awaits her husband that she long waited to prepare herself for; through the purification and healing process of entrainment. (Faithfulness-Blue Sapphire, Peace-Amethyst, Purity-Diamond, Love-Rubies, Happiness-Citrine, Prosperity-Green Aventurine) These are just examples because every bride's adornment is different.

Crystals used as a Weapon of Protection

The Ring as the Sword

The Ring that represents the sword that we wear on our finger with the crystal/or gemstone works in sync and in full alignment with the Word of God coming into full manifestation through the declaration of scriptures, your intentions, through prayer, meditation, and relationship with Christ. It also works in conjunction with what we decree and declare out of our own mouths for righteousness' sake to bring forth deliverance, fruitfulness, and protection. When we decree and declare protection scriptures to work in conjunction with the crystals for protection, then the protection round about us will become even more powerful. Because the word of God is powerful.

Chapter 7: Crystal Grids: The Stone Which the Builders Rejected, the Same is Become the Head of the corner:

*"**42 Jesus saith unto them, Did ye never read in the scriptures, The stone which the builders rejected, the same is become the head of the corner: this is the Lord's doing, and it is marvelous in our eyes?43 Therefore say I unto you, The kingdom of God shall be taken from you, and given to a nation bringing forth the fruits thereof." Matthew 21:42,43 (KJV)***

What are crystal grids? They could be used for healing, protection, prosperity, love, and manifesting anything you need help with. Crystal grids control the energy of groups of crystals and using crystals through sacred geometry, in order to create a shift in energy and bring about the desired change *and manifestation of our prayers and intentions. You don't always have to use sacred geometry, you can be creative yourself, or the Lord may show you the pattern to do the crystal grid in. They can also maintain the energy of a situation or anchor a specific type of energy. They shift the atmosphere and energy fields to bring forth manifestations through grace. Just like with Moses writing the 10 commandments on the tablet, he was shifting the geographical atmosphere in order that the Israelites would bring forth justice, righteousness, goodness, and love of the Father through grace that's released through the frequencies and vibrations released from the stone. We know the 10 commandments were written on the Sapphire stone, as stated earlier. So instead of men and women committing adultery, they would stay faithful to their spouses, instead of committing idolatry, they will keep their eyes focused on the Father and serve no other Gods, they will not want to steal, because of having the grace through the sapphire frequencies and vibrations released in the atmosphere in order to fulfill all the 10 commandments.*

*I remember I was driving and worshiping the Lord; I heard I'm the chief cornerstone which the builders have rejected. I said, Huh? He said, "Terika, in order to keep out demonic spirits and negative energies out of your house using crystals, what do you do?" I said you could place a black tourmaline and selenite in each of the four corners of your house, and he said, "Exactly." I am the stone that my builders have rejected, which have become the head of every cornerstone of the houses of people who utilizes the crystals and use crystal grids in order to keep away negative energies/demonic spirits. The Lord is going to reveal the truth back to his people for them to become protected. Other nations and nationalities know the benefits and protection of crystals. But the body of Christ doesn't, and the Lord is going to restore the use of crystal grids. The builders are those who accepted Christ Jesus as their Lord and Savior. They also are the ones who are preaching the Gospel. But they rejected the crystals or the stones, which is Christ himself. They will know the truth about the crystals because time is coming where you need them for protection because the spirit realm is real, and if gross darkness is increasing, more negative energy is going to increase. People will be more vulnerable to the enemy's tactics and their own weaknesses. But now the church must change their mindsets on crystals in order to be protected. It says in verse 43, "43 **Therefore say I unto you, the kingdom of God shall be taken from you, and given to a nation bringing forth the fruits thereof."** **Matthew 21:43 (KJV)***

Since crystals have always been reported for the wrong, and not the good, people have been vulnerable and still suffering from the same negative energies (demonic influences). It's just like watching the news, and how they show nothing

but evil things going on in the communities, they rarely show the good that happens in the communities, unfortunately. Why it brings forth fear, that's why I rarely watch the news at all. He said the kingdom was taken from them and given to a nation bringing forth fruits thereof. Some of us in the body of Christ has not brought forth real, genuine fruit. He said the kingdom of heaven should be taken and given to a nation bringing forth fruitfulness. I believe the kingdom of heaven is being given to people who are bearing fruitfulness (love, joy, peace, patience, etc.) with the use of crystals and those bearing fruit without the use of crystals, whether saved or unsaved. The crystals releases grace in order to help us be whole and complete.

The Lord showed me while proofreading this book that I had the same meaning for onyx (Joseph) and jasper (Benjamin) on the priest breastplate. So, I went and looked at the benefits of them. And surprisingly, I found out that black onyx protects you, your household, and city from crime. Just one stone can work to break the spirit of crime, just like the one in the book of Daniel tearing down the kingdom within King Nebuchadnezzar's statue. **(Read Daniel Chapter 3)** *Just that one stone tore down kingdoms. But, imagine if you do a crystal grid, it will really impact and prevent crime. One day, I had two family members, one from my mother's side of the family and the other from my father's side of the family to contact me. This particular day in the morning of June 17th at 11:52, one of my family members sent a message on Facebook saying that one of our family members stated and wanted people to know, " I'm going out on a limb here, but I think we as adults should to start a prayer chain for our youth. It's getting worse and worse! We had 3 innocent kids shot and killed this week alone in St. Louis." I instantly thought about black onyx that was shown to me that morning. Then, later on, that day, while driving, I picked up my friend from work and one of our closest friends called and said, she wanted to pray against the crime in St. Louis and she wanted to see if she can find one person to pray with her to come against it. But out of respect of her beliefs that crystals open up portals to Satan, I stayed in my lane. Even though I wanted to scream and say in excitement, "Do you not know if you do a crystal grid using black onyx, it can help protect neighborhoods from crime!" Just one onyx stone by itself can protect a neighborhood. We know this by another story in Daniel, which I will speak on later.*

Crystal Grids on your Altar

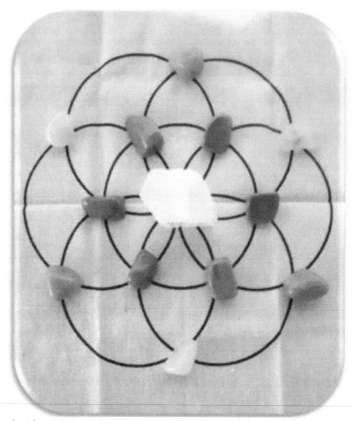

I have another book that is going to come out that will explain crystal grids, and I just wanted to go over the functions of the crystal grids and the scriptures for it.

"Now I have prepared with all my might for the house of my God the gold for things to be made of gold, and the silver for things of silver, and the brass for things of brass, the iron for things of iron, and wood for things of wood; onyx stones, and stones to be set, glistering stones, and of divers colours, and all manner of precious stones, and marble stones in abundance." 1 Chronicles 29:2 (KJV) *The picture showed is a crystal grid used to bring forth healing of the heart, forgiveness, and, most of all, love. The*

main stone is a clear quartz crystal generator  *, the second set* of stones is rhodochrosite , the third layer is rose quartz

and green aventurine . Which are all crystals assigned to the heart chakras. The clear quartz generator is to send forth the prayer not only to the Father, and his angelic force, and his other beings to accomplish the task at hand, but to universe, the sun, the moon, the stars, the earth and nature, the clear quartz sends out the primary goal of the reasons the crystal grids are being used, along with the energies and intentions of the surrounding crystals to accomplish the task at hand of each crystals assignment with the use of sacred geometry. But you don't have to use sacred geometry with your crystal grid. You can make a crystal grid without the use of sacred geometry. **You can subscribe to my website in order to get information on the next two books coming out very soon *called "Becoming the Father's Treasures, Christ Rocks!" and "Birthing and Manifesting Promises of the God through Crystal Grids"*The first book is on crystal benefits and affirmations along with prayer and the next book after that will be on crystal grids. You can subscribe to my website at www.spreadingjesusrocks.com or www.crystalkingdomrocks.com**

Putting crystal grids at the altar at your home brings forth manifestations of prayers and intentions, they bring the higher heavens down here on earth. They link heaven and earth together because they're in the Father. So, when you pray at your altar with your crystals, they bring forth the purpose and manifestation at which you are asking the Lord for, in general prayer, except they help manifest it quicker in half the time it would have took in prayer. I will talk about this in another book I'm writing about on crystal grids, as mentioned earlier.

So, if they used crystal grids back then, it should still be in use now. They bring forth manifestations through dimensions quicker verses prayer requests, without the use of crystals. Each crystal has a purpose of manifesting different things in the realm of the spirit, spiritually, mentally, emotionally, and physically. They cut the time down in half of what we do in prayer and fasting, even instantaneously sometimes. We have had long prayers, years of prayer, and no answer, "Why?" We have rejected Christ himself the rock by the rejection of the use of crystals by their different functions and characteristics of himself. They manifest our prayers along with the word of God because, as the angels do, they hearken unto the word of God that is spoken and manifest the prayer asked. They

manifest our prayers according to our needs, and at that time, what the Lord allows to be released at that time for blessings.

"**Therefore, it shall be when ye be gone over Jordan, that ye shall set up these stones, which I command you this day in mount Ebal, and thou shalt plaister them with plaister. And there shalt thou build an altar unto the Lord thy God, an altar of stones: thou shalt not lift up any iron tool upon them. Thou shalt build the altar of the Lord thy God of whole stones: and thou shalt offer burnt offerings thereon unto the Lord thy God: And thou shalt offer peace offerings and shalt eat there, and rejoice before the Lord thy God. <u>And thou shalt write upon the stones all the words of this law very plainly.</u>**"
Deuteronomy 27:4-8 (KJV)

This is another example that our altars should have crystals and gemstones on them, along with crystal grids. It's all part of the ancient paths. The stones manifest the word of God if written on them, wow! So how much will they fulfill the word of God through prayer or intention?

"He made it according to the instructions that Moses, the Lord's servant, had given the Israelites, as it says in the Law of Moses: "an altar made of stones which have not been cut with iron tools." On it, they offered

burnt sacrifices to the Lord, and they also presented their fellowship offerings." Joshua 8:31 (GNT)

*Crystal grids manifest your prayers in a shorter time span than regular prayers alone. Crystals bring forth manifestations of what we want them to do for us because they are living beings. It's not surprising that Jesus disappeared, or shapeshifted when the stones were thrown at him. **(John 8:59 KJV)** That shows forth manifestation. His intent was to be hidden; instead, he was definitely hiding in a different dimension by the stones being thrown at him, which made him disappear because of his intentions, and as part of his covenant with them. You don't have to speak to them if you choose not to, all you have to do is hold them and speak to them through your mind's eye and your thoughts. You tell them what you want for them to do or manifest in your life, in order to bring forth righteousness, deliverances, positivity, and blessings. They make a covenant with you, which I explain in scripture later on.*

*You will need the crystal grids during different seasons and changes in your life. It will be times where you use just crystals for particular purposes for healing, for restoration, for cleansing, for health, to forgive someone, for clarity, blessings, etc. Seasons in your life can range from a day to 6 years, etc. It's just different transitions you go through in life. So, using specific stones for different purposes while meditating, being around you, or by using crystal grids is vital and essential. **Ecclesiastes 3:5 NIV** explains this, **"time to scatter stones and a time to gather them, a time to embrace and a time to refrain from embracing,"***

Remember, can subscribe my website for the release date for my upcoming books on crystal grids, which is very soon to come out.

The Rock is a weapon

*There are few instances where rocks and stones were used as a weapon. One of the times a rock was used as a weapon was David versus Goliath. I love this because it shows how small a tiny rock packs a lot of power to kill the giants (sins, weaknesses, strongholds, bad habits, familiar spirits, demonic spirits (negative energy), curses, etc.) that we might suffer from in our lives. We see Goliath used two instances where size doesn't matter, David was just a little kid, and he had a small stone, and he defeated a person over 3 times his size and more. The giant mocked David because of his size (how many times have thoughts from the enemy, or negative energies come against us to mock us and tell us negative things and thoughts contrary to whom God says we are, and we can do.) I loved the statement of David when the Giant mocked him, he stated in **1 Sam. 17:46 NIV, "You come against me with sword and spear and javelin, but I come against you in the name of the LORD Almighty, the***

God of the armies of Israel, whom you have defied." *The Rock that he held was the Lord Jesus, whenever Christ spoke, things manifested as we see in the beginning in Genesis and throughout the bible, because Christ is the manifested word. This is what the crystals manifest when we speak the word of God.* ***"For who is God save the Lord? or who is a rock save our God?" Psalms 18:21 (KJV)*** *This is how Daniel knew who the Rock was in King Nebuchadnezzar's dream* ***(Daniel 2 (KJV)*** *because he knew this scripture passage David quoted. So, then it said in* ***1 Sam. 17:49 (KJV) Reaching into his bag and taking out a stone, he slung it and struck the Philistine on the forehead. The stone sank into his forehead, and he fell face down on the ground. This is similar to what happened in the book of Daniel, which we will talk about in a moment.***

So what are some of these things that can be giants in people's lives, some may be the spirit of drunkenness, habitually drinking of alcohol consumption in large amounts, loving to eat candy, gluttony, unforgiveness, bitterness, pride and some of these things can lead to unhealthy lifestyles or can harm the body, and can perhaps damage you spiritually. For instance, a person who may want to break the addiction to alcohol may want to use amethyst and carnelian; these

two break bad habits and addictions. Amethyst can also be used to prevent someone from getting drunk, intoxicated, and prevent the spirit of drunkenness and the negative energies (or demonic spirits) within it, if its put into wine or an alcohol beverage or if it is placed somewhere on your body, you will not get drunk or have a headache. <u>Amethyst comes from a Greek word, amethystos, that means "not drunk."</u> This is a fact for me because I tested it just to see if the benefits stated were real one time, for this book's sake and as a testimony to someone who can benefit from this, that wants to get a breakthrough in that area. Some people may just be a small percentage but because of their body weight may quickly get intoxicated easily or vice versa by drinking alcohol. But to know that amethyst does this, is a miracle. Now the results may be different for another person, this is not to encourage drinking or anyone to get drunk, even though there is nothing wrong with drinking wine, or an alcoholic beverage, the bible talks about not getting drunk and we see that in the Testament of Judah its speaks on the consequences of being drunk and what spirits it may bring and it can prevent you for making the right decisions or correct judgments in different situations. I just thought this was so profound and a supernatural experience because it prevents the spirit of drunkenness by counteracting it and protecting you through your aura from the spirit of drunkenness or negative energies or demonic spirits attached to it if significantly consumed. This is deliverance. You see in the book of revelation, the woman representing Babylon being drunk with the saints' blood (Rev.17:6 KJV)

Carnelian helps you overcome abuse, bad habits, like eating junk food, it helps promote positive life choices, breaking destructive, negative behavioral patterns, and destructive life choices. It detoxes your liver and other organs. Another great benefit of carnelian is, it breaks procrastination. It pushes you to move forward with a project you have to do or goals you need to pursue. I have witnessed this for myself. It helps you to manifest your positive desires, dreams, goals, whether business ideas, career-wise, birthing forth creativity, etc. This is so amazing! Of course, this happens through faith by the grace the crystals release through Christ. With Amethyst, I didn't need faith at all; I just couldn't get drunk because of the frequencies and vibrations released within my auras that attached itself to me through the neurons in my body physically. There are

crystals that help suppress your appetite like Apatite . I mean, even the smallest of one of these packs a lot of power. Amazing we see this in the book of Daniel, we are about to talk about.

King Nebuchadnezzar had a dream that troubled him, he gathered all the wise men, astrologers, and magicians together to have the dream interpreted, so he told them to be able to tell him the dream he had and interpret it, or basically, he would kill them. They told him that it was impossible. So, while he was going to sentence them to destruction, Daniel humbly asked the king if he could give him time to receive the dream and bring the interpretation of the dream to the King himself and the king granted his request in **Dan.2 :19-49 (KJV)**

"19 Then was the secret revealed unto Daniel in a night vision. Then Daniel blessed the God of heaven.

20 Daniel answered and said, blessed be the name of God forever and ever: for wisdom and might are his:

21 And he changeth the times and the seasons: he removes kings, and setteth up kings: he giveth wisdom unto the wise, and knowledge to them that know understanding:

22 He revealeth the deep and secret things: he knoweth what is in the darkness, and the light dwelleth with him.

23 I thank thee, and praise thee, O thou God of my fathers, who hast given me wisdom and might, and hast made known unto me now what we desired of thee: for thou hast now made known unto us the king's matter.

24 Therefore Daniel went in unto Arioch, whom the king had ordained to destroy the wise men of Babylon: he went and said thus unto him;

Destroy not the wise men of Babylon: bring me in before the king, and I will shew unto the king the interpretation.

25 Then Arioch brought in Daniel before the king in haste, and said thus unto him, I have found a man of the captives of Judah, that will make known unto the king the interpretation.

26 The king answered and said to Daniel, whose name was Belteshazzar, Art thou able to make known unto me the dream which I have seen, and the interpretation thereof?

27 Daniel answered in the presence of the king, and said, The secret which the king hath demanded cannot the wise men, the astrologers, the magicians, soothsayers, shew unto the king;

28 But there is a God in heaven that revealeth secrets, and maketh known to the king Nebuchadnezzar what shall be in the latter days. Thy dream, and the visions of thy head upon thy bed, are these;

29 As for thee, O king, thy thoughts came into thy mind upon thy bed, what should come to pass hereafter: and he that revealeth secrets maketh known to thee what shall come to pass.

30 But as for me, this secret is not revealed to me for any wisdom that I have more than any living, but for their sakes that shall make known the interpretation to the king, and that thou mightest know the thoughts of thy heart.

31 Thou, O king, sawest, and behold a great image. This great image, whose brightness was excellent, stood before thee; and the form thereof was terrible.

32 This image's head was of fine gold, his breast and his arms of silver, his belly and his thighs of brass,

33 His legs of iron, his feet part of iron and part of clay.

34 Thou sawest till that a stone was cut out without hands, which smote the image upon his feet that were of iron and clay, and break them to pieces.

35 Then was the iron, the clay, the brass, the silver, and the gold, broken to pieces together, and became like the chaff of the summer threshing floors; and the wind carried them away, that no place was found for them: and the stone that smote the image became a great mountain, and filled the whole earth.

36 This is the dream; and we will tell the interpretation thereof before the king.

37 Thou, O king, art a king of kings: for the God of heaven hath given thee a kingdom, power, and strength, and glory.

38 And wheresoever the children of men dwell, the beasts of the field and the fowls of the heaven hath he given into thine hand, and hath made thee ruler over them all. Thou art this head of gold.

39 And after thee shall arise another kingdom inferior to thee, and another third kingdom of brass, which shall bear rule over all the earth.

40 And the fourth kingdom shall be strong as iron: forasmuch as iron breaketh in pieces and subdue all things: and as iron that breaketh all these, shall it break in pieces and bruise.

41 And whereas thou sawest the feet and toes, part of potters' clay, and part of iron, the kingdom shall be divided; but there shall be in it of the strength of the iron, forasmuch as thou sawest the iron mixed with miry clay.

42 And as the toes of the feet were part of iron, and part of clay, so the kingdom shall be partly strong, and partly broken.

43 And whereas thou sawest iron mixed with miry clay, they shall mingle themselves with the seed of men: but they shall not cleave one to another, even as iron is not mixed with clay.

44 And in the days of these kings shall the God of heaven set up a kingdom, which shall never be destroyed: and the kingdom shall not be left to other people, but it shall break in pieces and consume all these kingdoms, and it shall stand forever.

45 Forasmuch as thou sawest that the stone was cut out of the mountain without hands, and that it will break in pieces the iron, the brass, the clay, the silver, and the gold; the great God hath made known to the king what shall come to pass hereafter: and the dream is certain, and the interpretation thereof sure.

46 Then the king Nebuchadnezzar fell upon his face, and worshipped Daniel, and commanded that they should offer an oblation and sweet odours unto him.

47 The king answered unto Daniel, and said, Of a truth it is, that your God is a God of gods, and a Lord of kings, and a revealer of secrets, seeing thou wouldest reveal this secret.

48 Then the king made Daniel a great man, and gave him many great gifts, and made him ruler over the whole province of Babylon, and chief of the governors over all the wise men of Babylon.

49 Then Daniel requested of the king, and he set Shadrach, Meshach, and Abednego, over the affairs of the province of Babylon: but Daniel sat in the gate of the king." Dan.2 :19-49 (KJV)

We see first that the stone was cut out without hand, so that shows that the Rock is Christ cause no one cut it out, it supernaturally cut itself out (manifestation), and in psalms David talks about the stone being Christ, "**For who is God save the Lord? or who is a rock save our God**?" **Psalms 18:21 (KJV)** This scripture is another reason how Daniel knew the rock was Christ Jesus. The high places are in Christ and in the Father. That's why the Father was upset with other people making carved images of different Gods or deities whom they sang and worshipped in the high places, as a meeting place of worshipping false idols because the high places is Christ himself and he doesn't want to share his glory with any other deity other than the Trinity. Because the high places where most of the time mountains, or hills, or large rocks stacked on top of each other and other tall places. What are in the mountain's crystals. A lot of them have open portals connected to them in the mountains. Why? Because of the high vibrations

crystals, stones, and rocks transmit out that make open portals. Why? Because crystals are multidimensional beings. Also, some rocks are attached to different angels to co-labor with them to bring forth manifestations. We see this when Joseph laid his head on the stone and called, "El-bethel" and he saw the angels ascending and descending upon the son of man, which is Christ (Read Genesis the 28th chapter). So, we see they opened portals and also can connect you with angels. You just have to use discernment and to test the spirits, to see if it is of God or not.

So, let's go back to the stone that was cut out without hands it was packed with a lot of power and destroyed and shattered every kingdom including King Nebuchadnezzar's Kingdom which is Babylon, it destroyed other kingdoms like Persia, Greece, Rome, etc., because it is Christ himself the Living Rock. The same way Christ destroyed those kingdoms, is the same way we are to use them to break the Kingdom of Darkness by using the crystals for the highest good, which is love. Will it be times you have to fight for what you want, yes. Is it times where you have to decree and declare the word of God in order that justice is served, absolutely, and for protection absolutely, but make sure it's in love. But, out of all, this love is who Christ is. Christ himself is the rock/stones/crystals/gemstones. Psalm 118:22 *The stone which the builders refused becomes the headstone of the corner. (Matthew 21:14 KJV)*

If you look at each characteristic, functions, and how the crystals help you offensively and defensively, then you see they all are birthed out of love. You have Rhodochrosite and Amethyst, Pink Quartz, and Ruby Zoisite, which teaches you to love yourself and forgive others so that you can be set free and others (others who may thing negative of you that you know or don't know) are set free, that is love. If you have a crystal that helps breaks soul ties and generational curses that is birthed out of love because The Father doesn't want you to suffer from curses, or generational curses, then that's love. If you have crystals that, even if a person accidentally is thinking something negative about you, but it's not having an impact on you or your family because the crystal protects you from their words and thoughts, that's love. If you have been having people wanting you to fail but can't because the crystals break those words through prayer instantaneously through faith, that's birth out of love. When you have had problems with anger through certain triggers, and now you see those triggers no longer work, and you are calmer than what you were, that's a crystal birthed out of Love, which is the Father's Heart and who Christ is. Therefore, the crystals are love because they protect you, and counteracts your weaknesses just like Christ Jesus if you would let them.

When Jesus says to bless those who curse you, that's what he means, because the reason people feel drained out of warfare coming against witchcraft is because they are not operating out of love but anger, and they think that it's bringing justice , that same anger we are giving out it is hitting us right back. There has to be a balance in your emotions. We have to pray that the Father set them free from negative words or spells that may have been put on them. There are crystals that protect a person from ill thoughts and negative words, and it won't touch you. That's why we bless and not curse. Christ wants the witches and warlocks saved also. So, you pray against any spell that was put on them or evil rituals to be broken of them. Pray that love will fill their hearts, and they will feel the love of the father and that he will heal them. Pray in tongues for them in love and not hate, and I bet you see some results. Now it may be times where you have to stand up and fight and decree and declare things to be broken in order to stop curses or certain attacks. You just have to be led by the spirit, and the crystals will help guide you also. That's birthed out of love from the Father's Heart. He wants to bring forth" righteousness, peace, and joy in the Holy Ghost "(Romans 14:17 KJV) and salvation for all mankind. We have to help others not be prejudice towards others, whether in the church or out. We can learn from one another and learn to discern what's right from wrong. So, we know the crystals are meant to be used to destroy the kingdom of darkness the same way it destroyed the kingdoms within King Nebuchadnezzar Statue.

Chapter 8: Gates, Chakras, Wheels, Energy Centers

You may be wondering what the differences in these are? Well, all four (gates, chakras, wheels, and energy centers) are the same. I just want people to see the different terms, that all four mean the same thing, just from other people's perspectives of what they are. **"Go through, go through the gates; prepare ye the way of the people; cast, cast up the highway; gather out the stones; lift up a standard for the people. "Isaiah 62:10 (KJV)** *It's saying*

let the crystals minister to the individual and its body. Our aura has 7 different layers which correlate to the 7 main chakras within our body.

As we saw in the book of Jeremiah the wheels are the gates or chakras. Each stone reconfigures the gates and purges the gateways from negative energy (or demonic spirits). Even what's in our bloodline. So when it is saying," go through the gates, prepare the way for the people, cast up, cast up the highway" **(Isaiah 62:10 (KJV)),** *he's talking about the higher gates or chakras from the heart up because that's how you go into ascension from the heart gate and up through the crown and further up. That's how you get Christ consciousness or the mind of Christ; I am feeling this as I am typing. This is where you go into higher dimensions and travel through dimensions. When he says to gather out the stones, he means to get every stone assigned to each gate within the body and place them on the body or have them hold the stones in their hands. Starting at the root chakra and move up to the mind's gate and beyond. He's saying cleanse out the gateways within the persons being in order to break the strongholds or weaknesses within the gates.*

*** Please Note: You will need a Crystal Healers Certifications License to lay crystals on people's body ****Each crystal is assigned to release impartation of the seven spirits of God and the word of God. To impart healing. They help correct wrong thinking. They take the old nature, sin nature, or weaknesses, and replaces it with the new nature, the right way of living, the right way of thinking, physical health to the body, they release and give the body grace to do what it could not do at first. So, if a person is always lashing out and is*

assigned lepidolite   that brings forth calmness because it balances the left brain and right brain hemispheres. A person will be more at peace and make the right choice to be calm and make the right choices through the entrainment process. The crystals become one with you so you can have life more abundantly. By removing the restraints and strongholds that have been keeping you bound from the enemy. For example, it's like saying to a person, give them

rose quartz   to meditate with, so they can forgive and not hold a grudge. Rose quartz is assigned to the heart wheel/chakra. Rose quartz reminds a person to forgive people and release the past. It reminds you not to hold a person responsible for the pain you feel any longer because it's keeping you the feelings of hatred, anger, and revenge. Which are negative thoughts that drain you negatively. The different gateways are attached to each gate, chakra, wheel, or energy center. So, whether you feel more comfortable calling them chakras,

wheels, energy centers, or gates, they are the beginning entrance of the gateways or spiritual tunnels within our own spiritual bodies. Some people may refer to the gateways being vortexes as well. If one of these wheels, chakras, energy centers, or gates are inactive, underactive, or overactive, it can affect us physically, mentally, emotionally, and spiritually. But, if they are balanced, you feel balanced, perfect, rested, at peace, full of life, strength, and vibrant. As stated earlier, the crystals are assigned to each wheel to bring them into balance. To cleanse the gateways, vortexes, or spiritual tunnels held within us.

*That's why in the Book of Jeremiah **(Jer.18:1-6 KJV),** it talks about remodeling and transforming us through our wheels by getting them back into full balance and alignment, which we know that one of the ways is by the use of crystals. They protect the gates and purifies, and detoxes our bodies physically, mentally, emotionally, and spiritually. They purify our aura and protect our aura by the removal of negative energies (demonic spirits and influence). They bring forth grace in order for us to be ye perfect as our Father in heaven is perfect. **(Matthew 5:48 KJV)** I am going to show you different ways and signs on how you can tell that they are imbalanced by what I have learned and by research.*

The Crown Wheel (Chakra, Energy Center, Gate) - *located at the top of your head, this is associated with your sense of enlightenment and awareness and knowing that you are part of a higher purpose and the plans of the Father. The Mind of Christ, some say the Consciousness of Christ. It deals with knowing your place and why you were created on this earth. It gives you the mind of Christ and what Jesus would do.*

Color: Violet
Physical areas assigned to: Brain Pineal Gland, Hair, Nervous System
Out of Balance Physical Signs: Headaches
If Underactive: Can't focus or concentrate on the present moment or task at hand. You are unable to see other people's perspectives. You may feel disconnected, unhappy, depressed, feel miserable, withdrawn, unconcerned, or uninterested.
If Overactive: Unbalanced, frustrated, aggravated, disappointed, destructive, inconsistent, Delusional, too much drama and negativity in your life. Lack of compassion
To bring into balance: Meditate, wear the color purple, be thankful, get involved in helping others or volunteering. Practice love to help or serve others sincerely.
If Balanced: Deeper understanding and knowledge. You are more aware and open to the realm of the spirit; you are enlightened, ascension, peaceful, loving.

Mind's Eye Third Eye Wheel (Chakra, Energy center, Gate) *- Located at the center of your forehead. It deals with imagination, intuition, inner wisdom, and insight.*

Related to see deep within your heart to get the wisdom that's needed to manifest the vision or outcome, or ideas, or on how to accomplish things or goals, or what to do in life to bring forth positive outcomes. It helps give the bigger picture and have a favorable view of the future.

Color: Indigo

Physical areas assigned to: Brain, Pituitary Nervous system, hypothalamus, eyes, brain, and heart

Out of Balance Physical Signs: Headaches

Underactive: Hesitant, Undisciplined, feel unworthy, detached, shows too much empathy, lack of inspiration, intuitive guidance, or discernment. You may feel like your mind is clouded.

Overactive: Egotistical, Controlling, too much Pride, Overwhelming imagination, bossy, critical judgmental, plotting, sneaky, or cunning behavior, or deceitful. No peace, a lot of mind chatter.

To bring into balance: Keep a dream journal, meditate, or wear the Color Blue. Keep your eyes focused intently on the Lord! Listen to and honor messages your body sends to you an inner knowing on what to do to bring a positive outcome.

If Balanced: Good leadership, clear sight, highly spiritually attuned with the voice of the Lord, non-attached, highly aware in the realm of the spirit. Guided and know the voice of which direction to go and what to do. You are free of addictions.

The Throat Chakra - (Wheel, Energy center, Gate) deals with communication and you speaking your truth to others of your truth from the heart and mind with clarity. And it deals with expression and creativity. It also deals with learning to listen with compassion and understanding. It deals with releasing and breathing.

Color - Turquoise

Physical Areas it is assigned to - the throat, thyroid, neck, mouth, jaws, and ears, respiratory system.

Out of Balance Physical Signs: Sore throat or laryngitis, stiffness or pain in your neck, colds, sinuses, and allergies

Underactive - Quiet, inability to speak up or set boundaries, or stand up for yourself, fearful, dishonest, wishy-washy, frightened, or nervous

Overactive - Overly talkative, not knowing when to stay quiet, talking all the time. Strict, toxic masculinity, dominant, arrogant, frustrations builds, and you lash out. You may act as if you know it all.

To Bring into Balance - Drink tea or lemon water. Sing. Listen to lovely music, or you can wear turquoise.

Balanced - Content, speaks up easily, verbally creative, communicative, artistic, centered, and balanced when it comes to talking (not cutting people off or getting loud), spiritual, and content. Expressive

The Heart Wheel - (Chakra, Energy center, Gate)

Deals with the love of all things and creations, friends, family, spouse, compassion for others, friendship, compassion for all creation, and love for yourself.

Color: Green
Physical Areas Assigned to: Thymus, heart, chest, lungs, shoulders, arms, hands, and upper back, blood pressure, lymph, and immune system.
Out of Balance Physical Signs: Tense, pain in the upper chest, or in your back. You may feel the tightness of shoulders, or overly flexible shoulders.
If Underactive, feelings of unworthiness, fears rejection, fear of loneliness, lack of self-compassion or self-love, lack of compassion, or lack of love for yourself and others. Self-pity, stagnant, suspicious, or skeptical.
If Overactive – you're dramatic, critical, overprotective, difficulties adjusting to change. You also are dominating
How to get back into balance: Go outside and breathe in the fresh air deeply. Meditate on the Father, Jesus, or Holy Spirit. Love yourself, talk in the mirror, and tell yourself how much you are loved by God and tell yourself you love yourself and everything about yourself. Love others (children, family, friends, etc.), creation, nature. Wear pink or green because they are the colors of the heart chakras. Stretch your chest, upper back, arms, hands, shoulders, arms.
Balanced: You are very calm, you have trust, you feel compassion, you are full of love, You're a giver, or generous to others. Positive attitude. You are balanced. You love yourself and honor who you are. You are not guarded but open to other people's ideas.

The Solar Plexus Wheel - (Chakra, Energy Center, Gate)
Deals with your will power, thoughts, and feelings about yourself. And your relationship with yourself.
Color: Yellow
Physical Areas assigned to: Stomach, sides of the body, liver, intestines (Digestion) abdomen, mid-back, deals with processing your blood sugar.
Out of physical balance signs: Digestive issues and abdominal pain
If Underactive: Inability to commit or follow through on plans and goals. Insecurity issues, jealousy, confusion, depression, low self-esteem. You may feel like you don't know your worth or the greatness that's within you. (Everything that the Father made was good and serves a purpose, and have greatness within)
If Overactive: Overachiever, demanding, conceited, entitled, think you're superior to others, privileged, critical, and judgmental.
To bring into Balance - meditate on the fire in the fireplace, meditate on a candle flame, or go around the bonfire, go outside and enjoy the sunlight. Wear the color yellow. Eat foods easy to digest. Strengthen your core. Do core exercises.
Once Balanced: You're more intelligent, energetic, respectful, friendly, joyful, and calm.

The Sacral Chakra Wheel- (Chakra, Energy center, Gate)
Deals with your emotions, creativity, pleasures, and senses. It deals with intimacy. It is related to your one on one relationships and creativity. It deals with your relationships with others.

Color: Orange

Physical areas it's assigned to - spleen, reproductive organs (uterus and ovaries) urinary tract, hips, kidneys, adrenal glands

Out of physical balance signs: You may feel pain and stiffness in your lower back and hips, sexual and reproductive issues, you may feel overwhelmed. You may have a lack of imagination, and your creativity has stopped. You may not have creativity at all if it is inactive.

If Underactive: Procrastination, Shy, fear, anxiety, Self-Pity, irritated, holding grudges, unforgiving, clingy, bitterness, feel like you are stuck emotionally. You may feel like you are stuck in an emotional state, and you can't get out — victim mentality.

If Overactive: Selfish, bullying mentality, intimidate, manipulative, overindulgent, reactive. Addictions (alcohol, cigarettes, drugs, sugar, etc.)

To bring into Balance: Wear the color orange, and dance because it restores happiness and joy. Move and stretch your hips. Drink plenty of water (86 minimum ounces), swim, take a soothing bath, journal, go to therapy,

Once Balanced: Emotionally Balanced, you feel creative, friendly, joyful, Intuitive, and Empathetic.

The Root Wheel (Chakra, Energy Center, Gate)
Color - Red

Deals with survival. It deals with your forefathers, ancestral line, DNA. It helps you to feel grounded and at peace. It also deals with how you feel protected and secure. It deals with who you are as a being. It can be blocked by ego.

Physical areas it is assigned to - legs, thighs, and feet. Lower Sexual Reproductive organs, rectum, tailbone

Out of Balance Physical Signs: may have stiffness or pain in your legs and feet.

If Underactive - You may feel tired, weak, hopeless, meek, passive, ungrounded, lethargic

You may not feel physically stable. You may feel stagnant. Clumsiness. Everything feels as if it's all hitting you at once, or it may feel chaotic all at once.

If Overactive - You want things your way. You typically are aggressive, angry, and resentful. You may want everything perfect; you may be controlling; you may be greedy and have addiction issues. Murmuring and complaining all the time.

To bring back into balance: Connect with nature or the earth. Stretch and do leg exercises in order to strengthen your legs. Walk your yard barefoot, walking in the sand or walk in the park, mainly walk and sit in the grass or lay there on the grass. Meditate in your yard. Eat Fruits and Vegetables, or you can wear the color red.

Once Balanced - Healthy, you feel fruitful (love, joy, peace, patience, kindness, goodness, self-control), respectful, you are productive, happy, calm, joyful, intelligent, show enthusiasm, affectionate. Confident, know your purpose. Feel grounded have energy; you are secure.

Chapter 9: Crystals are the Living Word

"Upon this Rock I will build my church"
(Matthew 16:18 KJV)

"And I say also unto thee, That thou art Peter, and upon this rock I will build my church; and the gates of hell shall not prevail against it. And I will give unto thee the keys of the kingdom of heaven: and whatsoever thou shalt bind on earth shall be bound in heaven: and whatsoever thou shalt loose on earth shall be loosed in heaven." (Matthew 16:18,19 KJV)

I want to show you another side of crystals. They are the Living Word themselves. There are different scriptures assigned to different crystals because they are a fulfillment of different crystals, characters, nature, and functions, and benefits.

Therefore, they are the Living Word. So, when you behold or wear an individual crystal, the word of God that fulfills that crystal's personality, character, or nature becomes alive and active. In other words, it comes to life. You start to become the living word of God in different situations in your life that are a fulfillment of the crystal's personality, character, and functions, etc. This is done by faith. So, if you have faith to practice the word and have gotten breakthroughs, how much more breakthrough will you get with a crystal which is the part of the written word. Just like Jesus, The Word made flesh. The word of God becomes who you are.

So, I want to elaborate more on Matthew 16:18,19 **KJV.That thou art Peter, and upon this rock I will build my church" (Matthew 16:18KJV)**

Let's use Amethyst again.
So what Christ is telling Peter is, you will live the scriptures that fulfill the character, nature, and benefits of amethyst, which reflects who I am in amethyst. Amethyst personality and character - Amethyst don't let anything bother her. She's a peaceful stone, she has much wisdom and understanding, and knows how to maneuver and avoid chaos and drama. She is patient. She sees things as how Christ sees things.

Amethyst removes negative thoughts, fear, anxiety, worry and stress. It gives you peace and calmness. And makes you more aware, and to see more clearly. Amethyst helps you put on the mind of Christ.

Scriptures that manifest Amethyst character is:
"Therefore I tell you, do not worry about your life, what you will eat or drink; or about your body, what you will wear. Is not life more than food, and the body more than clothes? Look at the birds of the air; they do not sow or reap or store away in barns, and yet your heavenly Father feeds them. Are you not much more valuable than they? (Matthew 6:25, 26 KJV)

So, when bills are overdue, you are not worried because this scripture is taking place in your life by you wearing it, having it in your pocket, or, most of all, meditating with amethyst. Now you're living (Matthew 6:25,26 27 KJV) And when you keep washing her back with her own word, and she gets stronger.
You will begin to remember everything is the Father's and that he takes care of them because Psalms 50:11 becomes a reality of your thoughts; therefore, you know in reality, that everything is the Lords.
"I know every bird in the mountains, and the creatures of the field are Mine." (Psalms 50:11 KJV)

*You know will know, all of a sudden, that he will feed you because he feeds the birds and you are his. He already knew when you would get behind on the bills. **(Matt. 6:26 KJV)** Therefore you know that he already made provision, so you are at ease, and resting in his arms.*

You will be patient while paying off the bills because the scripture has been activated, and you are now living it (James 1:4KJV) and even around your atmosphere around you. You will have much patience and peaceful because these scriptures are manifesting and are becoming who you are.

But let patience have her perfect work, that ye may be perfect and entire, wanting nothing. (James 1:4KJV)

Peace I leave with you, my peace I give unto you: not as the world giveth, give I unto you. Let not your heart be troubled, neither let it be afraid. (John 14:27KJV)

Amethyst is good for Artists, Poets, Singers, Song Writers, and Inventors, because it removes distractions and gives you clarity, creativity, peace, discernment, understanding, and wisdom. By being still, it keeps you focused.

Be still and know that I am God. (Psalms 46:10KJV)

***Artists, Inventors, Designers, Prophetic Singers:* "The word of the LORD came to me saying, "What do you see, Jeremiah?" And I said, "I see a rod of an almond tree." (Jeremiah 1:11KJV)**

***Song Writers, Singers:* For the Lord had caused the army of the Arameans to hear a sound of chariots and a sound of horses, even the sound of a great army, so that they said to one another, "Behold, the king of Israel has hired against us the kings of the Hittites and the kings of the Egyptians, to come upon us." 2 Kings 7:6 (KJV)**

***Artists, Inventors, Designers:* And the LORD answered me, and said, Write the vision, and make it plain upon tables, that he may run that readeth it.**

***Inventors, Artists, Designers:*" I wisdom dwell with prudence, and find out knowledge of witty inventions." (Proverbs 18:12 KJV)**

***Singers:* O sing unto the LORD a new song: sing unto the LORD, all the earth. (Psalms 96:1 KJV)**

***Artists, Poets, Singers, Song Writers, and Inventors:* "My heart is inditing a good matter: I speak of the things which I have made touching the king: my tongue is the pen of a ready writer." (Psalms 45:1 KJV)**

"and the gates of hell shall not prevail against it."
(Matthew 16:18 KJV)

If someone tries to start drama, chaos, confusion, it will just roll off, your back, you will have wisdom and strength to turn the other cheek because the following scriptures have become part of you through amethyst. It will also give you what to say in order to stop the drama, chaos, confusion, or whatever negativity is coming your way.

*You will know the strategies because **Psalms 23:5 KJV** have begun to you be a reality of who you are. It gives you the wisdom and understanding on how not to get into confrontation with another individual, but to be at peace and show love. It also lets you know to remember the other person may just so happened to have a bad day that day. **(Matthew 5:44 KJV)** When your mind says, "No." You begin to hear and feel the wisdom of the scripture, **"better a patient person than a warrior, one with self-control than one who takes a city."(Proverbs 16:32 NIV)** You are reminded of **(Philippians 4:13 KJV)** and utilizes it. And it becomes a reality of your thoughts and actions, and you showed love.*

"Thou preparest a table before me in the presence of mine enemies: thou anointest my head with oil; my cup runneth over." (Psalms 23:5 KJV)

"But I say unto you, love your enemies, bless them that curse you, do good to them that hate you, and pray for them which despitefully use you, and persecute you" Matthew 5:44 KJV

"I can do all things through Christ which strengtheneth me." (Philippians 4:13 KJV)

"Thou hast enlarged my steps under me, that my feet did not slip." (Psalms 18:36 KJV)

"For thou hast girded me with strength unto the battle: thou hast subdued under me those that rose up against me." (Psalms 18:39 KJV)
"I can do all things through Christ which strengtheneth me." (Philippians 4:13 KJV)
Now you are fulfilling the word of God through the grace of the living word within Amethyst.

Amethyst protects you from warfare and spiritual attacks.

"So shall they fear the name of the LORD from the west, and his glory from the rising of the sun. When the enemy shall come in like a flood, the Spirit of the LORD shall lift up a standard against him. '(Isaiah 59:19)

"For thou hast girded me with strength unto the battle: thou hast subdued under me those that rose up against me." (Psalms 18:39 KJV)

"for though the righteous fall seven times, they rise again, but the wicked stumble when calamity strikes." (Proverbs 24:16 NIV)

"And I will give unto thee the keys of the kingdom of heaven: and whatsoever thou shalt bind on earth shall be bound in heaven: and whatsoever thou shalt loose on earth shall be loosed in heaven." (Matthew 16:19 KJV)

Just as Jesus has given us the authority to bind and loose, so does the crystals have the power to do the same as well, they are keys to unlock life and happiness because each of them has specific living scriptures within them. Because they are the living word, of whom is Christ Jesus. Amethyst binds stress, fear, worry, insomnia, doubt, unbelief, agitation, frustration, anger, etc. and loose peace, calmness, wisdom, understanding, strategies, and creativity .Just as we are washed by the water of the word, they get stronger when we decree and declare the word of God that manifest who they are over them. Even with life trials and tribulations, they will seem not to bother you as much as it uses too. Even pray in tongues if you have the gift of praying in tongues. (Romans 8:26 KJV, 1 Cor.14:4-17KJV, Ephesians 6:18 KJV, Jude verse 20)

"Peace I leave with you, my peace I give unto you: not as the world giveth, give I unto you. Let not your heart be troubled, neither let it be afraid." (John 14:27KJV)

"Everyone then who hears these words of mine and does them will be like a wise man who built his house on the rock. And the rain fell, and the floods came, and the winds blew and beat on that house, but it did not fall, because it had been founded on the rock. And everyone who hears these words of mine and does not do them will be like a foolish man who built his house on the sand. And the rain fell, and the floods came, and the winds blew and beat against that house, and it fell, and great was the fall of it." (Matthew 7:24-27 KJV)

So, we see that the crystals are a fulfillment of different scriptures, and they are the living word just as Christ himself. That's why he's the living Rock. So, know we see a fulfillment of Matthew 7:24, 25 KJV.

So, this is one of the main reasons you need crystals, if sometimes you have a hard time fulfilling the word of God. Then choose something that is the living word and of whom Christ Jesus is, which is the Rock (crystal), that helps you in that particular area in your life at that time.

Chapter 10: Idolatry

What is Idolatry? Idolatry is making things in a figure, carved image, and calling it by another deity or person name that you see as a God. Talking to it as a deity, for example, carving a crystal and naming it "Isis," which was one of the Gods of Egypt, and you bow down and worship it by its name and talk to it by the name you gave it. Or some people carve things unto how they passed ancestors look and call it by their ancestors' names. They bow down and worship it and commune with it as if it's alive.

"**16 Lest ye corrupt yourselves, and make you a graven image, the similitude of any figure, the likeness of male or female,**

17 The likeness of any beast that is on the earth, the likeness of any winged fowl that flieth in the air,

18 The likeness of anything that creepeth on the ground, the likeness of any fish that is in the waters beneath the earth:

19 And lest thou lift up thine eyes unto heaven, and when thou seest the sun, and the moon, and the stars, even all the host of heaven, shouldest be driven to worship them, and serve them, which the Lord thy God hath divided unto all nations under the whole heaven.

20 But the Lord hath taken you, and brought you forth out of the iron furnace, even out of Egypt, to be unto him a people of inheritance, as ye are this day.

21 Furthermore the Lord was angry with me for your sakes, and swear that I should not go over Jordan, and that I should not go in unto that good land, which the Lord thy God giveth thee for an inheritance:

22 But I must die in this land, I must not go over Jordan: but ye shall go over and possess that good land.

23 Take heed unto yourselves, lest ye forget the covenant of the Lord your God, which he made with you, and make you a graven image, or the likeness of anything, which the Lord thy God hath forbidden thee.

24 For the Lord thy God is a consuming fire, even a jealous God.

25 When thou shalt beget children, and children's children, and ye shall have remained long in the land, and shall corrupt yourselves, and make

a graven image, or the likeness of anything, and shall do evil in the sight of the Lord thy God, to provoke him to anger:

26 I call heaven and earth to witness against you this day, that ye shall soon utterly perish from off the land whereunto ye go over Jordan to possess it; ye shall not prolong your days upon it but shall utterly be destroyed.

27 And the Lord shall scatter you among the nations, and ye shall be left few in number among the heathen, whither the Lord shall lead you.

28 And there ye shall serve gods, the work of men's hands, wood and stone, which neither see, nor hear, nor eat, nor smell.

29 But if from thence thou shalt seek the Lord thy God, thou shalt find him, if thou seek him with all thy heart and with all thy soul.

30 When thou art in tribulation, and all these things are come upon thee, even in the latter days, if thou turn to the Lord thy God, and shalt be obedient unto his voice;

31 (For the Lord thy God is a merciful God;) he will not forsake thee, neither destroy thee, nor forget the covenant of thy fathers which he swore unto them." Deut. 4:16-25 (KJV)

Many of People have stated that using crystals is a form of idolatry, that is far from the truth because it's here on earth to bring forth the spiritual realm into the physical realm and vice versa, it helps take our spiritual being to react in the realm of dimensions in the universe, heaven, and in the realm of the spirit. Idolatry is putting anything before the Lord. In order to bring heaven down, we must interact through the kingdom. We see back in the book of Joshua when the Israelites went about serving other Gods, Joshua renewed the covenant with the Lord for him and the Israelites. **"And Joshua recorded these things in the Book of the Law of God. Then he took a large stone and set it up there under the oak near the holy place of the LORD Joshua said to all the people. This stone will be a witness against us. It has heard all the words the LORD has said to us. It will be a witness against you if you are untrue to your God." Joshua 24:26,27 NIV**

It means the crystals or stones have heard the word of the Lord. Crystals are part of the Kingdom of God. We haven't even scratched the surface of bringing forth the kingdom because of man's tradition stating what we should not do or touch because of its idolatry. We see even Jesus talks about those who overcome would receive a white stone with a new name written on it. **"He who has an ear, let him hear what the Spirit says to the churches. To him who overcomes**

I will give some of the hidden manna to eat. And I will give him a white stone, and on the stone a new name written which no one knows except him who receives it." Rev. 2:17 (KJV) There are many different kinds of white stones, Girasol quartz , *scolecite* , *selenite* ,

white jade . *Why did he choose white stones? For one, it is said that white contains all of the colors because it is the primary source of light. White stones are the most comfortable stones to work with. And they also represent the moon. The moon and night reveal mysteries being revealed. It says a new name was written on it, and this is a mystery to us. White stones bring forth purity, purification, clarity, peace, rest, innocence, and healing in all ways. The white stones or more diverse to do things than other stones. These people overcame the trials, tribulations, and temptations of Satan and evil influence. They are brought forth pure and innocent. They were pure and holy before the Lord; they stayed righteous. So even if Christ will give the people who overcome, a stone must not be idolatry because he wants a person to have a stone all to themselves that they can look at any time they want with a new name written. Wow! Talk about awesome. So, it can't be idolatry because he trusts a person to have; they own stone as a personal gift from him.*

We see in Zachariah and Ezekiel they communed with angels. The majority of us in the body of Christ are not talking with these angels or other beings that the Father has assigned to us. Beings are anything that is alive, whether seen or unseen. The dictionary says existence. Psychics will probably call them guides. Everything alive has consciousness. We know that ancients in the ancient times, talked or communed with stones also to get directions. Because they understood they were alive. Unfortunately, they carved them into other Gods, which the Lord speaks against, which is what he originally teaches that idolatry is, but because of his mercy, he still gave answers of truth because he is the Father of all spirits whether an evil person or good person. He loves mankind, but they also were lead unto the deception of they own hearts, we learn that when it came to Laban, he learned through divination that the LORD (the Father) prospered him by having Jacob around, we know the Lord talked to him through dreams but also Laban used divination, and the Lord spoke to him, and it wasn't with the Urim and Thummim it was through images.

"And Laban said unto him, I pray thee, if I have found favour in thine eyes, tarry: for I have learned by experience that the Lord hath blessed me for thy sake.*" Gen 3:27(KJV)* *Experience if you look in other bible*

translations, it means divination. The Reason why Rachal took those images from Laban was that Laban would speak to the images it would reveal the truth. People from other nations would look through a mirror that had images on it or just the images itself, and it would reveal the truth, which is the spirit of truth that comes from God. That is why Rachel took the images because her Father images would tell her where Jacob and his daughters were, and it would speak the truth. Yes, Satan can speak the truth, but who allows him to, the Father does. Satan can also speak lies, but who lets him speak lies the Father does according to his purpose. Satan can only do what the Father allows him to do, as we see in the book of Job. Was it to say the image was bad, no because it spoke the truth, if something speaks the truth, maybe it's just plain and simple the spirit of truth? But the belief that the deities that were carved were speaking to him into made it perverse and corrupt. The reason why Laban would use the images for divination because it was doing what it was made to do, which is, to tell the truth. But Laban found some more images that told him where Jacob and his daughters where. This is why the Lord himself, through the crystal or stones, speaks truth, not the deity himself. The same thing when he said don't worship the idols in high places, high places where mountains were, which has gemstones and crystals in them. They are made up of the fullness of Christ with their own structure without being carved.

*The Lord is the owner of the spirit of truth and lies, in all things. He does whatever needs to be done in order for his divine will to come forth. He's the controller of the lying spirits as well, just as Satan also is the Father of lies himself. But the Lord speaks the truth, righteousness, and life, and his word. If he does send a lying spirit out, it is for a purpose that he has ordained, because he still knows the end from the beginning. He is outside of time. But Satan can only do what the Heavenly Father allows him to do. We know the Lord sent a lying spirit among the prophets of the king of Israel, that told the king of Israel that he would win the battle when in fact it was a lie and the king hated coming to the Prophet Micaiah because he always prophesied evil against him in **1 Kings 22: 18-25(KJV)***

"18 And the king of Israel said unto Jehoshaphat, Did I not tell thee that he would prophesy no good concerning me, but evil? 19 And he said, Hear thou therefore the word of the Lord: I saw the Lord sitting on his throne, and all the host of heaven standing by him on his right hand and on his left. 20 And the Lord said, Who shall persuade Ahab, that he may go up and fall at Ramothgilead? And one said on this manner, and another said on that manner. 21 And there came forth a spirit, and stood before the Lord, and said, I will persuade him. 22 And the Lord said unto him, Wherewith? And he said, I will go forth, and I will be a lying spirit in the mouth of all his prophets. And he said, Thou shalt persuade him, and also prevail: go forth, and do so. 23 Now therefore, behold, the Lord hath put a lying spirit in the mouth of all these thy prophets, and the Lord hath

spoken evil concerning thee.24 But Zedekiah the son of Chenaanah went near, and smote Micaiah on the cheek, and said, Which way the Spirit of the Lord from me to speak unto thee?25 And Micaiah said, Behold, thou shalt see in that day, when thou shalt go into an inner chamber to hide thyself. So, we see the Lord can use whatever and whoever wants in order to get his point across." 1 Kings 22: 18-25(KJV)

Laban would always speak to an image, and it would speak the truth. Rachel had enough of that, and that's why she hid it because the Lord put it on her heart to do so. Even though it looked evil in Laban's eyes for the images to be stolen, it was right in the eyes of the Lord, that's why he put it on Rachel's heart to do so. In the book of Jasher, it talks about the images speaking the truth if a question was asked through the stars. Satan can speak the truth, but it can be partial or twisted and manipulated. When we get crystals, it is not to say that making it into an image is wrong, but when we give it a name beside the Lord, it becomes a problem, and when we worship that name or deity, that is not part of the Trinity, it becomes idolatry.

Crystals speak truth through the Father and through the stars too. The stars prophecy of the coming of Jesus. Just like the original zodiac does, before they perverted it and changed the pictures and meaning. All these things we have turned away from that is called evil that is actually part of the kingdom.

Apostle Paul and the Mirror

The Lord showed me Paul mirror scryed. When you scry, you foretell the future or get prophetic visions using a crystal ball or other reflective object or surface. *How do I know that Paul mirror scryed? The Lord revealed it to me because this was a topic that many people will bring up from this book, especially when they find out that Joseph water scryed. He showed me a person that was looking in a black obsidian mirror while I was spending time with him in prayer around 4 am in the morning, I said Lord that's scary that looks like witchcraft because he showed me black obsidian and a person looking through it (mirror scrying). But all I could think was its a black mirror, so that's evil. Now that I know the good meaning of black is a mystery, truth, elegance, and wealth, etc. I see how ignorant I was. I said to myself, Father, you are going to have to prove it to me, LORD, so I know it's you and not myself. The next day me and my husband went to a church that night, and the Pastor was talking about looking in the mirror and prophesying over yourself as part of communing with the Father.*

He also told us to tell the Father what you wanted in the mirror; I was about to fall out of my seat. I go to this church even though it's a couple hours

away because he is a great Prophet of the Lord, when I need confirmation from the Lord I go there because he's always on target and it comes to pass what he speaks. He flows heavily in the glory realm. I told my husband, "You will not believe this, but he just confirmed what I was telling the Father to confirm." Even on my way there, I was just looking at the stars in the sky and how beautiful they are. **"Day unto uttered speech" (Psalm 19:2 KJV), talking of the clouds, the signs throughout the day of his language, "night unto night he showeth forth knowledge" (mysteries) (Psalm 19:2 KJV). They have no speech; they use no words; no sound is heard from them. Yet he tells us to look up and think on things above and not beneath. Yet their voice goes out into all the earth, their words to the ends of the world. In the heavens God has pitched a tent for the sun." (Psalm 19:2-4 (KJV))** *That was a night of mysteries revealed. So, since the Lord confirmed about mirror scrying with a black obsidian, I said okay, Lord, you are going to have to confirm this. I saw that morning in a vision he showed me the evil queen or witch in Snow White, and how she was talking to the Mirror and entrapped evil spirit talking back to her, it told her the truth, but at the same time I heard, for now, we see through a glass, darkly; but then face to face: now I know in part; but then I shall know even as also I am made known. So, I am saying to myself, Lord, where is that in the bible, I can't remember, and so I googled it and google brought up the scripture* **1 Cor. 13:12 (KJV).**

That scripture itself reveals the mysteries of Christ, it talks about knowing the dreams and visions, having tongues of angels, prophesying, yet if you don't have love, then you are nothing. That mirror spoke truth through a demon or evil spirit, and the evil queen reflected him. You notice the evil queen broke the governmental scriptures of love, once, Snow White came on the scene, "Why?" It spoke truth, and she got upset, acted contrary to the principles of love because she was all about herself. The evil queen was known as the most beautiful out of all the women at that time, till Snow White was born. The Lord showed me this is something that was perverted and that its original intent was to have face to face encounters with the Father. Black obsidian is the stone of prophecy and truth. It reveals your negative nature but also your positive nature; it gives you strength to overcome your negative nature or carnality. It also is known as the stone of truth. Some people use amethyst because of how strong black obsidian is. So, look at Laban situation, he talked to the images it revealed truth that's how he found Joseph, that why Rachael hid the idols. Again I ask the Lord for confirmation again, So I he had two people called me within that week who wanted to have face to face with the Father Jehovah (Yahweh, Yod Hey, Vav, Hey) I said okay Lord you are revealing things, I never told them what he revealed, but I knew it was the confirmation I needed. People in different cultures knows the use of the black obsidian mirror, and they see it as normal and are some of the nicest people you would ever meet. Even those that scry with crystals or crystal balls. They are so kindhearted and sweet. I'm just telling the truth. Joseph water scryed. They

are regular human beings like you and me. Yes, you have those who subjected themselves to Satan or evil forces. Light versus darkness. One thing I cannot do and will not do is lie in order to say what other people or religious leaders will want me to say. I will only speak truth. We give so much credit to the devil, and we need to stop it, we cannot be afraid of what the Heavenly Father Jehovah has made. The earth is his; the crystals are his. It's time to move in dimensions. Let's read **1 Corinthians 13 (KJV).**

"1Though I speak with the tongues of men and of angels, and have not charity, I am become as sounding

brass, or a tinkling cymbal.

2 And though I have the gift of prophecy, and understand all mysteries, and all knowledge; and though I have all faith, so that I could remove mountains, and have not charity, I am nothing.

3 And though I bestow all my goods to feed the poor, and though I give my body to be burned, and have not charity, it profiteth me nothing.

4 Charity suffereth long, and is kind; charity envieth not; charity vaunteth not itself, is not puffed up,

5 Doth not behave itself unseemly, seeketh not her own, is not easily provoked, thinketh no evil;

6 Rejoiceth not in iniquity, but rejoiceth in the truth;

7 Beareth all things, believeth all things, hopeth all things, endureth all things.

8 Charity never faileth: but whether there be prophecies, they shall fail; whether there be tongues, they shall cease; whether there be knowledge, it shall vanish away.

9 For we know in part, and we prophesy in part.

10 But when that which is perfect is come, then that which is in part shall be done away.

11 When I was a child, I spake as a child, I understood as a child, I thought as a child: but when I became a man, I put away childish things.

12 For now we see through a glass, darkly; but then face to face: now I know in part; but then I shall know even as also I am known.

13 And now abideth faith, hope, charity, these three; but the greatest of these is charity." 1 Corinthians 13 :1-13(KJV)

Let's see how the wicked queen broke all these laws in scripture; of course, number one she was evil.

Let's look at these scriptures:

Verse 1 "Though I speak with the tongues of men and of angels, and have not charity, I am become as sounding brass, or a tinkling cymbal." 1 Corinthians 13:1 (KJV)

The evil queen was loud, angry, and mean. If she probably spoke with tongues, it would be tongues of demons, if she had the gift of tongues. She had no love at all except for herself.

Verse 2 "And though I have the gift of prophecy, and understand all mysteries, and all knowledge; and though I have all faith, so that I could remove mountains, and have not charity, I am nothing."

1 Corinthians 13 :2(KJV)

She had the mirror, which was the gift of prophecy she communed with and evil spirit, and she reflected it. The evil spirit knew knowledge and truth; she had faith to do evil and move mountains. She knew she can manipulate or put a spell on someone in order to kill them.

Verse 3 "And though I bestow all my goods to feed the poor, and though I give my body to be burned, and have not charity, it profiteth me nothing." 1 Corinthians 13 :3 (KJV)

She never fed the poor or done none of these in this verse.

Verse 4 "Charity suffereth long, and is kind; charity envieth not; charity vaunteth not itself, is not puffed up," 1 Corinthians 13:4 (KJV)

She was impatient. She was not kind. She was filled with envy and jealousy; she vaunteth herself or boasted about herself; she was full of pride.

Verse 5 "Doth not behave itself unseemly, seeketh not her own, is not easily provoked, thinketh no evil;" 1 Corinthians 13:5 (KJV)

She behaved unseemly, inappropriate, rude, she was seeking her own fleshly desires and wanted to be the only one noticed.

Verse 6 "Rejoiceth not in iniquity, but rejoiceth in the truth;" Corinthians 13:6 (KJV)

She rejoiced in sin, witchcraft, poisoning someone so she can be known as the only beautiful person. She did not rejoice that Snow White was much prettier than her; she got angry."

Verse 7 "Beareth all things, believeth all things, hopeth all things, endureth all things." 1 Corinthians 13 :7 (KJV)

She did not bear (protect) or support Snow White, and she was her enemy, she didn't have faith and hope that people would still notice her beauty, she did not want to endure that she had a possible competitor.

Verse 8

"Charity never faileth: but whether there be prophecies, they shall fail; whether there be tongues, they shall cease; whether there be knowledge, it shall vanish away." 1 Corinthians 13 :8 (KJV)

The wicked queen/witch did not have love, the only love she had was for herself; therefore, she tried to kill Snow White, which she did for a moment, but tables turned back on her, and she died.

Verse 9

"For we know in part, and we prophesy in part." Corinthians 13:9 (KJV)

She knew in part of her own destiny and Snow White destiny by an evil spirit in the mirror.

Verse 10

But when that which is perfect is come, then that which is in part shall be done away." Corinthians 13:10 (KJV)

The evil queen never became perfect because she was filled with her own evil or fleshly desires.

Verse 11

"When I was a child, I spake as a child, I understood as a child, I thought as a child: but when I became a man, I put away childish things." Corinthians 13:11 (KJV)

She was very childish by pouting and getting upset that she wasn't the fairest and beautiful at all because she screamed and lashed out and was trying to compete.

Verse 12

"For now, we see through a glass, darkly; but then face to face: now I know in part; but then I shall know even as also I am known." Corinthians 13:12 (KJV)

Though she looked through a glass dimly, she was face to face with an imprisoned spirit or demonic spirit, so therefore she knew what she reflected was of that evil spirit. Too bad she could have been face to face with Jesus, who is the reflection of the Father. She would have known and fulfilled the commandments of love because Christ is Love.

Verse 13

"13 And now abideth faith, hope, charity, these three; but the greatest of these is charity." Corinthians 13:13 (KJV)

All these things, the evil queen never knew or pursued, but faith, hope, and love (charity) was wrapped in one person, which was Snow White.

Charity is the same as LOVE

*From what I have found out mirror scrying will show you only what you need to know at that time. That's why Paul said," we know in part, and we see in part," **(1Cor. 13:9 KJV)** because Christ would reveal what he needed to know at that time about himself or a situation. You may say, "Well, Terika, didn't you say that people called for face to face encounters with the Father, why are you saying Christ himself now?" The reason is because we have to remember Jesus already came on earth and said if you see him, then you have seen the Father **(John 14:9 KJV)** before his crucifixion. He visited Paul on the road to Damascus, and Paul was blinded. **(Acts 9:1-19 KJV)** It's so funny that he got blinded because the Father said if you shall see me, you shall not live because of the fire, the light, the glory frequency, and vibration he carries. Yet his son blinded Paul, cause of the light coming from him. So, the mirror was another avenue to use where you can commune with the Father without having to suffer death. **The Father told Moses, "you cannot see my face, for no one may see me and live." Exodus 33:20 (NIV)** If you know that you are one with the Father through Christ himself, the mirror will tell and show you your carnal nature and who you are in Christ or what Christ wants you to reflect. Through that relationship of who Christ himself is, we become a reflection of the Father. Because if you see Christ, then you have seen the Father. A good example is with Simba in the Lion King, Simba's Father passed away, and the monkey showed Simba who he was. He looked into the water and saw himself, but then he saw a reflection of his father, and his Father spoke to him. And told him remember who you are, which Simba reflected his Father, then you see the Father going into the heavens in the cloud, saying, "Simba remember who you are, Simba Remember who you are." So, you see manifestation, that he saw his Father. Though he didn't see his Father, he was very much alive in the realm of the spirit. Then the Father showed in self not only in the water, but he walked away as a spirit in the clouds. That's how we get the so great a cloud of witnesses. We see with Joseph that he water scryed by what he told his steward.*

"1And he commanded the steward of his house, saying, Fill the men's sacks with food, as much as they can carry, and put every man's money in his sack's mouth.

2 And put my cup, the silver cup, in the sack's mouth of the youngest, and his corn money. And he did according to the word that Joseph had spoken.

3 As soon as the morning was light, the men were sent away, they and their asses.

4 And when they were gone out of the city, and yet far off, Joseph said unto his steward, Up, follow after the men; and when thou dost overtake them, say unto them, Wherefore have ye rewarded evil for good?

5 Is not this it in which my lord drinketh, and whereby indeed he divineth? ye have done evil in so doing.

6 And he overtook them, and he spake unto them these same words." **Genesis 44:1-6 (KJV)**

The bible hit and misses in plenty of places because of translation, people know this, but it should be in the back of someone's mind that there are some hit and misses of what it says to do and not to do. Man, still had control of what was put in the Holy bible and what was taken out of it. People quote the scriptures below:

"18For these nations, which thou shalt possess, hearkened unto observers of times, and unto diviners: but as for thee, the Lord thy God hath not suffered thee so to do." Deut. 18:14,15 KJV

15 The Lord thy God will raise up unto thee a Prophet from the midst of thee, of thy brethren, like unto me; unto him ye shall hearken;

"9 When thou art come into the land which the Lord thy God giveth thee, thou shalt not learn to do after the abominations of those nations.

10 There shall not be found among you anyone that maketh his son or his daughter to pass through the fire, or that useth divination, or an observer of times, or an enchanter, or a witch.

11 Or a charmer, or a consulter with familiar spirits, or a wizard, or a necromancer.

12 For all that do these things are an abomination unto the Lord: and because of these abominations the Lord thy God doth drive them out from before thee.

13 Thou shalt be perfect with the Lord thy God.

14 For these nations, which thou shalt possess, hearkened unto observers of times, and unto diviners: but as for thee, the Lord thy God hath not suffered thee so to do.

15 The Lord thy God will raise up unto thee a Prophet from the midst of thee, of thy brethren, like unto me; unto him ye shall hearken;" Deut. 18:9-15 (KJV)

It shows the reason why the Lord didn't want them to go outside the camp because if they would of went outside the camp to these people , they could start learning things outside of the Lord's will and start to serve other gods, and he only wanted the Israelites to know his ways, then he said he would raise up a prophet to speak unto them. Necromancy it talks against (where you talk to those who have passed away), yet Jesus talks to Moses and Elijah. Which is what the Father said not to do, but we are in new testament now. Out with the old in with the new. If we haven't fulfilled the previous roles of Joseph, Paul, better yet Daniel, how can the latter rain come about if we haven't fulfilled the old yet? That's something to think about. It talks about not seeing magicians, yet the priest performed it with the woman's belly swelling and thigh rotting, and Daniel was again the Head of the Magician. He had to fulfill that role in order to get it. That's why it's so much confusion in the body of Christ. It still was up to man to determine what would be put in the bible and what should be taken out. Were they perfect people who wrote the bible, No. Moses wasn't even perfect? The King James even manipulated some of the things in the bible, unfortunately, because there were many people doing witchcraft and giving themselves over to Satan and other evil influences in those times, he put all the psychics in the same brackets of witches and warlocks. That's not fair or right at all. Some psychics were Christians themselves. So, in order for you to have truth, you have to have a relationship with the Father, The Son, and Holy Spirit. That's how truth was revealed to me.

We don't worship crystals. We honor them and acknowledge that they are living beings, and we co-labor with them to bring Christ's kingdom, and they work with us to become perfect as the Father is perfect by counteracting our weaknesses. The priest still used crystals for divination with the Urim and Thummim and had crystals at the altar.

The disciples cast lots (some people know as cleromancy) to make decisions which is where you can use stones, or crystals to determine the will of the Father so much of these things are in the bible, and people overlook it and don't put the pieces together because they never knew the original intent of the purposes the Father created them for. **"The Lot is cast into the lap, but the disposing thereof is of the Lord." Prov 16:33 (KJV)**The disciples use stones to cast lots to know the will of the Father. As the disciples did when it came to pick another

Apostle to replace Judas. **23 And they appointed two, Joseph called Barnabas, who was surnamed Justus, and Matthias.24 And they prayed, and said, Thou, Lord, which knowest the hearts of all men, shew whether of these two thou hast chosen,25 That he may take part of this ministry and apostleship, from which Judas by transgression fell, that he might go to his own place.26 And they gave forth their lots, and the lot fell upon Matthias; and he was numbered with the eleven apostles. Acts 1:23-26 (KJV)**

In the book of Leviticus chapter 16, the Lord commanded Moses to cast lots upon 2 sheep goats, one lot for the Lord, and one for a scapegoat. In the book of Jonah, the desperate sailors cast lots to see whose god was responsible for creating the storm: **"Then the sailors said to each other, 'Come, let us cast lots to find out who is responsible for this calamity.' They cast lots and the lot fell on Jonah." Jonah 1:17 (KJV) Wow! The Spirit of Truth!** Now, of course, we know some streams are demonic streams, like the OUIJA BOARD. THAT IS A NO! NO! I have had people tell me horrific detailed stories that they have had with the use of that and overtimes past, and it has produced nothing but pure evil because it comes from the demonic realm.

If the Lord showed his face in the mirror, showed different signs, or given you prophecies, are you going to be scared whether he release it through a mirror or crystal? Because he is restoring these truths back unto him. If you are a business owner struggling with finances and the Father gave you a detailed prophecy through a black obsidian mirror or regular mirror on how another business owner can get their breakthrough by meeting someone at 2 pm by Schnucks door. He tells you to tell them to wear a black and white suit because he informed that person, that they will invest 1 million dollars into their business and will be wearing a black and white suit. How will you react? Would you react like the wicked queen or witch in Snow White? By pouting withholding the prophecy, would you get jealous, would you get angry, or would you put these childish things away and trust that if he's giving you this prophecy to give to someone when you cheer for them, your breakthrough will come.

Just one crystal can lead a whole entire group on which way to go, just like in **Matthew 3:9 (KJV) "And think not to say within yourselves, We have Abraham to our father: for I say unto you, that God is able of these stones to raise up children unto Abraham."** He's saying just as the crystals help the priest give prophecies of the Lord by the Urim and Thummim, and the crystals can give prophecies to people themselves and show the people how to have faith like Abraham and to give the word of the Lord for each day if they wanted to. Just one crystal is needed to guide a person and can show the way of the Lord because it's in him. Again, it's not the crystal that's evil but the person and their intentions

on what they use it for, evil or good. It's not used to control people. So, is this idolatry? No, it's another tool the Father used to commune with people.

*If I carve a crystal into a lion, I know its symbolic for the Lion of Judah, who roars. But I don't bow down or sing to it, I may look at it as a remembrance that Christ roars on my behalf, and as he roars on my behalf, so also I should roar against the enemy as Christ himself does because I am one with Christ Jesus. Why because he gave me the power to do so **(Luke 10:19(KJV))** and that particular crystal that I used could impart and increase the power that break curses or keep away demonic spirits ,negative energies, evil entities, like black*

tourmaline  *, or amethyst* *, or snowflake obsidian*

, etc. Because that's the characteristic, the crystal reflects of Christ, whether it's carved or not. If I make an image into Buddha, who have passed away and believe that he is my God and say I worship you, Buddha, you are my God, then that becomes a problem because if you are born again believer in Christ, then Buddha is not your God, Christ is. Now Buddha may have had some profound wisdom like Christ, but he is not Christ himself, he had excellent characteristics too, but so do people in general, because we all have a piece of Christ himself without being born again, but when you are born again, you are one with him.

The Holy Spirit starts to lead and guide you through his word, his word is what starts to be built up in your spirit man and even in your soul, but the Father wants the soul to be under subjection unto Holy Spirit, or your higher self, which is part of the crystals/stones/gemstones duty, because it imparts the perfect vibrations into your soul which come into perfect alignment of the frequency and vibrations Holy spirit has been longing for years to be built within every born again believer himself and even those in other cultures. Crystals also ministers under subjection of the Holy Spirit also because now they are in contact with Christ DNA within you. They begin to minister to you according to what the Father wants them to, and they are cheering you on, to lead you on the right road through Christ himself. But they also help others to learn how to love, to be patient, to be cheerful, and to have life.

Again Job, "Speak to the earth, and it shall teach thee." The crystals are part of the earth for us to speak to and are birthed from it. (Job12:8 KJV) "The beast (animals) shall teach us" (Job12:8 KJV) It is talking about nature in its own original creative form. We haven't even interacted with nature or been able to commune with animals, and the bible tells us to do it. But because we repeat what everyone is saying in the pulpit and don't get me wrong, they do it out of the sincerity of their heart so that we don't be led astray, and we don't even know the true meaning behind biblical scriptures. How do we find this out? Through relationship with the Father through his son. We have to remember we're the Heavenly Father's children as well. We, as his children or Sons of God, gets revelation as well. We know they have to sound the alarm if they see a brother fall or think they have fallen. But a brother can't fall if they are obedient to the word of God and obey the Father's instruction. It completely tells us what we can do and what we should not do. You have to have discernment of knowing what the scripture as a whole is saying. We are to interact with the universe, the sun, the moon, the stars, the earth, and we have not because we have been closed-minded. The universe is what helps bring forth the kingdom of God. It's quite simple, and it's good versus evil.

Idolatry was making idols and giving them a name and worshipping that deity and specifically stating that you are worshipping them and burning incense to them. Calling them out purposely by name and deity and stating you worship them. We see even in the new testament people had engraved on their altar to the unknown God in acts chapter 17. Paul had to correct them, and they were religious leaders themselves out of other nations. They had idols themselves in the land, and it grieved Paul. **29 "Therefore, since we are God's offspring, we should not think that the divine being is like gold or silver or stone— an image made by human design and skill. 30 In the past, God overlooked such ignorance, but now he commands all people everywhere to repent. Act 17:29,30 (KJV)** *We see that people made images of people, animals, etc. and worshipping them as a God. I hate to say it, but again we see that much in the church, pastors wanting people to serve them and be under them, and to go along with their preaching so they can feel good. Now that's idolatry. We see the bible speaking against divination, but we clearly see Joseph divined. Divination is not idolatry is another way Holy Spirit or messengers of the Lord can communicate with people.*

It's clear that the Lord didn't want Israel to seek prophesy or divination from other countries, so they don't worship the other countries Gods that they served, he knew the Israelites could start doing other countries practices which could lead them to not worshipping God but the God they worshipped in their countries. **7 For so it was, that the children of Israel had sinned against the Lord their**

God, which had brought them up out of the land of Egypt, from under the hand of Pharaoh king of Egypt, and had feared other gods,

"8 And walked in the statutes of the heathen, whom the Lord cast out from before the children of Israel, and of the kings of Israel, which they had made.

9 And the children of Israel did secretly those things that were not right against the Lord their God, and they built them high places in all their cities, from the tower of the watchmen to the fenced city.

10 And they set them up images and groves in every high hill, and under every green tree:

11 And there they burnt incense in all the high places, as did the heathen whom the Lord carried away before them; and wrought wicked things to provoke the Lord to anger:

12 For they served idols, whereof the Lord had said unto them, Ye shall not do this thing.

13 Yet the Lord testified against Israel, and against Judah, by all the prophets, and by all the seers, saying, Turn ye from your evil ways, and keep my commandments and my statutes, according to all the law which I commanded your fathers, and which I sent to you by my servants the prophets.

14 Notwithstanding they would not hear, but hardened their necks, like to the neck of their fathers, that did not believe in the Lord their God.

15 And they rejected his statutes, and his covenant that he made with their fathers, and his testimonies which he testified against them; and they followed vanity, and became vain, and went after the heathen that were round about them, concerning whom the Lord had charged them, that they should not do like them.

16 And they left all the commandments of the Lord their God, and made them molten images, even two calves, and made a grove, and worshipped all the host of heaven, and served Baal.

17 And they caused their sons and their daughters to pass through the fire, and used divination and enchantments, and sold themselves to do evil in the sight of the Lord, to provoke him to anger.

18 Therefore the Lord was very angry with Israel, and removed them out of his sight: there was none left but the tribe of Judah only.

19 *Also Judah kept not the commandments of the Lord their God, but walked in the statutes of Israel which they made.*

20 *And the Lord rejected all the seed of Israel, and afflicted them, and delivered them into the hand of spoilers, until he had cast them out of his sight.*

21 *For he rent Israel from the house of David; and they made Jeroboam the son of Nebat king: and Jeroboam drave Israel from following the Lord, and made them sin a great sin.*

22 *For the children of Israel walked in all the sins of Jeroboam which he did; they departed not from them;*

23 *Until the Lord removed Israel out of his sight, as he had said by all his servants the prophets. So was Israel carried away out of their own land to Assyria unto this day.*

24 *And the king of Assyria brought men from Babylon, and from Cuthah, and from Ava, and from Hamath, and from Sepharvaim, and placed them in the cities of Samaria instead of the children of Israel: and they possessed Samaria, and dwelt in the cities thereof.*

25 *And so it was at the beginning of their dwelling there, that they feared not the Lord: therefore the Lord sent lions among them, which slew some of them.*

26 *Wherefore they spake to the king of Assyria, saying, The nations which thou hast removed, and placed in the cities of Samaria, know not the manner of the God of the land: therefore he hath sent lions among them, and, behold, they slay them, because they know not the manner of the God of the land.*

27 *Then the king of Assyria commanded, saying, Carry thither one of the priests whom ye brought from thence; and let them go and dwell there, and let him teach them the manner of the God of the land.*

28 *Then one of the priests whom they had carried away from Samaria came and dwelt in Bethel, and taught them how they should fear the Lord.*

29 *Howbeit every nation made gods of their own and put them in the houses of the high places which the Samaritans had made, every nation in their cities wherein they dwelt." 2 Kings 17:8-29 (KJV)*

The Father didn't want the Israelites to bring and serve other gods in the high places. Why? Because the high places were mountains made out of crystals which is part of the earth, that has been since the earth began Jesus is the living rock of all living rocks, he doesn't want to share his seat with anyone unless it's the Father or the Holy Spirit because they are the three in one of the Holy Trinity. The crystals and stones are also as we know alive and have their own consciousness because, in the book of Job, it says, "**8 Or speak to the earth, and it shall teach thee: and the fish of the sea shall declare unto thee. 9 Who knoweth not in all these that the hand of the Lord hath wrought this? <u>10 In whose hand is the soul of every living thing, and the breath of all mankind.</u>**" *Job 12:8-10 (KJV)*

When Jesus stated that if you have :no doubt in your heart and tell the mountain to be thou removed and cast into the sea, it shall obey you," (Matt.21:21) that's what he meant, the actual mountain. However, what are the mountains made out of? Rocks, gemstones, crystals, etc. So, if you tell a crystal or gemstone to perform a task according to what the Father created it to do, it is going to obey you because it flows from the Father Heart, through Jesus unto you, and becomes one with you as a gift of the Father. The reason for this is because we are all one in Christ Jesus himself. Just as Jesus is a gift to us, so is the crystals a gift, because they are made out of Christ and is a gift of the Father to us.

Crystals also work in conjunction with the word of God, and they hearken, just like the angels, to the voice of the Lord. They also do what you tell them to do through relationship with them through Adonai. I see crystals as my own friends, and you have a relationship with them, just like you have a relationship with your own friends, families, or sisters and brothers in Christ. After you have communed with the Father, Son, and Holy Spirit, you can commune with the crystal; I say the name of the crystal, for example, "Black Tourmaline, what's on the Fathers agenda to-do list today, or how would the Lord expect me to react in this situation. Or I may say, "Citrine, what is a new design can I do for this necklace or what's a new way to decorate this house." Citrine, I need new designs for this floor plan or a new design for a house? They are here to co-labor with us and to help us because we need help with different situations in life. They are assigned to do different things for us according to what the Father has instructed for them to do, just like the angels. We are able to interact and engage with them just like we engage with the Father, the Son, and Holy Spirit, angels, and the so great a cloud of witnesses that are cheering us on, even our ancestors. They are here to assist all mankind to bear fruit and receive healing through Christ as a gift of the Father to all creation like flowers, animals, to help bring life and prosperity, and healing to even the world, through Christ Jesus. Speak unto the crystal, and it shall teach you. How do we do that? Is it by force? No, it is by love.

I can actually say a friend loveth at all times, and a brother is born for adversity is what the scripture states.

So, we know the Trinity (Father, Son, and Holy Spirit) loves at all times and is born for adversity for the sons and daughters of God to fight on our behalf. So are the angels, crystals, and the universe, sun, moon, and stars on our behalf as well. When you are weak or need help, Holy Spirit will show you which crystal will help you in different situations, and even the crystal itself will show you which crystal you need because they are all alive and like the angels they give messages. Just like when you hear the name of individual angels or see them, it's the same for crystals. We are supposed to do these things because it's part of the kingdom principles. Unfortunately, we haven't even tapped into the fullness of the kingdom of God because we are not operating how we suppose to because, unfortunately, all the negative stories heard about people using crystal for wrongdoing and nothing but the wrong way have been shown in media. When do people proclaim using them in the right way? It's just like how on the news they expose all negative things going on in the communities, but they rarely show the good things that are happening in the community.

We are not even flowing in these things in the church. We can't commune with angels, or bring up seeing angels, without saying make sure you don't worship them, which is useful for those who are new to Christ to know; but those who have an intimate relationship with the Lord and honestly read the word of God, should know these things. We suppose to commune with angels like in Zachariah, I'm not just talking about talking with angels in dreams or you recognize an angel while interpreting your dreams. Or just a person saying I see Moses or Elijah or another being. I'm not talking just about seeing an angel lay hands on someone and appear, then you see them, and they smile. I'm talking about face to face as you would talk to the Father, the Son, the Holy Spirit, your family, friends, pastor, coworker, business partner, etc. Same goes for the crystals, the earth, the animals, and the trees, that have their own consciousness. Because the word of God said, "the trees clap their hands before the son of God" **(Isaiah 55:12).** *Zachariah communed with the Jesus and an angel at the same time.*

"7 Upon the four and twentieth day of the eleventh month, which is the month Sebat, in the second year of Darius, came the word of the Lord unto Zechariah, the son of Berechiah, the son of Iddo the prophet, saying, 8 I saw by night, and behold a man riding upon a red horse, and he stood among the myrtle trees that were in the bottom; and behind him were their red horses, speckled, and white.

<u>9 Then said I, O my Lord, what are these? And the angel that talked with me said unto me, and I will shew thee what these be.</u>

10, These are they whom the Lord hath sent to walk to and fro through the earth.

11 And they answered the angel of the Lord that stood among the myrtle trees, and said, We have walked to and fro through the earth, and, behold, all the earth sitteth still, and is at rest.

12 Then the angel of the Lord answered and said, O Lord of hosts, how long wilt thou not have mercy on Jerusalem and on the cities of Judah, against which thou hast had indignation these threescore and ten years?

13 And the Lord answered the angel that talked with me with good words and comfortable words.

14 So the angel that communed with me said unto me, Cry thou, saying, Thus saith the Lord of hosts; I am jealous for Jerusalem and for Zion with a great jealousy.

15 And I am very sore displeased with the heathen that are at ease: for I was, but a little displeased, and they helped forward the affliction.

16 Therefore thus saith the Lord; I am returned to Jerusalem with mercies: my house shall be built in it, saith the Lord of hosts, and a line shall be stretched forth upon Jerusalem.

17 Cry yet, saying, Thus saith the Lord of hosts; My cities through prosperity shall yet be spread abroad; and the Lord shall yet comfort Zion, and shall yet choose Jerusalem.

18 Then lifted I up mine eyes, and saw, and behold four horns.

19 And I said unto the angel that talked with me, What are these? And he answered me, These are the horns which have scattered Judah, Israel, and Jerusalem.

20 And the Lord shewed me four carpenters.

21 Then said I, What come these to do? And he spake, saying, These are the horns which have scattered Judah, so that no man did lift up his head: but these are come to fray them, to cast out the horns of the Gentiles, which lifted up their horn over the land of Judah to scatter it." Zachariah 1:17-21(KJV)

We see the scriptures underlined is Zachariah communing with an angel sent to work with him, teach and guide him because he called him Lord. In Greek, Lord means "teacher or master," and in Hebrew, it means "Lord God."

Angels were sometimes referred to as lord or guides (lord Greek meaning is a teacher, master, in Hebrew its God) but we know it was an angel sent to Zachariah to guide him and commune with him in order for Zachariah to complete

the Lord's task, I guess that's why some people call them guides, (this is not new age it's the new testament) This is to break religious mindsets and to tell the truth. We see the scriptures in underline is the Lord communing and guiding Zachariah also. So, we see Zachariah interacting with the Lord and the angel at the same time.

Apostle Paul communed with the Angel of the Lord and did what the angel told him to do in order to fulfill Christ mission. He served the angel by being obedient to what the angel of the Lord told him to do. It wasn't idolatry; it was bringing forth Christ Kingdom and mission, that the collaborated with the angel. It's all part of bringing forth the Kingdom of God. I'm sure the angel was like a friend; Paul had to consult with the angel in order to know the Fathers will or the next step to take for the mission and his ministry.

"22 And now I exhort you to be of good cheer: for there shall be no loss of any man's life among you, but of the ship. 23 <u>For there stood by me this night the angel of God, whose I am, and whom I serve,</u> 24 Saying, Fear not, Paul; thou must be brought before Caesar: and, lo, God hath given thee all them that sail with thee. 25 Wherefore, sirs, be of good cheer: for I believe God, that it shall be even as it was told me. 26 Howbeit we must be cast upon a certain island." Acts 27:22-26 KJV

It's time for us to move into real dimensions of the kingdom; these are just the minor things we supposed to have been tapped into or supposed to do. The majority of believers have not even tapped into these realms. Everything in creation that lives is loved and has a purpose. Everything in creation is here to help engage in the realm of the Kingdom of Light for Christ in order to defeat the evil deeds of the enemy that has been corrupted by Satan and the fallen angels. Just as angels and the so great a cloud of witnesses (those who have passed and went to heaven and come down to teach others) came to give us more in-depth insight and messages of the Father, Christ Jesus, and the Holy Ghost, so do crystals because they are, after all, made out of Christ the Head of all Rocks. Just as the angels hear the word of the Lord and perform them, so do the crystals. If anyone states you are committing idolatry, that is further from the truth. If your relationship with the Father through Christ Jesus is first in your life, and you ask your friends, family, loved ones, pastors for advice or a situation all the time or talking to them every day, then that is saying you are idolizing them too. And committing idolatry. Why? You are communing with them also and building a relationship with them. We are to have relationships because we need each other.

We talk to the Father, Jesus, and Holy Spirit always first and foremost. If you are a born-again believer in Christ, and you're asking the Lord for confirmation or an answer about a particular situation. Let's say the Lord did not confirm the answer like he did other times before. It can be that it's not time to reveal it yet or the answer may come through other avenues to confirm or answer

your question through signs when you walk out of the house or drive; you may see a license plate that has an answer to your question by the car in front of you. Or a driver of a car speeds up and the license plate speaking prophetically, or someone may drive a car with his name on it. You know that's the Lord communicating with you through discernment. You know his voice versus the enemy's voice. You may need advice on something, and you have asked too many people, and each one of them gave a different answer, or it may be a group of people that gave similar opinions and another group of people that gave different answers, so you may indeed get confused. But, then someone who ultimately don't know about the situation that you meet in a store and hold a conversation with, while waiting in line and all of a sudden they bring up a solution without even knowing that they gave you a solution to a problem, then you know that's the Lord's kingdom at work.

The Father knows the end at the beginning, and they are performing the book that is written of them, and you are performing the book that is written of you also. Or you may go on the internet, and something just stand out and pop out at you. The angels may flicker the light to confirm a thought you just had at the same time you finished that thought, to let you know you are right or the Lord may send a bird to confirm an answer or to simply let you know he loves you and hears your concerns. Or your 9-month-old just say, "pray" out of nowhere. You may get the answers to the question through a person in a completely different culture, or country, even religion to give you the knowledge or provision needed.

I remember I needed some clothes for my children to start back to school, and I wrote it in my journal. The same week my aunt, who is a Jehovah Witness, called me to ask if I had got the kids some school clothes, and I said, I didn't have the money. She said Jehovah had put it on her heart to ask me. This is to show that Christ is in all through the Father (Adonai, Yahweh, Jehovah, Yod Hey Vav Hey, etc.) because he is in all. If I didn't answer that call being prejudice and saying they of the occult of the devil, unfortunately like some people do, I could have missed the blessing because of the spirit of pride. Truth be told, they think those in the church are evil and in the dark, because that's what they have been told, and we have been taught that they are evil. You have Buddhist that think Christians stole meditation from them. So, you have all these religions having different pieces of the truth but not the whole truth because of what they have been taught in that culture or religion. Bottom line Christ wants all things to be one with him in his righteous way to bring forth the gospel and healing to the nations, and people, so they can get healed set free and delivered. He wants to be mankind's Lord and Savior. Christ said honor all men and love brotherhood. But we see, unfortunately, why people leave religion or the church altogether and just keep a relationship with The Holy Trinity or whoever they have a relationship with as their own God. Because of mankind's own view. Christ is all in all and want men to be subject unto him and his way.

Chapter 11: "I am the vine; you are the branches." John 15:5 (NIV)

New Meditation Technique: Yota Meditation (Not To be confused with Yoga Meditation)

As stated earlier, when I asked the Father if Yoga was of him while driving, A car pulled up in front of me while driving. It was a Toyota, and the license plate had on it <u>My Yota</u>. It was a Toyota, but it was their own Toyota; that's why it had My Yota. As I stated before, the Father talks to me through different license plates on people's cars to relay messages, prophetic messages, or answers to my questions. He was saying Terika, that's why the T was there to get my attention because my name starts with a T. So instead of Yoga, it was Yota. So, he was saying Yoga techniques are of me. Yoga techniques are good for every individual, and it's all about who the person give themselves to. Are you giving yourself up to an evil spirit or a good spirit? Are you doing yoga through The Father, the Son, and Holy Spirit? Or are you doing it through the devil, demons, or evil entities? So, if someone is doing yoga and can tell you what chakras are off in your body and they seem off, evil, or wicked, it's not the yoga information that they learned that's evil; it's the individual themselves. Now, if they give themselves over to demonic spirits, yes, it can

influence them, and yes, possess them if that's who they give themselves up to. I can tell a person which of their chakras are off balance by what I learned and researched. But I'm not evil, and I am a Son of the Most High God. In the kingdom of God, there is no gender. You may say some people look evil that do yoga because of their muscular built or self-discipline they learned through yoga or the yoga techniques that may be hard or difficult, but the person isn't evil. They just are disciplined in the techniques and structures of the body. Yoga is really based off of John 15:5

*You hear of people programming the crystals, and they do what you tell them to do, well this is true because of **Job 5:23 NIV** and because John 15:1-8 when Jesus says you will ask me, the Rock (crystal) what you will, and it would be done unto you. How many times have we meditated on the scripture and asked Jesus (Yeshua) to do something, and it didn't happen? A lot of times. I know it would be times, I'm trying to get clear focus on the Lord, and I couldn't get clear focus because of so many distractions, so I would ask him to remove it, but my mind was still chattering with distractions. Versus, if I would have held a black tourmaline in my hand and breathed in and out during meditation, it would have quickly decluttered my mind by instantly removing the distractions. I break down John 15:1- 8 below, and afterward, I go over the Yota Method based off of John 15:5 (KJV).*

"*1 I am the true vine, and my Father is the gardener. 2 He cuts off every branch in me that bears no fruit, while every branch that does bear fruit he prunes so that it will be even more fruitful. 3 You are already clean because of the word I have spoken to you. 4 Remain in me, as I also remain in you. No branch can bear fruit by itself; it must remain in the vine. Neither can you bear fruit unless you remain in me.*

5 "I am the vine; you are the branches. If you remain in me and I in you, you will bear much fruit; apart from me, you can do nothing. 6 If you do not remain in me, you are like a branch that is thrown away and withers;

such branches are picked up, thrown into the fire and burned. 7 If you remain in me and my words remain in you, ask whatever you wish, and it will be done for you. 8 This is to my Father's glory, that you bear much fruit, showing yourselves to be my disciples." John 15:1-8 (NIV)

If you consecrated the crystal back unto the Father, meaning if you prayed to the Father or Jesus whichever makes you feel comfortable, then you would see Christ as being the rock (crystal) himself, and Christ is the vine within us along our spinal cord and the 7 main chakras then you can see yourself as a tree of life. Because in Christ, there is life. That's where I am the true vine, and you are the branches comes in at. I give details on how to understand John 15:1-8 NIV This is a crystal meditation version.

"I am the true vine, and my Father is the gardener. 2 He cuts off every branch in me that bears no fruit, while every branch that does bear fruit he prunes so that it will be even more fruitful. John 15:1-2 (NIV)

Jesus is saying I am the conduit or spine (vine) that align the chakras (Wheels, energy centers, or gates) within the body. My Father (the gardener) is the source in which I remove sin, carnality, weaknesses, and negative energy as you breathe me in and exhale the negative thoughts, distraction, fear, etc. My Father is the source in which I remove and break habits and remove any demons that may try to influence or attach itself to you through your aura or bloodline. As I remove these things from you, through me the crystal itself, I release the characteristics of me through your aura and gateways during meditation. And by the crystals character being imparted to you through synchronization, my character, and nature becomes one with you on a much grander scale. Meaning more fruitfulness is being multiplied back to you through you being in sync with the crystal. Therefore, you are being who the father initially intended for you to be before sin entered the world, except you are your own unique character.

"You are already clean because of the word I have spoken to you." John 15:3 (NIV)

This means you are already clean because the Father has already started pruning and cutting off rotten branches through Christ the Rock (Crystal) removing all negativity, and unfruitfulness. The purifying of your body and your aura by you being one with me and meditating on my word as affirmation and declarations over yourself. The true vine (Christ himself within you who holds all the chakras together within the spine) awakens and shift the Chakras into divine order and perfection by cleansing, balancing, and activating the Chakras through receiving the crystals frequencies and vibrations.

"Remain in me, as I also remain in you." John 15:4 (NIV)

Jesus is saying, "Remain in me, the protection of your aura or electromagnetic field through entrainment of the vibrations of the crystals. Soak in my presence, energy, and vibrations of who I am through the crystal and your body will begin to mimic and becomes one with the crystal through your aura through me Christ Jesus, the true vine and the door within you; becoming one with your aura to protect it and purify it.

"No branch can bear fruit by itself; it must remain in the vine. Neither can you bear fruit unless you remain in me." John 15:4 (NIV)

No branch attached to each Chakra can bear actual fruit unless it is connected to Christ the vine within, the chakras bear the crystal (Christ the Rock) fruits. (Not only that, you are getting detoxed, inside and out, and your body is receiving the minerals of the crystals. Jesus (Yeshua) is saying, I am the vine in which you breathe through, and you are the branches that grows out as you exhale out of both sides of the chakras, being purified and cleansed through me (the Rock in which you hold). Therefore, bringing you into balance.

"If you remain in me and I in you, you will bear much fruit; apart from me you can do nothing." John 15:5 (NIV)

If we remain in Christ Jesus, himself the vine (pillar) within us that holds the chakras within ourselves together and understand that he's the rock (crystal) in which we hold during meditation, you would bear much fruit of the crystals characteristics and nature that they vibrate and impart to you through entrainment. Remember, our body can start to mimic what surrounds it, depending on how sensitive you are in the realm of the spirit. If you have a green

aventurine.   it gives off vibrations of joy, so you will become joyful by receiving the joy it imparts unto you through its vibration. At the same time, fights for you by removing any negativity within you and imparting positivity. It brings forth prosperity. Therefore, you become joy in your own unique way, that the Father has intended as your true nature since the beginning of creation! Each crystal is assigned to our soul to counteract its weaknesses and release grace to do those things we could not do. It makes us free and breaks bondage. Apart from the crystal, you won't have the grace to bear fruit. That's why it's constant warfare during fast when you need deliverance, but at least if you have the crystal in whom Christ the rock is, we have grace during the fast. Or in our day to day lives. We must keep our armor on. Don't get me wrong it will be times when you don't have them on, but the crystal gives an extra level of grace. I can tell if I don't have my crystals on because it's a change in my attitude the way I think, etc. Therefore, I can tell which chakras are not aligned as well because, of course, the crystal protects them and balances them.

Jesus (Yeshua) is saying be still in me (the true vine, which I AM through the spine (vine) within you that align the 7 major and even minor chakras within the middle of your body) and breathe in deep and exhale through Christ the true vine within you, while I clean your chakras, your aura, and your physical, mental, and emotional body through the branches that birth forth the fruit of Crystals(Christ the rock) depending on their own characteristics, nature, and functions. Without Christ Jesus the Rock (crystal), you can do nothing. He is the missing link in Yoga in order to be whole. Yoga helps a lot, but how much more will it help you through Christ.

Jesus (Yeshua) is saying if you remain in me the true vine, you will bear much fruit because I am the rock of which you hold. Apart from me (the rock), you can do nothing because I am the Rock (crystal), the one who corrects the wheels as you breathe out the branches.

"If you do not remain in me, you are like a branch that is thrown away and withers; such branches are picked up, thrown into the fire and burned." John 15:6 (NIV)

Jesus is saying if you don't remain in him the vine, your chakras will not be balanced through the branches, which is yourself. Our body, mind, will, and emotions has to be balanced. <u>For example, if you are a person that always criticize and don't show mercy, you can come off as being too strict, harsh, and negative. But if you show mercy and forgiveness, sometimes, you become more balanced and know God's right judgment.</u>

"If you remain in me and my words remain in you, ask whatever you wish, and it will be done for you." John 15:7 (NIV)

Jesus is saying if you remain in me, the true vine, and my words (scriptures) remain in you, you can ask me, Christ, the rock (crystal), what you will and it shall be established through your intentions and covenant (Job 5:23 NIV) with the crystals according to the crystals benefits and functions that the Father has called, commissioned, and ordained for them to do.

"This is to my Father's glory, that you bear much fruit, showing yourselves to be my disciples." John 15:8 (NIV)

Jesus is saying I am the treasures or crystals of the Father's heart, and according to what the Father has created me to do as the crystal itself. Therefore, you will learn of me, through the crystals and know the Father's heart, through me, who is the way the truth, and the life, and the door to the Father. Jesus is saying through the crystals, and you will bear fruitfulness, their characteristic, and nature through Christ himself the Living Rock. Hallelujah!

Different Yota (Not Yoga) Meditation Techniques

We can have a healthy aura where the colors are clear, vibrant, and radiant without any tears, leaks, or dark brown, or black colors. On the other hand, we can have an unhealthy aura which have openings and dull, muddy colors within it, and you may see spots of black and brown within the aura; that's why it is vital that we breathe in and out of the chakras/wheels.

While meditating on the Lord and breathing in and out, he showed me a new meditation technique. So, I call it, "Yota Meditation," it's based off of John 15:5. I am the true vine, and you are the branches. He showed me during meditation a person as a tree, which they teach you in yoga. But this is a little different, he showed me while you breathe in deeply and hold your breath for a couple of seconds "all the while the breath is in me, the spirit of the Lord is in my nostrils" **Job 27:3 KJV** *then you breathe out and imagine you are breathing out branches from each of the 7 main chakras. But instead of the roots growing out of your legs and feet. Imagine the roots to start growing out of only your feet. You can do this technique with the minor chakras as well. With this method, imagination and breathing is very vital.*

Yota Meditation Technique #1 "Tree Method"

Yota Meditation Technique #1 "Tree Method" Cleansing your gateways just through inhaling and exhaling without the use of crystals.
Estimated time 3-5 min

***Before each exercise, rub your hands together for 30 seconds or more till they get hot, Now open your hands, you should feel a tingling sensation or electricity that's energy flowing through your hands. ***

1. Sit Indian style, or you can sit in a chair with feet flat on the floor, or you can stand. Breathe in (all the while breath is in me the spirit of the Lord is in my nostrils) and hold it for a couple of seconds, then breathe out any negative thoughts, feelings, frustrations, distractions, anger, etc. Repeat this method 3 or 4 times.

2. Tap your thymus a couple of times.

3. Inhale through the crown chakra and exhale imagining branches growing out of both sides of the crown chakra without leaves.

4. Inhale through crown chakra down to the 3rd eye and hold it for a few seconds at the 3rd eye, and exhale imagining branches growing out of both sides of the 3rd eye without leaves.

5. Inhale through the crown chakra, down through the 3rd eye, down through the throat chakra, and hold it for a few seconds at the throat chakra and exhale imagining branches growing out of both sides of the throat chakra.

6. Inhale through the crown chakra, through the 3rd eye chakra, through the throat chakra, through the heart chakra, hold your breath for a couple of seconds at the heart chakra and exhale imagining branches growing out of both sides of the heart chakra.

7. Inhale through the crown chakra, through the third eye chakra, through the throat chakra, through the heart chakra, through the solar plexus, and hold your breath for a few seconds at the solar plexus chakra, and exhale branches growing out of both sides of the solar plexus without any leaves on them.

8. Inhale through the crown chakra, through the third eye chakra, through the throat chakra, through the heart chakra, through the solar plexus, and through the sacral chakra, hold your breath for a few seconds at the sacral chakra, and exhale imagining branches growing out of both sides of the sacral chakra without any leaves on them.

9. Inhale through the crown chakra, through the third eye chakra, through the throat chakra, through the heart chakra, through the solar plexus chakra, and through the sacral chakra, through the root chakra, hold your breath for a few seconds at the root chakra, and exhale branches growing out of both sides of the root chakra without any leaves on them.

10. Inhale through the crown chakra, through the third eye, through the throat chakra, through the heart chakra, through the solar plexus chakra, and through the sacral chakra, through the root chakra, hold your breath for a few seconds at the root chakra, exhale out imagining the root chakra turning into the trunk (hips and legs)of the tree, down to the feet with roots spreading out of the feet down into the earth.

11. Inhale through the crown chakra, through the third eye, through the throat chakra, through the heart chakra, through the solar plexus, and through the sacral chakra, through the root chakra, hold your breath for as long as you can at the root, and exhale firmly as you feel the energy intensify going through the branches of each chakra, quickly going down through the trunk(hips and legs) through the roots that form in the feet that spread wide deep down into the earth quickly and very deep.

(Please note: It might feel like a vibration shock wave going down your body.)

12. Now imagine inhaling from the ends of your roots, up through your feet, up through your root chakra, and hold your breath for a few seconds. Then, exhale leaves and fruit growing out of both sides of your branches of your root chakra.

13. Inhale from the ends of yours roots, up through the feet to the root chakra, up through your sacral chakra, and hold your breath for a few seconds. Then, exhale leaves and fruit growing out of both sides of your branches of your sacral chakra.

14. Inhale from the ends of your roots up through your feet, up through the root chakra, up through your sacral chakra, up through your solar plexus, and hold your breath for a few seconds. Then, exhale leaves and fruit growing out of both sides of your branches of your solar plexus.

15. Inhale from the ends of your roots up through your feet, up through your root chakra, up through the sacral chakra, up through your solar plexus, up through your heart chakra, and hold your breath for a few seconds and exhale leaves and fruit growing out of both sides of your branches of your heart chakra.

16. Inhale from the ends of yours root up through your feet, up through the root chakra, up through the sacral chakra, up through the solar plexus, up through your heart chakra, and hold your breath for a few seconds. then exhale leaves and fruit growing out of both sides of your branches of your heart chakra.

17. Inhale from the ends of your roots, up through your feet, up through your root chakra, up through your sacral chakra, up through your solar plexus chakra, up through your heart chakra, up through your throat chakra, and hold your breath for a few seconds then exhale leaves and fruit growing out of both sides of your branches of your throat chakra.

18. Inhale from the ends of your roots, up through your feet, up through your root chakra, up through your sacral chakra, up through your solar plexus chakra, up through your heart chakra, up through your throat chakra, up through your mind's eye, and hold your breath for a few seconds. Then, exhale leaves and fruit growing out of both sides of your branches of your crown and imagine branches of fruit and leaves growing up and around like an arch finishing the top of your tree, which is you. Continue to feel your breath reach into heaven.

19. Inhale and exhale fruit and leaves growing out of both sides of your 7 main chakras 3 times or more until you feel fruitful, rejuvenated, and at peace.

Or you can repeat steps 1-18, then, step 19. (Please note you can use this technique using a crystal(s) in your non-dominant hand or both hands. However, you feel led by the spirit. You can also do this exercise without the use of crystals

in order to clear your chakras of any negative energies. It kind of reminds you of recycling.

To deep clean your chakras and gateways with the use of 1 Crystal

Estimated time 30 - 35 Min

repeat steps 1-18 7 times, then add step 19.

Yota Meditation Technique #1"Tree Method" with the use of 1 Crystal
Estimated Time 3 to 5 Minutes

This is the same method, but you just choose 1 crystal you are led to use. Hold it in your non-dominant hand with your hands open-faced upward resting on your thighs. If you are standing, just have your arms resting with your forearms bent with your hands open facing up. Do steps 1-19

Yota Meditation Technique #1 "Tree Method" To deep clean your chakras and gateways with the use of 1 crystal or more

Estimated Time 30-35 min.

**See Corresponding Crystals for Each of the 7 Main Chakras (Wheels, Energy Centers, Gateways) **

Repeat Steps 1-18, 7 times then, Step 19. If you are in standing position Hold it in your non-dominant hand with your hands open-faced upward resting on your thighs. If you are standing just have your arms resting with your forearms bent with your hands open facing up

Yota Meditation Technique #1 "Tree Method" with the use of 7 Corresponding crystals for each chakra
Estimated Time 30-40 min.

Repeat Steps 1-18, 7 times, then step 19. Each time use the corresponding crystals for each chakra starting with the corresponding crystal of the crown chakra which is Amethyst, and use for all the chakras for steps 1-18, Then find the corresponding crystal for the mind's eye, which is lapis lazuli for the second time around for steps 1-18 and repeat with each corresponding crystal on down, once you get to the 7th time, add step 19.

Estimated Time 30-40 min.

Corresponding Crystal for Each of the 7 Main Chakras (Wheels, Energy Centers, Gateways)

Crown Chakra: *Corresponding Crystals = Purple Crystals and White Clear crystals: Amethyst, Charoite, Clear Quartz, Lepidolite, Rutilated Quartz, Selenite*

Note: B, Frequency = 480HZ, Aura Layer = Ketheric Body

Third Eye Chakra: Corresponding Crystals: *Lapis Lazuli, Sodalite, Sapphire Iolite, Tanzanite, Dumortierite, Blue Kyanite, Blue Quartz,*

Note: A, Frequency = 426.7HZ, Aura Layer = Celestial Body

Throat Chakra: Corresponding Crystals: *Sodalite, Lapis Lazuli, Dumortierite, Blue Kyanite, Blue Quartz, Blue Apatite, Chrysocolla, Angelite, Celestite, Blue Lace Agate*

Note: G, Frequency = 384HZ, Aura Layer = Etheric Template

Heart Chakra: Corresponding Crystals: *Rose Quartz, Green Aventurine, Jade, Malachite, Peridot, Rhodochrosite, Rhodonite*

Note: F, Frequency = 341.3HZ, Aura Layer = Astral Body

Solar Plexus Chakra: *Corresponding Crystals: Citrine, Golden*

Tigers Eye, Imperial Topaz, Golden Calcite, Yellow Calcite

Note: E, Frequency = 320HZ, Aura Layer = Mental Body

Sacral Chakra: Corresponding Crystals: *Carnelian, Orange Calcite, Peach Selenite, Amber, Apricot Botswana Agate, Fire Agate*

Note: D, Frequency = 288HZ, Aura Layer = Emotional Body

Root/Base Chakra: Corresponding Crystals: *Red Jasper, Black Tourmaline, Garnet, Ruby, Hematite, Petrified Wood, Black Onyx*

Note: C, Frequency = 256HZ, Aura Layer = Etheric Body

Yota Meditation "Walking Trees" Based Off Mark 8:22-25 (KJV).

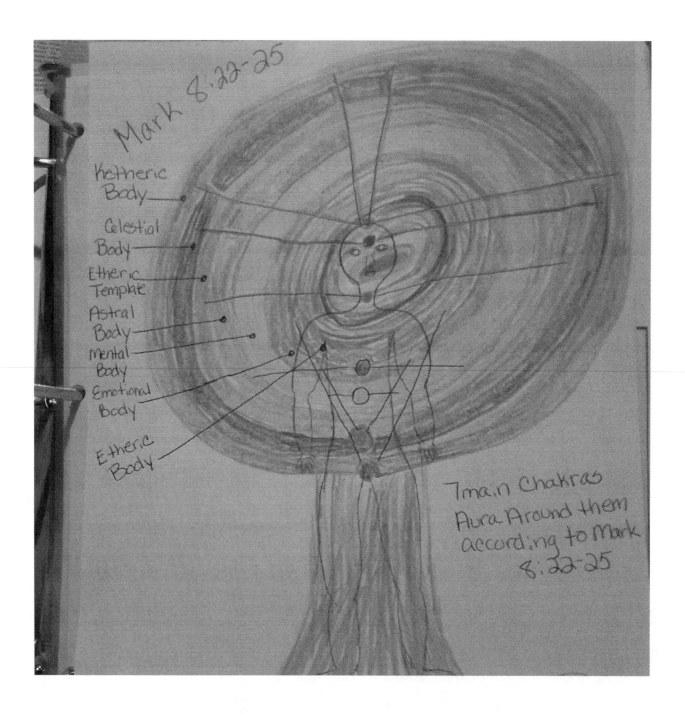

22 And they came to Bethsaida. And some people brought to him a blind man and begged him to touch him. 23 And he took the blind man by the hand and led him out of the village, and when he had spit on his eyes and laid his hands on him, he asked him, "Do you see anything?" 24 And he looked up and said, "I see people, but they look like trees, walking." 25 Then Jesus[c] laid his hands on his eyes again; and he opened his eyes, his sight was restored, and he saw everything clearly. Mark 8:22-25 (KJV)

We can have a healthy aura or an unhealthy aura which have openings and dull colors in it. That's why it is vital that we breathe in and breathe out of the chakras (wheels). I just want you to do the previous exercise so you can see the circle shape that appears around your 7 main chakras.

1. Go and stand in front of a mirror, preferably a dresser mirror. Get a measuring tape and measure your arms from your shoulder down to the tip of your finger of your most extended finger, and split them into 7 sections. Each one corresponding with each chakra going down, starting with the crown chakra, and the furthest section of your aura correlates with the crown chakra, which is the color violet. And as you go down, your chakras, their colors extend to the next furthest color of your aura until it comes close to the outside layer of your aura around your skin.

*2. Continue to stand in front of the same mirror, and inhale, while bringing your arms up straight, hands together, hold your breath for a few seconds. Now, exhale with your arms and hands still extended out, and bring them around, out all the way down to your thighs, do this three times this should be a shape of a circle around your upper body, and around your 7 main chakras. This is your aura around your body, which the blind man seen first in the spirit. Even though you don't see the aura, or you may see the aura. This is what the blind man saw the first time he started to see, which is the spiritual, and this is the aura he saw on each individual. The rest of the thighs and feet was the stump. The next time the man looked, he didn't see with the spiritual, he saw in the physical, which is his physical sight. And this is the fulfillment and the revelation of **Mark 8:22-25 (KJV).** The lower thighs of the men on down was the trunk of the tree he saw.*

Yota Meditation Technique #2 "Walking Trees" based off of Mark 8:22-25 (KJV)

Yota Meditation Technique #2 "Walking Trees" based off of Mark 8:22-25 (KJV) without the use of crystals.

Estimated Time 5-10 Min

Before each exercise, rub your hands together for 30 seconds or more till they get hot, Now, open your hands, you should feel a tingling sensation, or electricity, that's energy flowing through your hands. *

<u>1.</u> Go stand in front of a mirror, preferably your dresser mirror. Or you can sit and imagine this. Hold your arms up, extended up towards heaven with your hands closed over your crown chakra. I want you to imagine the color purple coming down through a golden circle above your head. Open your hands parallel to the sides of your face and inhale and see the color purple through your crown chakra and hold your breath for a few seconds, then exhale the color purple being extended out roundabout in the circle that you see in the mirror filling your body while your hands are still extended out towards the heavens. See your circle filled with purple.

2. Now I want you to spread your hands out and down a little further to be parallel to your mind's eye. And again, imagine seeing a golden circle above your head and inhale, and see the color energy indigo, going down through your crown chakra, through your third eye chakra, and hold your breath for a few seconds, and exhale the color indigo, filling the circle to the next aura layer you measured, which is called the celestial body.

3. Now I want you to spread your hands out and down a little further to be parallel to your throat chakra. Again, imagine seeing a golden circle above your head and inhale and see the color energy of light blue going down through your crown chakra, through your third eye, through your throat chakra, and hold your breath for a few seconds and exhale the color light blue filling the circle to the next aura layer you measured which is called the etheric template.

4. Now I want you to spread your hands out and down a little further to be parallel to your heart chakra. Again, imagine seeing a golden circle above your head, and inhale, and see the color energy of green going down through your crown chakra, through your third eye chakra, through your throat chakra, through your heart chakra, and hold your breath for a few seconds. Now, exhale the color green filling the circle to the next aura layer you measured, which is called the astral body.

5. Now I want you to spread your hands out and down a little further to be parallel to your solar plexus chakra. Again, imagine seeing a golden circle above your head, and inhale and see the color energy of yellow down through your crown chakra, through your third eye chakra, through your throat chakra, through your heart chakra, through your solar plexus chakra, and hold your breath for a few seconds, and exhale the color yellow, filling the circle to the next aura layer you measured, which is called the mental body.

6. Now I want you to spread your hands out and down a little further to be parallel to your sacral chakra. Again, imagine seeing a golden circle above your head and

inhale and see the color energy of orange seen through your crown chakra, through your third eye, through your throat chakra, through your heart chakra, through your solar plexus chakra, through your sacral chakra, and hold your breath for a few seconds. Now exhale the color orange, filling the circle to the next aura layer you measured, which is called the emotional body.

7. Now I want you to spread your hands out a little further down, straight down to your thighs, so your hands can be where the root chakra is. Again, imagine seeing a golden circle above your head and inhale and see the color energy of red down through your crown chakra, through your third eye, through your throat chakra, through your heart chakra, through your solar plexus, through your sacral chakra, through your root/base chakra and hold your breath for a few seconds. Now exhale the color red, filling the circle to the next aura layer you measured, which is called the etheric body, which outlines our body.

8. Now with both hands laid down flat on both sides of your thighs. I want you to imagine seeing a golden circle above your head and inhale and see the color energy of all the colors go down through your crown chakra, through your third eye chakra, through your throat chakra, through your heart chakra, through your solar plexus, through your sacral chakra, through your root/base chakra, and hold your breath for a few seconds. Now exhale all the energies of colors of the rainbow going down through the trunk, down through the roots.

9. And repeat starting at roots back up again with the same colors but in the opposite order going up each chakra through the crown.

You can repeat this as many times as you like. Till you feel at peace, rejuvenated, and refreshed.

Yota Meditation Technique #2 "Walking Trees" based off of Mark 8:22-25 (KJV). with the use of crystals.

See Corresponding Crystals for Each of the 7 Main Chakras (Wheels, Energy Centers, Gateways)

You can place each corresponding crystal of each chakra in your pocket, or you can where a chakra necklace with each corresponding gemstones or gemstone beads of each chakra. You can repeat steps 1-9 as many times as you would like.

Corresponding Crystal for Each of the 7 Main Chakras (Wheels, Energy Centers, Gateways)

Crown Chakra: Corresponding Crystals = Purple Crystals and White Clear crystals: Amethyst, Charoite, Clear Quartz, Lepidolite, Rutilated Quartz, Selenite

Note: B, Frequency = 480HZ, Aura Layer = Ketheric Body

Third Eye Chakra: Corresponding Crystals: *Lapis Lazuli, Sodalite, Sapphire Iolite, Tanzanite, Dumortierite, Blue Kyanite, Blue Quartz,*

Note: A, Frequency = 426.7HZ, Aura Layer = Celestial Body

Throat Chakra: Corresponding Crystals: *Sodalite, Lapis Lazuli, Dumortierite, Blue Kyanite, Blue Quartz, Blue Apatite, Chrysocolla, Angelite, Celestite, Blue Lace Agate*

Note: G, Frequency = 384HZ, Aura Layer = Etheric Template

Heart Chakra: Corresponding Crystals: *Rose Quartz, Green Aventurine, Jade, Malachite, Peridot, Rhodochrosite, Rhodonite*

Note: F, Frequency = 341.3HZ, Aura Layer = Astral Body

Solar Plexus Chakra: *Corresponding Crystals: Citrine, Golden Tigers Eye, Imperial Topaz, Golden Calcite, Yellow Calcite*

Note: E, Frequency = 320HZ, Aura Layer = Mental Body

Sacral Chakra: Corresponding Crystals: *Carnelian, Orange Calcite, Peach Selenite, Amber, Apricot Botswana Agate, Fire Agate*

Note: D, Frequency = 288HZ, Aura Layer = Emotional Body

Root/Base Chakra: Corresponding Crystals: *Red Jasper, Black Tourmaline, Garnet, Ruby, Hematite, Petrified Wood, Black Onyx*

Note: C, Frequency = 256HZ, Aura Layer = Etheric Body

Yota Meditation Technique # 3 "Cactus"

Yota Meditation Technique # 3 "Cactus" - without the use of crystals.
Estimated time: 3 to 5 min

Before this exercise, rub your hands together for 30 seconds or more, till they get hot, Now open your hands, you should feel a tingling sensation, or electricity, that's energy flowing through your hands. *

1. Sit Indian style, or you can sit in a chair with your feet flat. Stand on the floor, with hands opened up on your lap. Or you can stand with hands to your sides. Breathe in (all the while breath is in me the spirit of the Lord is in my nostrils) and hold it for a couple of seconds, then breathe out any negative thoughts, feelings, frustrations, distractions, anger, etc. Repeat this method 3 or 4 times.

2. Tap your thymus a couple of times.

3. Inhale through the golden circle of light, down through the crown chakra, and exhale, imagining spikes coming out of all sides and throughout the crown chakra, outside the body, this is the crown and the top of the oval shield.

4. Inhale through the crown chakra, down to the 3rd eye, and hold it for a few seconds at the 3rd eye, and exhale (spines) spikes, coming out of all sides, and throughout the 3rd eye to outside your body roundabout.

5. Inhale through the crown chakra, down through the 3rd eye, down through the throat chakra, and hold it for a few seconds, at the throat chakra and exhale imagining spines (spikes) coming out of all sides and throughout the throat chakra to outside your body roundabout.

6. Inhale through the crown chakra, through the 3rd eye chakra, through the throat chakra, through the heart chakra, hold your breath for a couple of seconds at the heart chakra, and excel imagining spines (spikes) coming out of all sides and throughout the heart chakra, throughout the outside of your body roundabout.

7. Inhale through the crown chakra, through the third eye chakra, through the throat chakra, through the heart chakra, through the solar plexus chakra, and hold your breath for a few seconds at the solar plexus chakra, and exhale, imagining (spines) spikes coming out of all sides, and throughout the solar plexus, to outside your body roundabout.

8. Inhale through the crown chakra, through the third eye chakra, through the throat chakra, through the heart chakra, through the solar plexus, and through the sacral chakra, hold your breath for a few seconds at the sacral chakra, and exhale imagining (spines) spikes coming out of all sides, and throughout the sacral chakra, to outside your body roundabout.

9. Inhale through the crown chakra, through the third eye, through the throat chakra, through the heart chakra, through the solar plexus, and through the sacral chakra, through the root chakra, hold your breath for a few seconds at the root chakra, and exhale imagining (spines) spikes coming out of all sides and throughout of the root chakra to outside your body roundabout.

10. Inhale through the crown chakra, through the third eye, through the throat chakra, through the heart chakra, through the solar plexus, and through the sacral chakra, through the root chakra, hold your breath for a few seconds at the root chakra, exhale out imagining the root chakra turning into the trunk (hips and legs)of the tree, down to the feet with roots spreading out of the feet down into the earth.

11. Inhale through the crown chakra, through the third eye, through the throat chakra, through the heart chakra, through the solar plexus, and through the sacral chakra, through the root chakra, hold your breath for as long as you can at the root, and exhale firmly as you feel the energy intensify going through the branches of each chakra, quickly going down through the trunk(hips and legs) through the roots that form in the feet that spread wide down into the ground quickly and very deep.

(Please note: It might feel like a vibration shock wave going down your body. In some cases, it may feel like an intense rush energy.

12. Now imagine inhaling from the ends of your roots, up through your feet, up through your root chakra, and hold your breath for a few seconds. Then, exhale spines (spikes) coming out of all sides of your root chakra towards the outside of your body.

13. Inhale from the ends of yours roots, up through the feet to the root chakra, up through your sacral chakra, and hold your breath for a few seconds. Then, exhale spines (Spikes) coming out of all sides of your sacral chakra to outside your body roundabout.

14. Inhale from the ends of your roots up through your feet, up through the root chakra, up through your sacral chakra up, up through your solar plexus, and hold your breath for a few seconds. Then, exhale more spines (Spikes) coming out of all the sides and throughout your solar plexus to outside your body roundabout.

15. Inhale from the ends of your roots up through your feet, up through your root chakra, up through the sacral chakra, up through your solar plexus, up through your heart chakra, and hold your breath for a few seconds and exhale more spines (Spikes) coming out of all sides throughout your heart chakra to outside the body roundabout.

16. Inhale from the ends of yours root up through your feet, up through the root chakra, up through the sacral chakra, up through the solar plexus, up through your heart chakra and hold your breath for a few seconds then exhale spines (Spikes) coming out of all sides throughout your heart chakra to outside your body roundabout.

17. Inhale from the ends of your roots, up through your feet, up through your root chakra, up through your sacral chakra, up through your solar plexus chakra, up through your heart chakra, up through your throat chakra, and hold your breath for a few seconds then exhale spine (spikes) coming out of all sides throughout of your throat chakra to outside your body roundabout.

18. Inhale from the ends of your roots, up through your feet, up through your root chakra, up through your sacral chakra, up through your solar plexus chakra, up through your heart chakra, up through your throat chakra, up through your mind's eye, and hold your breath for a few seconds. Then, exhale spines (spikes) coming out of all sides and throughout the crown chakra roundabout and around like an arch finishing the top of your oval shield. Continue to feel your breath reach into heaven.

19. Inhale and exhale spines (spikes) coming out of all sides throughout of your 7 main chakras 3 times or more until you feel fruitful, and rejuvenated, and at

peace. **Or you can repeat steps 1-18 as many times as you would like, then, apply step 19**

You can also use this exercise by the uses of the tree branches in Yota Meditation Technique #1

***Please note the use of crystals for Cactus Yota meditation is below:

*******Step 20. This step is to be used with the crystals*******

20. Hold all the corresponding crystals in your dominant hand and imagine a white light surrounding them and inhale seeing a white glow around the crystals and as you exhale, see that white light turn into a shimmering golden light sealing your aura for protection.

Yota Meditation Technique #3 "Cactus" with the use of 1 Crystal
This is the same method, but you just choose 1 crystal you are led to use. Hold it in your non-dominant hand with your hands open-faced upward resting on your thighs. If you are standing, just have your arms resting with your forearms bent with your hands open facing up. **Do steps 1-20**

 Estimated Time: *3 to 5 Minutes*

Yota Meditation Technique #3 "Cactus" To deep clean your chakras and gateways with the use of 1 Crystal or more.
Estimated Time: 30-35 min.

**See Corresponding Crystals for Each of the 7 Main Chakra (Wheels, Energy Centers, Gateways) **

Repeat Steps 1-18, 7 times, then apply steps 19 and 20. *If you are in standing position Hold it in your non-dominant hand with your hands open-faced upward resting on your thighs. If you are standing, just have your arms resting with your forearms bent with your hands open facing up.* **Estimated Time:** *30-35 min.*

Cactus Yota Meditation Technique #3 with the use of 7 Corresponding crystals for each chakra

Estimated Time 30-40 min

Repeat Steps 1-18, 7 times, then steps 19 and 20. *Each time use the corresponding crystals for each chakra starting with the corresponding crystal of the crown chakra which is Amethyst, and use for all the chakras for steps 1-18, Then find the next corresponding crystal for the third eye, which is lapis lazuli for the second time around for steps 1-18 and repeat with each corresponding crystal on down that was shown earlier on a previous page),* **once you get to the 7th time, then add steps 19 and 20**.

Corresponding Crystals for Each of the 7 Main Chakras (Wheels, Energy Centers, Gateways)

Crown Chakra: *Corresponding Crystals = Purple Crystals and White Clear crystals: Amethyst, Charoite, Clear Quartz, Lepidolite, Rutilated Quartz, Selenite*

Note: B, Frequency = 480HZ, Aura Layer = Ketheric Body

Third Eye Chakra: Corresponding Crystals: *Lapis Lazuli, Sodalite, Sapphire Iolite, Tanzanite, Dumortierite, Blue Kyanite, Blue Quartz,*

Note: A, Frequency = 426.7HZ, Aura Layer = Celestial Body

Throat Chakra: Corresponding Crystals: *Sodalite, Lapis Lazuli, Dumortierite, Blue Kyanite, Blue Quartz, Blue Apatite, Chrysocolla, Angelite, Celestite, Blue Lace Agate*

Note: G, Frequency = 384HZ, Aura Layer = Etheric Template

Heart Chakra: Corresponding Crystals: *Rose Quartz, Green Aventurine, Jade, Malachite, Peridot, Rhodochrosite, Rhodonite*

Note: F, Frequency = 341.3HZ, Aura Layer = Astral Body

Solar Plexus Chakra: *Corresponding Crystals: Citrine, Golden Tigers Eye, Imperial Topaz, Golden Calcite, Yellow Calcite*

Note: E, Frequency = 320HZ, Aura Layer = Mental Body

Sacral Chakra: Corresponding Crystals: *Carnelian, Orange Calcite, Peach Selenite, Amber, Apricot Botswana Agate, Fire Agate*

Note: D, Frequency = 288HZ, Aura Layer = Emotional Body

Root/Base Chakra: Corresponding Crystals: *Red Jasper, Black Tourmaline, Garnet, Ruby, Hematite, Petrified Wood, Black Onyx*

Note: C, Frequency = 256HZ, Aura Layer = Etheric Body

Chapter 12: Similarities of Crystals

Christ the Rock and the Crystals

Christ	*Crystals/Stones/Rocks*
Christ - Ministers to us, guides us, teaches us, and gives the word of who he is himself and which way to go; and gives insight and help guide us in the way that we should go.Ps.32:8 (KJV) I will instruct you and teach you in the way you should go, I will counsel you with my loving eye on you.	*Crystals - Ministers to us, guides us, teaches us, and gives the word of the Trinity (Father, Son, and Holy Spirit), and gives insight and help guide us in the way that we should go.(Job 12:8 (KJV)) Or speak to the earth, and it will instruct you..* *"Go through, go through the gates; prepare ye the way of the people; cast, cast up the highway; gather out the stones; lift up a standard for the people."* *Isaiah 62:10 (KJV)*
Christ - God's Greatest Gift (John 3:16) to creation	*Crystals - God's Treasure to Creation*
Christ - Chief cornerstone rejected	*Crystals - Many people reject crystals because of people using them for evil purposes versus good purposes, and lacks the knowledge that crystals have health benefits, spiritual benefits, and helps you spiritually, mentally, and emotionally, physically, They also protects your home from negative energy (demonic spirits) if you place crystals in the four corners of your house, depending on crystals you use." For example, black tourmaline and selenite protects from negative spirits altogether, or black onyx and selenite protects your house from harmful spirits and from crime. My people are destroyed because of lack of knowledge" (Hosea 4:6 KJV)*

Christ - Gives grace to us to do those things we couldn't (spiritually, mentally, and emotionally, and physically)	*Crystals - Give us and creation grace to do those things we want to do for the better (spiritually, mentally, and emotionally, and physically).*
Christ - Increase Fruitfulness (Love, joy, peace, patience, kindness, goodness, faithfulness, gentleness and self-control, etc. (Galatians 5:22-23 KJV)	*Crystals - Increase Fruitfulness (Love, joy, peace, patience, kindness, goodness, faithfulness, and self-control, etc. (Galatians 5:22-23 KJV)*
Christ is Perfect Spiritually, Mentally, and Emotionally (Deut.32:4 NIV) He is the Rock, he is perfect, his works are perfect, and all his ways are just.	*Crystals - Have perfect molecular Structure that gives off excellent vibrations, frequencies, energies of Christ through the neurons in our body to bring forth fruitfulness, discernment between right and wrong, and imparts just ways.*
Christ Mediator and door to the Father	*Crystals - Mediator through Christ between the Soul and the Spirit working in conjunction together to bring fruitfulness and perfection in a person, Be Ye Perfect as my Father in Heaven is perfect.*
Christ - Heal Physically, Mentally, and Emotionally, Spiritually	*Crystals - Heal Physically, Mentally, and Emotionally, Spiritually*
Christ - Removes distractions and keep you focused on the things you need to be focused on day to day	*Crystals - Removes distractions and keep you focused on the things you need to be focused on day today*

Christ - Deliverance - Luke 8:45-48 And Jesus said, Who touched me? When all denied, Peter and they that were with him said, Master the multitude throng thee and press thee, and sayest thou, Who touched me?And Jesus said Somebody hath touched me: for I perceive that virtue is gone out of me. And when the woman saw that she was not hid, she come trembling, and falling down before him, she declared unto him before all the people for the reason she had touched him and she was healed immediately. And he said unto her, Daughter, be of good comfort: thy faith hath made thee whole: go in peace.	*Crystals - Brings Deliverance through Christ Removes the negative things and imparts the positive things we need in our Electromagnetic field/aura through entrainment. Each crystal has a perfect repetitive molecular structure within them that is different from other crystals. For example, if you are a person who gets stressed or tensed a lot then Amethyst, Howlite, Rose Quartz, or Black Tourmaline, would be excellent because it relieves stress and can help calm you down instantaneously by working with your aura/electromagnetic fields. However, Amethyst, Howlite, Rose Quartz, and Black Tourmaline each have a different molecular structure even though they relieve stress and calm you down.*

Christ - Manifestation - Manifest your request through prayer, petition, declaration, meditation, intention, or communication. *Matt. 4:3 [3] And when the tempter came to him, he said, if thou be the Son of God, command that these stones be made bread. (Mark 11:23 (KJV)) For Verily I Say unto you, That whosoever shall say unto this mountain, Be thou removed and be thou cast into the sea; and shall not doubt in his heart, but believe those things shall come to pass, he shall have whatsoever he saith.*	*Crystals - Get things in order that is requested in your life that you need help with during prayer or meditation, or communication (Mark 11:23KJV)(Number 20:8-12KJV) Take the rod, and gather thou the assembly together, thou, and Aaron thy brother, and speak ye unto the rock before their eyes, and it shall give forth his water, and thou, shalt bring forth to them water out of the rock: so thou shalt give the congregation and their beasts drink. And Moses lifted up his hand, and with his rod he smote the rock twice: and the water came out abundantly, and the congregation drank and the beast also. And the LORD spake unto Moses and Aaron, because ye believed me not, to sanctify me in in the eyes of the children of Israel, therefore ye shall not bring this congregation into the land which I had given him.*
Christ - Manifestation (shape-shifted and disappeared, in and out of Dimensions) John 8:59 King James Version (KJV) *"Then took they up stones to cast at him: but Jesus hid himself, and went out of the temple, going through the midst of them, and so passed by."*	*Crystals - Gemstones disappear and come back to release more information or go back into other dimensions and returns. Or if you have finally manifested what the Father wanted you to bring forth, which is their vibration and frequency. Then, there is no longer use for them. They can disappear and appear maybe to*

	someone else who have need of it. They are supernatural.
Christ - Restores all the enemy stolen (Breaks Curses, corrupt and useless habits, evil soul ties, and blesses you.	*Crystals - Removes negative energy and imparts positive energy. Breaks curses, bad and useless habits, bad soul ties, and blesses you.*
Christ - Gives rivers of living. (John 4:13, 14 (KJV)) ¹³ *Jesus answered and said unto her, Whosoever drinketh of this water shall thirst again:* ¹⁴ *But whosoever drinketh of the water that I shall give him shall never thirst; but the water that I shall give him shall be in him a well of water springing up into everlasting life.* *(Ezek. 47:8) This water flows toward the eastern region, goes down into the valley, and enters the sea. When it reaches the sea, its waters are healed, and it shall be that every living thing that moves, wherever the rivers go will live. There will be a very great multitude of fish because the waters go there: for they will be healed, and everything will live wherever the river goes.*	*Crystals - Elixirs- healing water through its minerals of the crystals that are quartz or approved stones or crystals for elixirs (indirect method preferred use of making crystal elixirs) (Numbers 20:11) And Moses lifted up his hand, and with his rod he smote the rock twice: and the water came out abundantly, and the congregation drank and the beast also. They all ate the same spiritual food and drank the same spiritual drink; for they drank from the spiritual rock that accompanied them, and that Rock was Christ.1 Cor 10:3-5 NIV* *For Example: While writing the book When I found out that Moses lost going to the promised land because he didn't tell water to come out of the rock like the Father told him to through obedience. I spoke to my black tourmaline and said, "Black Tourmaline, I want water to come out. I'm thinking to myself it's not going to work." So, nothing happened but then my lips*

	got tight and my throat starting to drink water in the spirit even though I didn't see it, I drank from it spiritually and got drunk in the Holy Ghost. Laughter and joy-filled my belly, the more and more I drank from the living water flowing through Black Tourmaline. Shungite stone cleanses and purifies water. (I suggest using a tumbled Shungite stone within the water)
Christ - Jesus took our infirmities and bare our sickness (Matt 8:17) That it might be fulfilled which was spoken by Esaias the prophet, saying, himself took our infirmities, and bare our sicknesses so that we may be healed and whole.	Crystals - Take our infirmities and sicknesses and help treat or cure sickness through crystal therapy, so that we can be healed and whole.
Christ - Increases your spiritual gifts	Crystals - Increases your spiritual gifts
Christ - Births forth and increase the prophetic gift	Crystals - Birth forth and increase the prophetic gift
Christ - Birth forth and increase your talents	Crystals - Birth forth and increases your talents
Christ - Gives Peace to all creation because he is God all by himself, and all things consist and exist; without him, they can't function or operate.	Crystals - Give Peace to all creation that they need by the different facets, characteristics, attributes, and functions of the crystal
Christ - Protects all things	Crystals - Protects

Christ - Imparts Strength	Crystals - Psalm 62:7 In God is my salvation and my glory: the rock of my strength, and my refuge, is in God

Angels and Crystals Similarities

Angels	**Crystals**
Angels - Ministers the word of the Lord	Crystals - Ministers the word of the Lord (Job 12:8 (KJV), Matt. 3:9)
Angels - Heal, set free, and deliver	Crystals - heal, set free, and deliver
Angels - Gives strength	Crystals - Imparts strength
Angels - Gives Messages	Crystals - Gives Messages
Angels - Fights on our behalf	Crystals - Fights on our Behalf- Song 4:4 Your neck is like the tower of David, built with courses of stone, on it hang a thousand shields(shield of protection from crystals),all of them shields of warrior (crystal being warriors on our behalf to fight the enemy, with the power God gave to them to execute)(Is.33:15-16 (KJV))

Angels - helps you to shapeshift, go through dimensions, transport you from one place to another (astral projection or out body experiences), transports you in and out of dimensions.	*Crystals - Helps you to shapeshift, go through dimensions, transport you from one place to another (astral projection or out of body experiences), transports you in and out of dimensions.*

Crystals are Love

<u>Crystals are Love because Christ Himself is Love</u>

Let others know about the Father's heart, and Jesus love for them by gifting them with a crystal as a gift. For example, if you know someone is suffering from nightmares, insomnia, or stress, tell them, "Here is a gift of the Father from me to you, here's an amethyst which reflects who Christ is. And you tell them the benefits of amethyst, and how its beneficial for them to sleep, and be at peace and rest, along with its other benefits. Or you can purchase a necklace for them to protect their aura and thoughts from negativity or influences of the enemy, and to guard their heart. If they are having a hard time loving themselves or forgiving others, you can purchase for them stones of love. Or you can buy them a carved crystal heart to represent the Father's Love for them and Christ love for them.

Sincere love is my prayer that I and all may become, sincere love, is "Christ the Rock." Not love works because we think we may be rewarded from showing an outward love, but may we birth the genuine, sincere attributes and characteristics of each crystal we may possess and reap their benefits of the Father's gift to us. As we work together as one. May we birth forth the love, joy, peace, patience, kindness, goodness, faithfulness, and self-control. Which is what the different stones work to accomplish in our lives and all creations because they reflect Christ himself.

Purchase the book for someone else who needs to know about crystals in the Word of God and why Christ Calls himself the rock. Crystals birth for the promises of God and birth forth who we truly to be if work in alignment with them through faith in order for you to be a better you. They help to break you out of bondage, or our negative ways of thinking, they are love.

You may purchase some of these gifts at www.crystalkingdomrocks.com or www.spreadingjesusrocks.com

Crystals are Love

Chapter 13: How to Cleanse, Program (Make a covenant with them), and Activate Crystals.

"For you will have a covenant with the stones of the field, and the wild animals will be at peace with you. "Job 5:23 NIV

Caution: Some crystals are harmful, so make sure you read about them before you use them, especially if you are going to use them for an elixir to bring healing to your body. Indirect methods of making crystal elixirs are best

1. Running water

Water neutralize any negative energy stored inside the crystal or gemstone and return it back to the earth. You can use your regular faucet water. But it's best to use natural spring water because it is natural with no added chemicals. Pat dry when complete.

Approximate time: 1 minute per crystal

Use this for quartz stones or hard stones **do not use with stones that end with ite like selenite, angelite, kyanite, tanzanite, etc. these are soft stones. Or that may be brittle like kyanite or breakable. You can do research on the ones not to run in water.**

2. Himalayan Salt

You can submerge your crystal in Himalayan Sea Salt overnight. Then you can rinse it off in water weather faucet or spring water. Then you can pat dry crystal.

Approximate time: Anywhere from 6 to 48 hours

3. Saltwater

Salt has been used throughout history to absorb unwanted energy and banish negativity.

If you're near the ocean, consider collecting a bowl of fresh saltwater. Otherwise, mix a tablespoon of sea, rock, or table salt into a bowl of water.

Make sure that your stone is completely submerged and allow it to soak for a few hours to a few days' time. Rinse and pat dry when complete.

Approximate time: up to 48 hours

Use this method for hard stones, such as like clear quartz, amethyst, rose quartz, etc. You can use this for hard stones as well **do not use with stones that are soft or end with ite like selenite, angelite, kyanite, tanzanite, etc. These are soft stones. Or chalky, brittle kyanite, or breakable. You can do research on the ones not to run in water.**

4. Brown Rice

This method can also be used to draw out negativity in a safe and contained setting. It's especially beneficial for protective stones, such as black tourmaline, black obsidian, jet, amethyst, etc.

To do this, fill a bowl with dry brown rice and bury your stone beneath the grains. Dispose of the rice immediately after cleansing, as the rice is said to have absorbed the energy you're trying to eradicate.

Approximate time: few hours to 24 hours - This method can be used on any stone

5. Natural light

Although ritual cleansing is often centered around specific points in the solar or lunar cycle, you can set your stone out at any time to cleanse and recharge.

Set your stone out before nightfall and plan to bring it in before 11 a.m. This will allow your stone to bathe in the light of both the moon and sun.

Prolonged exposure to direct sunlight may weather the stone's surface, so make sure you return for it in the morning.

If you're able to place your stone directly on the earth. This will allow for further cleansing. Wherever they are, ensure they won't be disturbed by wildlife or passersby.

Afterward, give the stone a quick rinse to remove any dirt and debris. Pat dry.

Approximate time: 10 to 12 hours.

This method can be used on most tumbled stones

Don't use this for vibrant stones, such as amethyst, in sunlight, soft stones, such as celestite, halite, and selenite, that may be damaged by inclement weather.

6. Beans

You can put them in uncooked beans for a few hours to be cleansed. Then throw away the beans because it holds negative energy

7. Incense or Sage

You can use incense smoke, palo santo sticks, or sage to cleanse your stone in order to remove any imbalances or negative energy within the stone.

When you're ready, light the tip of the incense of your choice (incense sticks, palo santo sticks, sage, etc.) with the flame. Transfer the sage or incense stick to your nondominant hand and firmly hold stone and move it through the smoke for about 30 seconds. If you sense the stone still is heavy or need cleansing, you can cleanse it for a minute instead.

Approximate time: about 30 to 60 seconds per stone. This method can be used on any stone

8. Sounds

Different notes can cleanse and charge the crystals, and you can use singing bowls, keyboard, or a tuning fork. You can also sing to the crystal.

This can be accomplished singing, a tuning fork, keyboard, any musical instrument next to the crystal. It doesn't matter what key the sound is, as long as the sound emitted is loud enough for the vibration to consume the stone.

**Some people place one crystal within the singing bowl and use the sounds of the singing bowl to cleanse it as well and to charge it because of the vibrations released.

Approximate time 5 to 10 minutes. This method can be used on any stone

9. Use a large stone

Large quartz clusters, amethyst geodes, and selenite slabs can be great tools for clearing smaller stones.

Place your stone directly inside or on top of any of these stones. The larger stone's vibrations remove the negative energies and imbalances energies found within the stone.

Approximate duration: 6 to 24hours. This method can be used on any stone

10. Using Selenite Sticks

Selenite Sticks are high vibrational stone, and it cleanses other crystals and doesn't have to be cleansed; however, I still clear it sometimes through incense so it can be more productive. Besides, they are alive beings either way. But just how the angels need strength through prayer, singing, and the word of God. So do the selenite and crystals because they are alive beings themselves. Just how we need rest, they need rest too sometimes.

"a time to scatter stones and a time to gather them, a time to embrace and a time to refrain from embracing," Ecclesiastes 3:5 NIV

Approximate duration: couple of hours to 24 hours. This method can be used on any stone

11. Visualization

Take a few minutes to ground and center your energy, then pick up your stone and visualize your hands filling with white, radiant light.

See this light surround the stone and feel it growing brighter in your hands. See all the imbalances coming into alignment. Envision the impurities flushing out of the stone, allowing the stone to shine brighter and brighter as it is thoroughly purified.

Continue this visualization until you feel a shift in the stone's energy. Approximate time is :1 minute for each stone

12. Prayer can be on your number one list as well

Hold your hands over the crystals, and ask the Father, and the angelic host to cleanse the crystals of any negative energy, imbalances, any demonic spirits, or demonic influences that may have tried to attach itself to the stone. You should not be afraid of any crystal or negative energy or demonic spirits, you have authority to speak, and they have to go. You subdue them through your words.

My day to day prayer to consecrate and cleanse them is:

Father, I thank you for **name a crystal,** one of the treasures of your heart Father God. I pray that you will cleanse and purify and sanctify amethyst in Jesus name. I ask that you remove any imbalances, any old programming, or covenants this crystal has had with the previous owners or entities that I may not know of. I pray that you will remove all negative energies, or negative influences, or demonic spirits that may have attached itself to the crystal, in Jesus name. I ask you remove any negative technology in the realm of the spirit that I may not know of that is attached to it right now in Jesus name. I pray that any evil spell or incantations that has been prayed over this crystal or crystals be broken now in Jesus name. I pray that the anointing and the frequencies and vibrations of the Father, the Son, and the Holy Ghost restores this crystal(s) back to The Fathers original intent and purposes he had for it since the beginning of time. Jesus purifying sanctify this crystal in your blood because it is you, your property, through the Father Heart in Jesus name. Amen. Approximate time is 30 seconds or more.

There's no right or wrong way to say this prayer. You don't have to use this prayer; Holy Spirit may lead you to another way to pray over your crystal(s).

13. Himalayan Salt Lamp

You can place the crystals very close around a Himalayan Salt Lamp. It releases negative ions which purifies and remove negative energy from the atmosphere around it.

Duration of time: 3 Days

How to Make a Covenant or Program Your Crystals

Making a covenant with your stone or programming, it is crucial. You do this by setting your intention for your stone or multiple stones. This helps you connect with its energy, frequency, and vibration in order for you to restore your true self and your purpose by having your soul under subjection unto Holy Spirit or your higher self. This helps you to be free from bondage and receive the deliverance you may need or wanted. This helps you to be who the Father originally called, commissioned, and ordained for you to be, by it counteracting any weaknesses, negative thoughts, sin, or things that bring negative consequences in our life.

You may feel comfortable holding the stone in your hand as you meditate or placing it on your third eye (mind's eye). You can also lay down and allow the stone to rest on the corresponding chakras or the area of body that needs your attention.

Visualize the stone's energy becoming one with your own energy. You can also see it as becoming one with you as your armor on your body. Speak to the stone silently or verbally and ask for assistance or tell it what you need to be done, and it will do it according to what the Father sees fit for your life at that time. Thank and acknowledge the stone for its presence because it's alive just like the angels, then spend a few minutes in meditation and prayer with it. And that's your covenant and program with the crystal.

For example, I thank you Amethyst for being the Father's gift to me during this time and season; I ask that you remove stress, anxiety, and anger away. And that I will have peace, I ask that you remove and prevent distractions from me because this is what the Father called, commissioned, and ordained for you to do.

This is what I need assistance from you during this time and season, in Jesus name, amen. Remember the crystals bring heaven down to earth the bind and loose supernaturally.

How to activate the crystal, you can hold it in your hand and silently say be activated, or you can speak to it by name and say you are activated and tell it thank you and thank the Father for his gift to you. You can use a clear quartz to activate it. You can point to the crystal to activate it as well.

Research Resources, Books, Websites, and Credits

The book of Jasher :https://www.sacred-texts.com/chr/apo/jasher/index.htm SALT LAKE CITY: PUBLISHED BY J.H. PARRY & COMPANY1887. Is not this written in the Book of Jasher?" Joshua, 10:13 KJV

The Testament of Reuben, The Forgotten Books of Eden, by Rutherford H. Platt, Jr., [1926], at sacred-texts.com
The Testament of Levi, The Forgotten Books of Eden, by Rutherford H. Platt, Jr., [1926], at sacred-texts.com
The Testament Simeon, The Forgotten Books of Eden, by Rutherford H. Platt, Jr., [1926], at sacred-texts.com
The Testament of Judah, The Forgotten Books of Eden, by Rutherford H. Platt, Jr., [1926], at sacred-texts.com
The Testament of Issachar, The Forgotten Books of Eden, by Rutherford H. Platt, Jr., [1926], at sacred-texts.com
The Testament of Dan, The Forgotten Books of Eden, by Rutherford H. Platt, Jr., [1926], at sacred-texts.com
The Testament of Zebulon, The Forgotten Books of Eden, by Rutherford H. Platt, Jr., [1926], at sacred-texts.com
The Testament of Gad, The Forgotten Books of Eden, by Rutherford H. Platt, Jr., [1926], at sacred-texts.com
The Testament of Asher, The Forgotten Books of Eden, by Rutherford H. Platt, Jr., [1926], at sacred-texts.com
The Testament of Naphtali, The Forgotten Books of Eden, by Rutherford H. Platt, Jr., [1926], at sacred-texts.com
Reubens biblical Reference -https://en.wikipedia.org/wiki/Reuben_(son_of_Jacob)

The Testament of Joseph, The Forgotten Books of Eden, by Rutherford H. Platt, Jr., [1926], at sacred-texts.com

Websites Of information
10 Commandments written on sapphire: -Wikipedia
https://en.wikipedia.org/wiki/Tablets_of_Stone
African Green Garnet - https://ambergemstones.com/blog/african-jade-buddstone
African Green Garnet (African Jade, Grossular Agate) - http://thehealingchest.com/crystals-stones/jade-meaning/
Agate Benefits - http://www.gemstonebuzz.com/meaning/agate
Agate Benefits: https://www.plantshospital.com/benefits-agate-stone/
Agate benefits: https://www.healingwithcrystals.net.au/agate.html
Agate benefits-https://www.charmsoflight.com/agate-healing-properties
Agate benefits- https://www.crystalvaults.com/crystal-encyclopedia/agate
Andradite Garnet Benefits - https://www.crystalvaults.com/crystal-encyclopedia/andradite
Andradite Garnet Benefits - https://www.healingwithcrystals.net.au/garnet.html
Almandine Garnet benefits - https://www.healingwithcrystals.net.au/garnet.html
Amethyst Benefits - https://www.crystalvaults.com/crystal-encyclopedia/amethyst

Amulets Jewish Encyclopedia-http://www.jewishencyclopedia.com/articles/1445-amulet
Aquamarine Benefits - http://thehealingchest.com/crystals-stones/aquamarine-meaning/
Beryl Benefits-https://www.healingwithcrystals.net.au/beryl.html
Black Onyx Benefits- https://www.healingcrystals.com/Black_Onyx_Articles_73.html
Black Onyx Benefits - https://www.crystalvaults.com/crystal-encyclopedia/onyx
Black Onyx benefits-https://crystalbenefits.com/healing-properties-meaning-of-black-onyx-gemstone
Blue Lace Agate Benefits - https://www.gemrockauctions.com/learn/a-z-of-gemstones/blue-lace-agate-information
Blue sapphire - http://mapassion.co.in/blog/benefits-of-blue-sapphire-gemstone/
Blue Topaz Benefits - https://gemisphere.com/products/blue-topaz#
Blue Topaz Benefits - https://www.healing-crystals-for-you.com/blue-topaz-stones.html
Botswana Agate - https://www.crystalvaults.com/crystal-encyclopedia/botswana-agate
Bulls Eye Agate - https://www.charmsoflight.com/agate-healing-properties
Carbuncle aka garnet-https://www.crystalvaults.com/crystal-encyclopedia/garnet
Carbuncle (Garnet) https://www.energymuse.com/garnet-meaning
Carnelian Benefits - http://thehealingchest.com/crystals-stones/carnelian-meaning/
Coral Calcium https://coralcalcium.com/coral-calcium-health-benefits/
Crazy Lace Agate Benefits - https://www.astrolika.com/stones-crystals/crazy-lace-agate.html
Crazy Lace Agate Benefits - https://www.crystalvaults.com/crystal-encyclopedia/crazy-lace-agate
Dandelion benefitshttps://www.consciouslifestylemag.com/dandelion-root-tea-health-benefits/
Dandelion benefits - https://www.canuexplain.com/health/a-miracle-weed-that-regenerates-the-body-from-the-inside-out/
Emerald Benefits - https://www.healing-crystals-for-you.com/emerald-stones.html
Emerald Benefits -https://www.gemstoneuniverse.com/emeraldgemstonebenefits.php
Emerald Benefits-https://crystalbenefits.com/benefits-of-wearing-emerald-stone

Garnet Benefits - https://www.charmsoflight.com/garnet-healing-properties
Garnet carbuncle- https://shop.atperrys.com/blogs/healing-crystals-blog/healing-crystal-handbook-garnet
 gold benefits- https://www.dazzlingrock.com/blog/2019/01/health-benefits-wearing-gold-jewelry/
Golden Beryl and Heliodor Benefits- https://gemisphere.com/products/golden-beryl#product-details-scroll
Golden Beryl and Heliodor Benefits - https://www.healingcrystals.com/Golden_Beryl_Articles_13815.html
Golden Beryl and Heliodor Benefits - https://www.crystalvaults.com/crystal-encyclopedia/heliodor
Golden Beryl and Heliodor Benefits-
 Green sapphire benefits https://www.astrospeak.com/article/everything-you-need-to-know-about-green-sapphire-stone
Grossular Garnet - https://www.crystalvaults.com/crystal-encyclopedia/grossular
Hessonite (Grossular Garnet) Benefits - https://medium.com/@hessonite.org.in/health-benefits-of-wearing-hessonite-or-gomed-stone-f11130536fc1

Jasper Benefits - https://www.crystalvaults.com/crystal-encyclopedia/jasper
Morganite Benefits - https://www.crystalvaults.com/crystal-encyclopedia/morganite
Onyx Benefits-https://www.crystalvaults.com/crystal-encyclopedia/onyx
Orange/Padparadscha sapphire benefit - https://astrokapoor.com/products/padparadscha-orange-sapphire-ceylon/
Pearl benefits -https://www.ratnajyoti.com/Benefits-of-pearl
Pearl benefits https://www.gempundit.com/blog/pearl-stone-benefits/
Pink Sapphire benefits -https://gemisphere.com/products/pink-sapphire#
Pyrope Garnet benefits - https://www.crystalvaults.com/crystal-encyclopedia/pyrope
Pyrope Garnet benefits - https://www.healingwithcrystals.net.au/garnet.html
Red Beryl and Bixite Benefits - https://www.healingwithcrystals.net.au/beryl.html
Red Coral Gemstone https://www.gemstoneuniverse.com/top-red-coral-moonga-gemstone-benefits.php
Red Garnet Benefits - http://thehealingchest.com/crystals-stones/garnet-meaning/
Rhodolite Garnet Benefits - https://www.healingwithcrystals.net.au/garnet.html
Rubies benefits spiritually and emotionally ttps://www.crystalvaults.com/crystal-encyclopedia/ruby
Ruby physical health benefits: https://www.infocuriosity.com/top-10-benefits-of-ruby-gemstone/
Sapphire stone benefits:https://www.healingcrystals.com/Blue_Sapphire_Articles_59.html Silver Benefits-https://www.huffingtonpost.com/entry/9-silver-benefits-and-uses-backed-by-science_us_5797d100e4b0b3e2427d2c65
Spessartine Garnet - https://www.healingwithcrystals.net.au/garnet.html
Tsavorite - https://www.healingwithcrystals.net.au/garnet.html
Topaz benefits: https://www.gempundit.com/blog/astrological-benefits-of-yellow-topaz-gemstone

Topaz:Yellow, Golden, and Imperial Topaz, Blue Topaz, Clear Topaz, White Topaz, Brown Topaz, Rutilated Topaz ,Pink Topaz, Purple Topaz,Silver Topaz Benefits - https://www.crystalvaults.com/crystal-encyclopedia/topaz

Yellow Sapphire Benefits - https://docs.google.com/document/d/1tEHjm-IWCrH-u6uuGOF5yA3xSnLLT0eMUuM1rDeGj8Q/edit

 Yellow Topaz Benefits - https://astrokapoor.com/products/yellow-topaz/

Yellow Topaz Benefits - https://eluneblue.com/yellow-topaz-meaning/

Yellow Topaz Benefits - https://www.sitarejewels.com/benefits-of-wearing-yellow-topaz-gemstone/

About the Author

T.R. Green is from St. Louis, MO. She's been a born-again believer in Christ Jesus for 10 years. She has ministered in purity, singing, choir, dancing, and encouraging others. She has ministered and encouraged others to have a relationship with the Father, the Son, and Holy Spirit. She has encouraged people to believe in who they are. She has had many remarkable experiences with the Father, the Son, and Holy Spirit. She flows in healing through Christ Jesus and is a certified crystal healer. She has her own small business selling crystals, making crystal jewelry, and as being a certified crystal healer in order to help her clients heal with crystals through Christ Jesus. She has an awesome husband and three awesome and amazing children. She believes in being who you are and for you to recognize the greatness that lies within you. She believes for you to know why you have been chosen to live for such a time as this. Her small business is called Crystal Kingdom, Bringing Wholeness into Reality. The website is www.crystalkingdomrocks.com and www.spreadingjesusrocks.com. You can help spread the word of this book or by purchasing it as a gift to someone else. You can also donate to the business as well, for it to expand if you'd like.

Upcoming Books by T.R Green Coming soon!

Becoming the Father's Treasures, Christ Rocks!
(Goes over benefits, affirmations, and scripture manifestations and affirmation of different crystals)

Birthing and Manifesting Promises of God through Crystal Grids
(Manifest your prayers, intentions, inheritance, and covenant blessings through Crystal Grids)

T.R. Green Business Website Information:

®

www.crystalkingdomrocks.com

or

www.spreadingjesusrocks.com